100

Rod MacKenzo
443 15th St
Bellingham, Wa. 98225
206-734-9351

AAPC fall Meeting 10/20-21/89
St Mary's at Toledo, Wa.
Sam was one of the resources on the
Evangelical understanding of Pastoral Counseling.

PROPERTY OF
BEAVERTON CHURCH OF
THE NAZERENE LIBRARY

D1006361

Theology & Therapy

The Wisdom of God in a Context of Friendship

Theology & Therapy

The Wisdom of God in a Context of Friendship

Samuel Southard

WORD PUBLISHING
Dallas · London · Sydney · Singapore

THEOLOGY AND THERAPY

Copyright © 1989 by Samuel Southard. All rights reserved. No portion of this book may be reproduced in any form, except for brief quotations in reviews, without written permission from the publisher.

Unless indicated otherwise, all Scripture quotations in this volume are from the Good News Bible, the Bible in Today's English Version. Copyright © by the American Bible Society, 1976. Used with permission. Those identified RSV are from the Revised Standard Version of the Bible, copyright 1946, 1952, 1971 by the Division of Christian Education of the National Council of the Churches of Christ in the USA. Used with permission. Those identified KJV are from the King James Version.

Library of Congress Cataloging-in-Publication Data

Southard, Samuel.
    Theology and therapy.

    Includes index.
    1. Pastoral counseling.   2. Counseling.   3. Theology,
Doctrinal.   I. Title.
BV4012.2.S66   1989   253.5   89–9072
ISBN 0-8499-0682-2

Printed in the United States of America
9 8 0 1 2 3 9 AGF 9 8 7 6 5 4 3 2 1

Contents

Contents

Preface

An eminent clinical psychologist at the Menninger Clinic, Paul W. Pruyser, was troubled by his observations of ministers and theological students who were trained for Christian counsel in the clinic: "They manifested, and sometimes professed, that their basic theological disciplines were of little help to them in ordering their observations and planning their meliorative moves."[1]

Is it therapeutically possible to order observations and plan therapy around basic theological disciplines? Yes, if the discipline of theology shows us the continuing relationship between God's design and our disorder. The relationship is established through the incarnation of God in Christ. This union of divinity and humanity is basic for theologies that may be called "incarnational" or "mediated."[2] Whatever the label, the theology is a sympathetic and systematic inquiry into the relation of God's will to our will.

A biblical label would be "wisdom." Wisdom is reflection upon human possibilities and limitations in the light of God's revelation. It is guided both by realistic observations of ourselves and explanations of our attitudes and behaviors that are drawn from revealed knowledge of God's original intentions for his creation. The context for the wisdom of God is the power of his love shown in understanding of the self and others—both friends and strangers.

The communication of power and wisdom will take many forms, the most intimate being friendship. Jesus presented this bond of understanding as basic for the knowledge of God's will.

> I call you friends, because I have told you everything I heard from my Father. (John 15:15)

It is a relationship of choice (v. 16), with preferential commitments that call for sacrifice (v. 13), built upon values that may be risky in this world (v. 14), and equalitarian in full sharing of the highs and lows of life (v. 15).

This context for wisdom includes many elements of modern therapy, such as shared respect, empathy, mutual understanding. But there is an emphasis upon sacrifice, spiritual values, and commitment in friendship that makes it the relation of choice for edifying conversations about God's will in relation to ours, and of ours in relation to each other.

This redemptive friendship is *therapon* (from whence, "therapy"), the Greek term for "highly personal, sympathetic, confidential acts of service."[3] Through this service, Jesus as the *therapon* of God mediates divine redemptive love (Matt. 8:7; 4:2; Mark 1:34; 3:10; Luke 14:3). The revelation of sacrificial love is more than intuitive understanding. It is also a proclamation, an announcement that the kingdom of God has come to us through his Son, Jesus the Messiah. This good news (*kerygma*) enlightens and heals all who hear and believe.

Christian counsel is that special form of therapy in which healing attitudes are shaped by the message of the kingdom of God. What are the shaping forces? In part they are basic Christian doctrines such as the Trinity and the Incarnation. In the first eleven chapters I will use case studies to show the congruence of specific theological teaching with therapeutic concern. This is an aspect of Christian counsel that partially fulfills the biblical requirement of wisdom.

The other shaping force of wisdom is the intimate relationship which facilitates friendship. It is implicit and explicit knowledge of God and knowledge of self in a direction which facilitates emotional and spiritual growth.[4] Chapters 12–15 will explore this possibility through strategies for friendship that are authoritative for the church and therapeutically sound when they combine empathy with confrontation. My hope is that wisdom presented in the context of friendship will be a stimulus to both holiness and wholeness.[5]

EDITOR'S NOTE: All of the conversations that appear in this book are from real case studies. Differences in style, tone, and details reflect the individual personalities of the participants. With the notable exception of the author's own, names and identifying details have been altered in order to protect the privacy of the participants.

NOTES

1. Paul Pruyser, *The Minister as Diagnostician* (Philadelphia: Westminster Press, 1976), pp. 27–28.
2. Therapy cannot be correlated with "propositional" theologies that state dogma apart from a knowledge of human difficulties. Also, mediated theologies cannot be correlated with "non-theologies" which despise the mind and depend upon special emotional states as signs of God's direct and absolute guidance of an isolated individual.
3. Thomas Oden, *Kerygma and Counseling* (Philadelphia: Westminster Press, 1976), p. 148. The New Testament emphasis upon service led LeRoy Aden to define pastoral care as "a response of love to the neighbor in need in response to what God is and does for us!" LeRoy Aden, "Pastoral Care and the Gospel," in LeRoy Aden and J. Harold Ellins, eds., *The Church and Pastoral Care* (Grand Rapids: Baker Book House, 1988), p. 39.
4. "Knowledge" in theology is more than cognition. It is personal insight and awe before the mysterious revelation of God. See Rudolph Otto, *The Idea of the Holy* (London: Oxford University Press, 1923). Geoffrey Wainwright describes the knowledge of God, theology, as intellect in the service of existential vision and commitment, *Doxology* (New York: Oxford, 1980). The knowledge of self grows with the knowledge of God, for the purpose of human knowledge is to know clearly what it means to be human in answer to a higher calling. See Gerhard Ebeling, *Word and Faith* (Philadelphia: Fortress Press, 1963), pp. 305ff.
5. I use "stimulus" because the study is exploratory rather than complete. There are some notable defects in balance and comprehensiveness. All but one of the case studies is about counsel by males. The concepts of maturity are partially based on psychological studies, which are notoriously male-oriented toward autonomous thinking, clear decision making, and responsible action. I have difficulty balancing an emphasis upon structure and cognition with intuitions and personal exceptions. (The problems of male-oriented research studies are reviewed by Carol Gilligan, *In A Different Voice* [Cambridge: Harvard University Press, 1982], pp. 6–19.)

The cultural context is western, rational, middle-class. My brief contacts in East Asia have warned me away from attempts to write as though images of care were the same in all cultures. See David and Vera Mace, *Marriage: East and West* (Garden City: Doubleday, 1960); Samuel Southard, *Family Counseling in East Asia* (Manila: Christian Literature Society of the Philippines, 1969); David Augsburger, *Pastoral Counseling Across Cultures* (Philadelphia: Westminster Press, 1986).

Introduction

Christian counsel is the wisdom of God presented in the context of friendship.

Wisdom is equated in the Bible with empathetic counsel: "A person's thoughts are like water in a deep well, but someone with insight can draw them out" (Prov. 20:5). The counsel is more than sympathetic intelligence and congruent feelings. Counsel that is powerful is the wisdom of God: "Old men have wisdom, but God has wisdom and power. Old men have insight; God has insight and power to act" (Job 12:12–13). Supremely, counsel is incarnate in the "wonderful counselor," Jesus Christ, who embodies both the wisdom and the power of God (Isa. 9:6; 1 Cor. 1:24).

Godly counsel is a combination of human and divine insight which is ultimately dependent upon the power of God to produce observable change in a person. It is rooted in knowledge beyond human understanding, but it is displayed in strong attitudes and actions which can be empirically verified: "The spirit of the Lord will give him wisdom and the knowledge and skill to rule his people" (Isa. 11:2).

Wisdom, counsel, understanding are multifaceted terms for a comprehensive approach to human dilemmas. The range and variety of usage may extend from psychological insight and motivation for change to philosophical and moral questions about reasons for suffering and purpose in life. Those who are called wise counselors will rely upon these diverse sources of human and divine wisdom: (1) "international" intelligence, (2) moral guidance, (3) prophetic insight, and (4) sacrificial spiritual power.

International Intelligence

Counsel includes a substratum of observations and conclusions on social order, interpersonal harmony, and personal integration which may be found in more than one culture. Biblical scholars such as G. Ernest Wright and J. Coert Rylaarsdam have noted the importance of this "international wisdom" in Proverbs and other wisdom sayings of the Old Testament.[1] It is "universal reason," insofar as one Near Eastern culture knew another. The universal purpose is proclaimed in the introductory phrases of Proverbs.

> Here are proverbs that will help you recognize wisdom and good advice, and understand sayings with deep meaning. They can teach you how to live intelligently and how to be honest, just, and fair. (1:2–3)

Counsel is an emphasis upon prudent, considered experience, and competent action to live decently with others and to master the various problems of life.[2]

The mastery of problems depends on two aspects of international intelligence. One is the collection of aphorisms, as in Proverbs:

> If you want to stay out of trouble, be careful what you say. (21:23)

These are wise sayings because they show knowledge of the way that God created us and intends for us to live with each other and with our environment. This is the supreme wisdom praised in Psalms.

> Lord, you have made so many things! How wisely you made them all. (104:24)

These collections of tested experiences for the solution of life problems form a traditional guide book which serves more as stimulus to reflection than as a final answer, since varying viewpoints on the same subject may be found in the aphorisms.[3]

The other aspect of international intelligence is individual sagacity in solving interpersonal problems. Solomon is extolled for this type of wisdom (1 Kings 3:16-28; 10:1-3). Prophets look forward to a ruler of this quality.

The Spirit of the Lord will give him wisdom. . . . He will not judge by appearance nor hearsay.   (Isa. 11:2-3)

The Gospels present Jesus' sagacious and prudent way of thinking as one of the attributes which drew people to him, and which preserved his integrity under attack. Some examples would be his

(1) realistic observations (the way Pharisees predict weather, Matt. 16:1-4; the way hypocrites fast, Matt. 6:16-19);
(2) practical classifications (the condition of soil before planting is like the varying conditions of readiness to hear the Gospel, Matt. 13:10-17);
(3) concise explanations (some Pharisees will not believe the healing of a blind man because it is a judgment upon their own blindness, John 9:39-41).

These characteristics of wisdom in Jesus' ministry are essential in Christian counsel.[4]

But, in times when middle and lower class people despair of any control over their lives in crowded, greedy cities, the way of the "wonderful counselor" seems too long and lacks power. They want Jesus the wonderworker. Instant success rather than mature thinking is desired by counselees who think obsessively, are socially inept, and often play "victim."

The inept individuals who are threatened by international intelligence say they want no worldly wisdom. They're wrong in their defensiveness about daily decisions, but they are partially right whenever their questions are about the ultimate meaning of life. Wisdom literature, built on a subfloor of international intelligence, does show the futility of knowledge about the relation of the self to the universe apart from the revealed knowledge of God. Questions concerning the meaning of life transcend wisdom as competent action in daily affairs. To receive answers to the ultimate questions of life we must humble ourselves before the Creator (Job 42:1-6). The New Testament assures us that God provides this wisdom "generously and graciously to all" (James 1:5).

The perspective upon meaning and purpose in life that comes through humility before God's revelation will temper and correct the "international wisdom" of prudent advice and competent action that may be considered wise in the context of one or more cultures.[5] Both Old and New Testament writers warn that without obedience to this transcendent awareness of reality, selfish and hedonistic humans may restrict their knowledge to the foolish worship of mortal sensations and fantasies (Rom. 1:18-23). It is this willfully myopic view of the world which the Apostle Paul denounces as "the world's wisdom" (1 Cor. 1:20-25).[6]

The warning presents an issue of quality control for counsel. Is it realistic to confine questions of motivation and purpose to psychological forces that we can observe, and to some extent control? Do we define any "God-talk" as projection of unconscious conflicts upon some mythological power that would perpetuate our dependent state? Or do we show implicitly or explicitly that there is power "beyond psychology" (to use a phrase of Otto Rank) to justify this decision? If so, how do we distinguish righteous dependence upon God from the hypocrisy that lives by repression, projection, displacement?

The impact of these questions upon counsel is shown in biblical warnings of deception and ignorance in the pursuit of wisdom—and awareness of our discomfort in trying to distinguish righteousness from hypocrisy, wisdom from foolishness:

> I was determined to learn the difference between knowledge and foolishness, wisdom and madness. But I found out that I might as well be chasing the wind. The wiser you are, the more worries you have; the more you know, the more it hurts.   (Eccles. 1:16-18)

> Never let yourself think that you are wiser than you are: simply obey the Lord and refuse to do wrong.   (Prov. 3:7)

Introduction

Moral Guidance

Intelligent awareness of the self is essential for anyone who claims knowledge of God:

> Whoever listens to the word but does not put it into practice is like a man who looks in a mirror and sees himself as he is. He takes a good look at himself and then goes away and at once forgets what he looks like. But whoever looks closely into the perfect love that sets people free, who keeps on paying attention to it and does not simply listen and then forget it, but puts it into practice—that person will be blessed by God in what he does.
>
> (James 1:23–25)

How do we perceive and describe ourselves? James warns against distortions and commends those who speak with self-control, take care of the needy, and avoid corrupting influences (James 1:16–27).

This is moral counsel. Like James, a counselor will discuss those attitudes and actions that demonstrate "perfect law that sets people free." The freedom is from social conformity and from rationalizations for selfishness, uncontrolled anger, and addictive desires (James 2–4).

A distorted view of self reflects dissonance between who we now are and how we were originally made. But who knows how we were originally made? The answer to that question is the beginning of wisdom (consider, for example, the questions of God to Job in Job 38).

Counsel that begins in the wisdom of beginnings ("genesis" or "etiology") will then trace original outlines in contemporary self-images. To what extent does a living soul conform in purpose and function to our Creator's intent?

How do we perceive, describe, evaluate the outline in ourselves and others? Wisdom discerns it in the "image of God" or the capacity for righteousness in a soul. The discernment is understood between persons through words or phrases that express purpose in life and effectiveness in function according to God's image.

Moral counsel is designed for explicit commitment to effectively function in the image of God (see chapter 4 for a description of "image of God"). Effectiveness is measured in terms that describe our relation to God, self, others.

The principle term for honest, purposeful living in all these contexts is "righteousness," contrasted with "wickedness." Psalm 1 describes inner strength of soul above social conformity (no sitting, standing, or walking with the wicked). The ideal is a passionate soul impelled toward righteousness despite the scorn of the self-righteous and the hatred of those who lay snares for the innocent.[7]

In Hebrew thought, morality requires emotional depth. This depth is expressed as a soundness of the soul that is known through character, attitude, and acts of wisdom in doing justice (1 Kings 3:9–12). The soundness is based upon unified functioning of thinking, willing, and acting. A passionate commitment is combined with powerful execution (Prov. 8:18). This morality is an affair of the heart (Ps. 90:12) that is full of pleasure (Prov. 2:10) or pain (Eccles. 1:18). The passions of the soul united with the power of God produce apt discernment and finely tuned discretion in decisions (Isa. 28:28–29).[8]

The shape of righteous action lies in the soul. Here the direction of life is formed so deeply that it may first be manifest in realistic dreams. When Solomon, the epitome of wisdom, dialogued with God in a dream, this was followed by the wisdom to rule justly (1 Kings 3:1–28). The message that emerges without conscious control through dreams is one test of true and false prophets. The true prophet is filled with strength of soul from God, and dreams of action that surely comes to pass. The false prophets show the deceitfulness of their hearts in fanciful dreams that are not rooted in reality (Jer. 23:25–32).

This judgment is one challenge for Christian counsel. Will any discussion of morality combine depth of soul with powerful, prudent action?

Another challenge for modern "physicians of the soul" will be the development of terms for righteousness and wickedness that unite deeper self-insight with observable changes in relationships—but as more than insight or relationships. Biblical wisdom would place these terms within a world-view that proclaims the knowledge of God as basic for any knowledge of self. Our interpersonal relations are developed out of the original model of God's relationship with us. The basis for "looking out for one another's interests" is Christ Jesus, who was so obedient in his knowledge of the Father's will, which he shared, that he willingly sacrificed himself for us (Phil. 2:5–11).

A third guideline from biblical wisdom is open commitment to a moral world-view in counsel. A righteous person is so passionately committed to moral living that it is obvious to others. But there are so many possibilities of distortion that both the perceptions of the counselee and the preconceptions of the counselor must be shared. Who is really wise? One who can share the lessons of life under the guidance of God, but always with awareness of self-deceit and selfishness. Equalitarian communication will combine humility with honesty in counsel built upon moral wisdom.

Prophetic Insight

Deeper stirrings of the soul, as with dreams and visions, require interpretation.[9] Who can show how subjective messages shape our expectations or explain our motivations? This is the calling of a prophet, one who sees souls in a state which is to come. Prophetic consciousness is a faculty of fellow-feeling, a long-term empathy (for examples, see Jer. 38:22; 2 Kings 8:13; Jer. 4:20). Prophetic wisdom is insight that persists.[10]

The historical fulfillment of prophetic insight is more than individual prediction and control. It is the unfolding of interdependent consequences of deep motives which are dimly perceived in the soul. From these shadowy outlines of things to come, the prophet counsels action and attitudes which will fulfill the will of God for individuals, families, tribes, and cultures (for an example of confrontive prophecy, see 1 Kings 22:13–28).

That which can be predicted with accuracy can be controlled for success. The control is not considered in prophecy to be a function of human movement as much as it is submission to the irresistible fulfillment of that which God intended. Personal choices with future consequences are accommodations to divine power rather than assertion of will according to the objectives of one person. For this reason, there are many warnings against pride in counsel. What does one person really know about another? All "prophetic" utterances must be evaluated, checked by peers, weighed for detection of the inevitable distortion caused by human attempts to control others (1 Cor. 13:1–4; 14:29; Matt. 7:1–5).

Prophets who adjust their counsel with humble acceptance of their own limitations will be blessed by wisdom and power from

God. The blessing is both the strength or capacity to produce righteousness and the staying power of attitudes and actions which bring forth the fruit of righteousness. This quality of prophetic counsel brings blessings over time to individuals and to groups. For this reason the prophet is spoken of as one who guards the people with "knowledge and understanding" (Jer. 3:15). His or her counsel leads to steadfastness by which one may progressively accomplish righteous and realistic purposes. This blessing radiates in all directions—to family, friends, and nation, and to sons and daughters (Gen. 48:3–4, 15ff.).

The consequences of prophetic vision for Christian counsel are social and historical. Godly counsel is offered in the context of social units, and righteousness is presented as a function of interdependent consequences of individual decisions. Furthermore, perceptible results over a period of time are crucial for determining the validity of counsel. Although the timeless unconscious is recognized as a major force in personal integrity, counsel is not bounded by interminable struggles for psychological individuation. Prophetic counsel interrupts ceaseless introspection with demands to consider present responsibility to others. There is limited time within which we may make prudent decisions for the future.

How do present decisions relate to future consequences? In wisdom literature, dream and action, motivation and consequences are one. Wisdom is not considered to be prophetic until the discernment of inner purpose is unfolded in congruent historical consequences.

Sacrificial Spiritual Power

The accurate fulfillment of dimly known prophecies is one guarantee of godly wisdom. In the New Testament, the faithful fulfillment of God's wisdom is personalized in Jesus Christ (Heb. 1:1–3). Divine will and human experience are united in Christ, the power and wisdom of God (1 Cor. 1:24).

The apostle Paul applies this faith affirmation to the imperfect interpretation of prophetic wisdom in the Corinthian church. He traces the distortions of self-deception and interpersonal divisiveness. This etiology is helpful to modern counselors who see people with co-dependent, obsessive tendencies. Their religion is often dysfunctional because of self-deception. They have a self-protective interpretation of reality that they use to justify their pursuit of unacceptable passions. The self-justifying system of thought contains defensive and repetitive beliefs: I'm not worthwhile; People won't like me if they know what I think; I must find security in a relationship.[11] Therapy includes shared appraisal of the person's interpretation of inner beliefs which promote self-protective views of work, health, finances, relationships. When a person is willing to consider reality from another point of view, defenses may be reduced enough for some openness and honesty to emerge from a traumatized self.

This is the direction of wisdom for Paul, but with this proclamation: "God has made Christ to be our wisdom" (1 Cor. 1:30). His sacrificial death is the power by which wisdom is revealed through vulnerability rather than self-deception, friendship rather than divisiveness. In contrast to the protective system of a lonely soul, Paul presents honest admission of faults, dedication to purposes beyond ourselves—with risk, joyous commitment to a fellowship that creates the sense of friendship that Jesus shared with his disciples on the night of his betrayal (1 Cor. 11:18–34).

This counsel from a wounded healer is foolish to self-protective people—unless they can be persuaded through love to see the world more deeply and accurately than a painfully inadequate self would permit. That deeper reality is God's intention to bring strength out of weakness, when weakness is honestly admitted. It is a return to our original design by God, in which it is no sin to be human. Sin is the stupid assertion that we can be more than limited human beings through powerful associations, angelic talk, mountain-moving faith, extractive relationships, perpetual assertions of autonomy (1 Cor. 13:1–6).

A nondefensive self is one benefit of the wisdom of the cross. Christ's life and death for others is the power-sign of our acceptance by God—if we will accept ourselves as finite creatures. Another benefit is the empowering of the self through open and loving relationships, characterized by Paul as "the body of Christ" (1 Cor. 1:29). Divisiveness is gradually overcome through the gift of graciousness toward one another that characterizes a life of gratitude for the wisdom and power that God has lavished upon us.

These are strong theological assertions. Do they really make a difference in the life of a counselee? To some extent we will never know, and should be cautious in our claims. There is an elusive, mystical element in the "hidden wisdom" of God that defies experimental verification (1 Cor. 2:7).[12]

Friendship

But there is another demonstrable characteristic of wisdom which is proclaimed by Jesus to the eleven disciples that remained with him: "I call you friends, because I have told you everything I have heard from my Father" (John 15:15). Friendship is the demonstration of love in a privileged, equalitarian relationship between disciples. It is privileged because of shared knowledge that may be very intimate. It is equalitarian because friends have the capacity to give and receive love in a nondefensive way. They appreciate the truth which is shared.

Friendship is not only a sign that self-deception is being overcome; indeed, friendship contains the indispensable ingredients of empathy, congruence, and positive regard that are antidotes for secrecy and deceit. Friendship is also the triumph of trust and specific self-giving over former trends toward divisiveness and competition.[13]

But what is distinctly Christian about this definition of friendship, which contains elements of any effective counseling relationship? Godly power will be evident in two ways: first, in the grace and forgiveness with which the quality of friendship is maintained despite disruptive and destructive forces; second, in the expansion of friendship toward strangers. It is self-giving to people who from a human point of view don't really deserve our loving attention. (Thus we move in Christian love from the initial restrictiveness of friendship toward universal benevolence.)

Friendship as modeled by Jesus is mutually fulfilling, but it includes self-giving that may end in self-sacrifice. This is the persuasive context for counsel that embraces the wisdom of God. One person is consistently willing to accept another with trust and respect if both of them can come to see ultimate reality in the same way—that God has created us to receive strength when we admit our weakness and are willing to love others as we learn to love ourselves.

But there is a supreme requirement of biblical friendship that I have not seen in modern counsel—sacrificial death. It is through the cross that Christ has made us the friends of God (Rom. 5:6–11).

Those who follow his commandment and example of love will receive power to befriend others at the risk of life itself (John 15:12–14). When inner obedience becomes sacrificial action, we can be called friends of God (James 2:22–24).

I don't remember hearing or reading about such an ultimate expectation of counsel, and would probably have repressed any rare reference to this kind of sacrifice. But I think that people would have come alive to my counsel if they knew in some quiet and unmistakable way that I would die for them. I wouldn't have been smarter, but I would have been more authentic.

Maybe this is why I always admired my mother's calling as a Red Cross nurse. During the flu epidemic of 1917 she volunteered for duty at an army hospital where one out of three doctors and nurses died. When I asked if she had been frightened, she gave a "head nurse" shrug and replied, "You don't think much about it. It's a risk you live with in caring for people."

I never lived with that risk in my calling. I've been willing to give up a little self-preoccupation to become empathetic, understanding and respectful of people in trouble. But there were positive benefits that outweighed my limited expenditure of time, attention, and pride. I never thought of literally walking as a friend with a comparative stranger through a valley of death. But that would be the authentication of wisdom for those who are transformed into friends of God.

The Contemporary Challenge

How authentic is wisdom in contemporary Christian counsel? As a basis for this exploratory study, I reviewed a hundred cases and verbatims collected from 1963–1985. They came from "lay shepherds," seminary students, pastors, several psychiatrists, and two Christian exorcists. In order of frequency, the writers were Baptists, Lutherans, Presbyterians, "neo-Pentecostal" or "charismatic," and Episcopalian.

The verbatims and cases contained more international wisdom and moral guidance than prophetic insight or sacrificial spiritual power. Most of the counselors had learned something about listening with compassion, but they seemed to lack reference points for the application of spiritual power or wisdom to specific difficulties. Perhaps their theological training concentrated so much upon God's design that it was not shaped toward awareness of specific human disorders.[14]

I kept wishing for something in Christian counsel like the training in diagnosis and prescription that I vaguely remembered from a year in medical school. As first-year students, we kept reading and hearing about the eight systems of the body: skeletal, muscular, nervous, and so on. Clinical medicine was built on those classifications.

Why didn't we have some similar system of theological classification for the soul?[15] When I transferred from medicine to theology, I found that moral or practical theologians had built a variety of systems for understanding human problems in the light of divine revelation (many of these are described in John T. McNeill, *A History of the Cure of Souls*).[16] But these were unknown or unused by the Christian counselors who handed cases to me in class or workshops.

I'd like to restore what was lost without losing anything we have gained from the theory and practice of post-World War II therapies. Yet in the process of becoming a new knower of old truths I found a faith-assertion that might be interpreted as dogmatic imperialism. The texts of moral or practical theology until the post-World War II period located the ultimate power and wisdom for a solution to human dilemmas with God. Most of the writers, going back to biblical authors, did not exclude the proximate benefits of human knowledge and caring, but in the last analysis the theological system was "the ground of being."[17]

I hope to avoid vain boasting with an admission that the full meaning or appropriation of God's wisdom was not very evident in the cases I studied. We probably need more long-term studies, or in-depth interviews with friends and relatives to fill out our investigation. In any case, it is difficult to demonstrate the continual primacy of divine indwelling over human potential as a solution to problems of motivation and direction for life.

Such an exercise in practical theology would call for both courage and curiosity. I'm asking for courage to state our basic way of thinking and commitment to God's wisdom and power, combined with curiosity as to identification in therapeutic dialogue. Curiosity opens our minds to the identifiable ways we live by what we believe. Courage sustains our continuing search for more evidence of this belief when our initial investigation is inconclusive.

To begin the study of wisdom through friendship I've shortened a popular term of the last forty years, "counseling," to "counsel".

Introduction

"Counseling" in the last half of the twentieth century came to the attention of many Christian counselors as an emphasis on technique. A sign of this preoccupation was the "nondirective" designation of the most popular therapy that influenced clergy in the 1950s. I affirm the importance of methodologically-oriented therapies which helped to free the ministry, lay and clerical, from nineteenth-century stereotypes of counsel as stern command or sentimental platitudes. But I also affirm that Christian counsel is shaped by the content of our commitments which lead to demonstration of care in our relationships. Counsel is more than a caring relationship. It is also a demonstration of content, the wisdom of God.[18]

In my investigation of cases and verbatims, wisdom and counsel sometimes consisted of explicit theological statements and sometimes was demonstrated as implicit attitudes based on theological commitments. As I reviewed cases with Christian counselors, some said that their theology was implicit. They thought to create a climate of expectation that God's power would be manifest in a conversation. The expectation might be seen by the way in which a counselor defined a crucial or crisis experience, responded to client's statements with certain emphases, or encouraged through non-verbal cues the development of specific subjects by the counselee. Sometimes I could sense the outline of this expectation in a verbatim and sometimes I could not. Other Christian counselors sought to be explicit at times about theology. I identified this in the moral and theological definition of problems; the explanation of the counselor's or counselee's attitudes as expressions of God's power; or the biblical and theological answers which were given to questions about sickness and death, evil and sin, forgiveness and hope, trust and love.

Would the implicit and/or explicit theology that was identified by Christian counselors be the same as biblical understandings of wisdom? The question is a difficult one when we compare the context and content of advice giving, moral instruction and prophetic exhortation of ancient Palestine with the varied expectations of modern therapy and theology. But we do know that biblical references to wisdom include both the power of God and sensitivity to personal relations and individual character. Some correlations of ancient and modern assumptions and methods are possible, so long as we speak more of direction and dedication than we do of dogmatic solutions or indifferent compromises. We seek with another an answer to the universal question, Who are we to answer the call of God, and how? This is the counsel of wisdom and revelation (Eph. 1:17).

NOTES

1. G. Ernest Wright, *The Old Testament Against Its Environment* (London: SCM Press, 1950), pp. 44–45; J. Coert Rylaarsdam, *Revelation in Jewish Wisdom* (Chicago: Univ. of Chicago Press, 1946), p. 72.

2. Georg Fohrer, *"Sophia,"* in Geoffrey W. Bromiley, tr. and ed., *Theological Dictionary of the New Testament* (Grand Rapids: Eerdmans, 1971) vol. 7, 476. R. B. Y. Scott found agreement among wisdom writers of the Old Testament on the following points: (1) The world as God made it is to be an orderly home for humans. (2) The basic moral issues are justice and mutuality, truth, concordance of profession and practice. (3) Personal commitment to worthy moral goals is a turning away from chaos toward an order that is again meaningful and good, and (4) the wise person is obligated toward this commitment. (5) The foundation of humane wisdom is reverence for God's creativity and guidance. *The Way of Wisdom in the Old Testament* (New York: Macmillan, 1971), pp. 227–29.

3. The variety of words may appear as a "hypnotic piling up of nouns," but they are arranged with care to stimulate in-depth comprehension (Gerhard Von Rad, *Wisdom in Israel* (Nashville: Abingdon Press, 1974), p. 25. Without this care, aphorisms may be taken out of context and abusively applied (Gordon Fee and Douglas D. Smart catalog these abuses in *How to Read the Bible for All Its Worth* (Grand Rapids: Zondervan, 1981), pp. 181ff.).

4. The sagacity of Jesus was masterfully portrayed in Otto Borchert's *The Original Jesus* (London: Lutterworth Press, 1933), a German book that waited sixteen years for publication and then appeared as a best seller at the same time that Hitler came into power. An American example of sensitivity to the thought of Jesus is Harry Emerson Fosdick's *The Man from Nazareth* (New York: Harper and Brothers, 1949).

5. Humility is the antidote for professional pride and the restrictive assumption of guilds in counseling. In *Professionalism and Pastoral Care* (Philadelphia: Fortress Press, 1985), Alastair P. Campbell presents three dangers of a professional model in counsel: inequality, intellectualism, individualism (p. 8). In counsel provided by pastors, Professor Campbell (New College, Edinburgh) suggests that these dangers be met by (1) care from the entire church, (2) the relating of our own story and our human presence with those in trouble, and (3) a passion for the truth (pp. 67–77). See also Kurt E. Farnsworth, "Christian Psychotherapy and the Culture of Professionalism," *Journal of Psychology and Theology,* Summer 1980, pp. 115–21.

6. E. D. Schmidt, "Knowledge," in Colin Brown, editor, *Dictionary of New Testament Theology* (Grand Rapids: Zondervan, 1976) II, 400ff.

Introduction

7. The dependence of this moral counsel upon the wisdom of a revelational world view would have been immediately detected in the ancient Near East, where other views of the world and society were dominant. The immobile, stratified and sophisticated society of Egypt was full of warnings against "the passionate." Such persons were continually corrected for raising questions and acting independent. The Egyptian ideal, in life and death, was the "silent man" who serenely followed the order established by priests for this life and the afterlife. Wright, *Old Testament*, p. 44. For the relation of Hebrew wisdom to Egyptian and Greek thought, see Robert Gordis, *Koheleth* (New York: Schocken Books, Third Editions).

   Although modern therapies seek to avoid prejudgment and condemnation through reduction of references to the counselor's moral convictions and a concentration upon the values of the client, the very phrases and thought forms of a counselor reveal some world view and ethical assumptions. See the evidence developed by Don Browning, *Religious Thought and the Modern Psychologies* (Philadelphia: Fortress Press, 1986).

8. Johannes Pedersen, *Israel: Its Life and Culture* (London: Geoffrey Cumberlege, 1926), pp. 128–32.

9. Although the New Testament unites wisdom and prophecy in Jesus, there were differences in the Old Testament. R. B. Y. Scott declared: "The prophet speaks from the standpoint of revelation, the wise man from that of reason working from the data of experience and observation." *The Way of Wisdom in the Old Testament*, p. 113.

   Distinctions between wisdom and prophecy may also appear in New Testament. For example, in his directions for life in answer to questions raised by a church (1 Cor. 7:1), Paul writes as one who "has God's Spirit" (1 Cor. 7:40). But on some matters he speaks with wisdom: "I give my opinion as one who by the Lord's mercy is worthy of trust" (1 Cor. 7:25); and on others he speaks as a prophet: "I have a command which is not my own but the Lord's" (1 Cor. 7:10). The wisdom he gives is not an order; it is a statement of personal preference (1 Cor. 7:6). The prophecy is to be obeyed (1 Cor. 7:10). Paul takes care to show which subject is under "permission" and which under obligation (1 Cor. 7:6, 12).

   The Pauline distinction is sometimes forgotten in the spontaneous declaration of "words of wisdom," by which one person in a charismatic group will diagnose the personal difficulties of another or give directions for decisions. The continual temptation is to use the power-phrase, "this is of the Lord," when it may in fact only be impulsive advice.

10. Wisdom persists, or fulfills insight, because the mystical vision of God in dreams and visions can be united with cognition—the hearing of the Word of God (e.g., Isaiah 6). In his book, *The Elusive Presence* (San Francisco: Harper & Row, 1978), Samuel Terrien examines the Old Testament accounts of God's presence in both auditory and visual metaphors and argues that hearing is dominant over sight.

11. For examples, see Anne Wilson Schaef, *Co-Dependents: Misunderstood— Mistreated* (San Francisco: Harper and Row, 1986).

12. Perception of the location of God's power through wisdom in human life will vary among denominations and periods of religious history. In the Anglican tradition of moral theology, the church was the active agent of reconciliation between statement and strategy. The Christian counselor in this tradition would think first of the revelation which God had delivered to the church in Christ. Secondly, there would be thought concerning the application of this truth through the intellect, training, and feeling of the counselor. Special emphasis would be placed upon "knowledge by connaturality," the ability to understand human consciousness as a receptor for the revelation of God. (See E. L. Mascall, *Theology and the Gospel of Christ* [SPCK, 1977], pp. 35–36.) Karl Rahner has expanded this correlation through the church to include everything done by the church in the relationship of faith with sociology, psychology, and cultural anthropology (Karl Rahner, *Theology for Pastoral Action* [New York: Herder and Herder], 1968). (For an explanation of "correlation," see p. 39.) Other Roman Catholic theologians, such as John Shea, relate statement to strategy by identifying the experiences of individuals, illuminating them with the Christian tradition and elaborating a style and strategy of action that will enable the experiences to be deepened. (For a discussion of Shea and others, see Robert Kinast, "How Pastoral Theology Functions," *Theology Today*, January 1981, pp. 425ff.)

The American Protestant tradition located transcendent power in individual religious experience. Don Browning has placed particular emphasis upon practical moral thinking in *Religious Ethics and Pastoral Care* (Philadelphia: Fortress Press, 1983), pp. 53ff.). A variation on this theme of the religious consciousness is an emphasis upon maturity, in which the content of the Christian faith is considered in the light of a phenomenological theory of adult development. An example of the use of this type of correlation is the "Religious Experience Inventory" of Alter (Margaret G. Alter, "A Phenomenology of Christian Religious Maturity," *Pastoral Psychology*, Spring 1986, pp. 151ff.). The most influential focus of correlation in the early days of the pastoral psychology movement after World War II was the writings of Seward Hiltner. Hiltner's emphasis was upon competence in the assessment of personality difficulties, awareness of psychological and theological resources that would serve the ego, and sensitivity to the way in which a counselee would appropriate these resources in an atmosphere of total acceptance. For an analysis of Hiltner's use of theology, see Brian H. Childs, "The Role of Theology and Theological Language in Pastoral Observation," *Pastoral Psychology*, Winter 1979, pp. 112ff.

On the American scene, psychological strategy seemed to dominate over any theological statements in the period of 1950–1970. In the 1980s, theologians such as Thomas Oden and pastoral psychologists such as Wayne Oates represented a resurgence of interest in theological statements. In a 1986 volume, Oates presented this purpose for *The Presence of God in Pastoral Counseling* (Waco, TX: Word Books, 1986): "to explore with you the difference it can make if you and I make the Presence of the Eternal God the central dynamic in our dialogue with counselees. In essence, I want to move from dialogue to trialogue in pastoral counseling" (p. 23).

Introduction

These statements recapture the classic dimension of worship in theology. For a discussion of theology as worship, doctrine, and life, see Geoffrey Wainwright, *Doxology* (New York: Oxford, 1980), pp. 1–12; and Mascall, *Theology*, pp. 46ff.

13. Friendship is described theologically, philosophically, and historically in Gilbert Meilaender, *Friendship: A Study in Theological Ethics* (Notre Dame: University of Notre Dame Press, 1981); and Benjamin Nelson, *The Idea of Usury* (Chicago: University of Chicago Press, 1969), pp. 136–65. See also Martin Marty, *Friendship* (Allen, Tex.: Argus Communications, 1980); John M. Reisman, *The Anatomy of Friendship* (Lexington, Mass.: Irvington, 1979).

    Popular presentations of friendship which supply the feminine dimension are Ruth Senter, *The Seasons of Friendship: A Woman's Search for Intimacy* (Grand Rapids: Zondervan, 1982); Kristine Johnson Ingram, *Being a Christian Friend: A Christian Friendship Can Help You Draw Closer to God* (Valley Forge: Judson, 1985); Dorothy Devers, *Christian Growth and Spiritual Direction through Faithful Friendship* (Washington, D.C., Church of the Savior, n.d.).

14. In my reading of the hundred cases and interviews by Christian counselors (1970–1980), I could find no consistent theological pattern or reason for theological statements. In some cases there was a demonstrable relationship between Christian assumptions and method of counsel, or between the belief system of the counselee and the responses of the counselor. In other cases, the correlation was quite clear when certain subjects were discussed, such as Christian commitment, death, sin, or guilt, but at other times in the same cases there was no demonstrable correlation. Furthermore there were many cases in which the methodology not only seemed more secular than Christian, but also unconnected by the counselor with any value assumptions.

    When I questioned lay counselors, theological students, and pastors about the relationship of methodology to theology, I received a variety of responses. Some defined theology as Christian love and equated Christian love with "unconditional positive regard." Others saw theology as relating to methodology only in the quotation of Scripture or the use of prayer. A few saw the connection only in evangelistic statements. Most of them felt that there was some connection, but few were ready to state the procedures that demonstrated their theological assumptions.

    Some substantiation for my impressions comes from questionnaire responses by 116 pastoral counselors and pastors in the Boston and Indianapolis areas. They reported that at a functional level, pastoral counseling was predominantly psychological and sociological, with little integration of spiritual perspectives (William H. McKain, Jr., "The Contributions of Paul Tournier to the Practice of Pastoral Counseling," Th.D. dissertation, Boston University School of Theology, 1978.)

15. The question was raised consistently by professors of pastoral counseling who provided articles on the future of Christian counsel in the 1980s and beyond. See Samuel Southard, "The Current Need for Theological Counsel," *Pastoral Psychology*, Spring 1984, pp. 94–105 which contrasts the call for theology in counsel by writers in the field of practical theology (1980)

with a preoccupation toward psychological methods and integration of psychology and religion in the first year *Pastoral Psychology* was issued (1950).

16. John T. McNeill, *A History of the Cure of Souls* (New York: Harper Brothers, 1951), includes Martin Buber's organization of the cure of souls based upon Ezek. 34:16, Acts 4:32, Eph. 4:4, 15–16 (p. 177). Sometimes the "classical" formulations, such as vindicating the justice of God amid pain, are "hard arguments for moderns to grasp," as Tom Oden admits in his review of theologies from Apostolic to Reformation periods, *Crisis Ministries*, (New York: Crossroad, 1986), p. 72.

17. I hope that all readers will make some contribution to more precise definitions of godly wisdom than I have given in these exploratory explanations. Some definitions of implicit theology have been given in the research of Jackson Caroll and Gerald Jenkins, "The Development of Religious Commitment— Some Exploratory Research," (*Journal of Pastoral Care*, 1973, pp. 236–52); Paul Schmidt, "The Character Assessment Scale: A New Tool for the Counselor," (*Journal of Pastoral Care*, 1980, pp. 76–83); H. N. Malony, "Differences in Pastoral Care As a Function of Religious Belief and Attitude Toward Human Behavior," (*Journal of Pastoral Care*, 1977, pp. 38–46). When explicit theological references are observed (as in Po Hong Wang's study of twenty-one Protestant ministers), the identified references, such as biblical quotations and prayer, were negatively related to effective pastoral counseling when "effective" was defined as unconditional positive regard, warmth, and congruence. ("Demographical, Perceptual and Religious Determinates of Pastoral Counseling," unpublished Ph.D. thesis, Fuller Theological Seminary, 1982).

18. Biblical wisdom may combine statement and strategy with a variety of themes. It may be the "counsel of righteousness" (Dan. 4:17; Jer. 23:18) which combines word and deed. It is conversation and fellowship (Ps. 55:14), understanding and might (Job 12:13). Always it discloses the purposes of the heart (1 Cor. 4:5). For a symposium on the Old Testament understanding of wisdom, see James L. Crenshaw's *Studies in Ancient Israelite Wisdom* (New York: KTAV Publishing House, 1976).

The *Tebunah* or "man of understanding" of Prov. 20:5 is a working model for wisdom in counsel. I look forward to some biblical exegesis of the conception of the wise man, the fool, wisdom, and stupidity in relation to Christian counsel.

In the formative days of pastoral psychology, a theologian, Albert C. Outler related the movement to "the ancient art of sympathy and shared wisdom." He affirmed the newer relation to modern psychology, but with an admonition, "What is wanted is a Christian *context* for counseling." Albert Outler, "A Christian Context for Counseling," *Journal of Pastoral Care* 2, 1 (Spring 1946), pp. 1–2. It appears from the absence of this emphasis in the 1950–1970 period that writers in the field were content with the operational definition of a founder of clinical pastoral education, Anton Boisen: "What term has the liberal minister of religion for his ministrations or for the object thereof? . . . the term 'counseling' is the non-medical equivalent of 'psychotherapy.'" Anton Boisen, "The Minister as Counselor," *Journal of Pastoral Care* 2, 1, p. 13.

PART I
WISDOM

How does wisdom guide counsel into deeper knowledge of both God and self? A theological system of mediated revelation will unite Word and "flesh," content of revelation and divine/human medium of communication.

But wisdom warns against the possibilities of hypocrisy and deceit in this process. The Old Testament contains the confessions of a wise judge who could not tell the difference between knowledge and foolishness (Eccles. 1:16) and a righteous patriarch who was shamed in his attempts to explain the ways of God (Job 38). The New Testament presents Jesus' correction of those who judge others without remedying their own faults (Matt. 7:1-5). He came into increasing conflict with religious counselors who were so inwardly contaminated that they had no balance or prudence in their guidance of self and others (Matt. 23:13-28). Paul asks if those who have "full content of knowledge and truth" are committing the sins which they emphasize in their self-righteous teaching (Rom. 2:17-24).

The answer of Paul was a systematic evaluation of human motivation and conduct, the Law, which stops human deception and deceit (Rom. 3:9-20). At the same time, God's love provides an inner dynamic beyond condemnation, which is the creation of a new self-in-relationship (Rom. 5:1-11). This is also a corrective to misplaced emphasis in righteousness or selective inattention to godly commands, for the "new being" sets the struggle of every human alongside the human struggles of Jesus. Here is reality-testing for prudent counsel. There can be constant comparisons between the old and new Adam, the human actuality and the divine/human example (Rom. 5:12-19).

With "all possible wisdom," the apostle Paul exhorts believers to judge their maturity by the life of Christ, a life they now share through the Spirit (Col. 1:28; Eph. 3:14-19). Knowledge of the Son of God is disciplined, coordinated growth within self and in relation

1

to others (Eph. 4:13–16). This is the work of the Spirit through the church, which codified the life and teachings of Jesus as a guide for eternal life and faithful living (John 20:30–31).

The Gospels and the Epistles are the measures (canon) of personal maturity, sacrificial friendship, spiritual wisdom. Upon this authoritative base the church developed systems of thought that would demonstrate God's design for our lives despite our deceit and indifference. The quality control for honest, abundant living should be found in the theologies developed in response to new configurations of ancient human dilemmas.

But although theologies are necessary as systematic and reflective measures of the life of Christ in relation to our purpose and problems as limited, fallible copies of God's original design, some systems of thought follow the way of wisdom and some do not.

What's the difference? The salient problem is an insistence in wisdom literature that all our attempts to know ourselves and God are only approximations of the divine disclosure. We live by faith that God has provided infallible guidance for us through his Son, displayed in human personality and perpetuated in his Spirit, but who can be sure of the application of truth to the problems of anyone, including ourselves?

Our difficulty with any conceived, articulated order of truth is the intransigence of the human heart, defended by plausible excuses of the mind. This is why many who are diligent in their "searching of the scriptures" cannot see or accept the living truth (John 5:39).

And this is why some theologies are defective in wisdom. They do not prepare counselors for realistic testing of mind and heart. They do not deal with the question, how do we receive and respond to God's revelation? This misses a consistent theme of wisdom, that human claims of righteousness may conceal as well as reveal the self.

Which theological system will provide comprehensive ways of detecting human deceit and encouraging a clear knowledge of self and God?

1

The Significance of a
Theological System

Some systematic presentation of the life of Jesus and his impact upon disciples is necessary for comprehensive, integrative approximations of righteousness and for the detection of deceits, disguises, and distortions of the truth about God, ourselves, and others.

There is an advantage and a danger in any system of thought. Analysis and synthesis are primary in attaining comprehensiveness and cohesion, but we must also recognize intuition and deep personal assumptions in the structuring of our response to sacred concerns. There is such an interplay of the rational and the experiential in our commitment to God with heart, mind, and soul that we must evaluate any organization of thought with questions like this: How much of our life is revealed and what is concealed as we formulate our knowledge of God?[1]

One system will concentrate upon mental processes and inhibit emotional life. Rational propositions will be proclaimed as the whole knowledge of God and assent to these intellectual formulations will be equated with saving knowledge of God and sufficient inquiry into the self.[2]

Another system will exclude rationality, and enthusiastically identify a knowledge of God's will with supposedly spontaneous human

3

sensations. The followers of this way will devalue any orderly proclamation of the Gospel or discipleship and concentrate upon systematic expectation of emotional and physical signs that God's power has instantly solved any problem.[3]

Both extremes in theology may be rejected by a third way of thinking that is organized around psychological knowledge. The propositions of theology are redefined into helpful explanations of human conditions. The knowledge of God becomes a useful part of the ego's search for self-realization and social integration.[4]

What is the significance of wisdom in any of these approaches to the knowledge of God and self? What is revealed and what is concealed about the self and about God? And why?

Direct and Mediated Revelation

Each of these theologies perpetuates some concealment. Propositional theology disguises personal preferences and avoidance of emotional conflicts under assurances that dependence upon dogma will solve all problems. Sensational theology either ignores or encourages the obsessive rationalizations with which troubled people justify their search for absolute assurance and final answers to obscure and complex problems of living. Self-realization theories with theological phrases obscure the fear of death and evil by limiting knowledge to that which humans can comprehend and possibly control.

I have singled out these overbalanced theologies (weighted either toward head or heart, God or humanity) because they are the most troublesome in counsel. When we discern one of these sets of assumptions, how do we assist ourselves and our clients toward more balance between head and heart, divine revelation and human response?

Start with some reflection on the client's characteristic way of thinking about God and self. Discern whether it is a conscious and coherent formulation or an unexamined arrangement of explanations for success and tragedy, living and dying. What is the dynamic reason that a client would rely upon a part of the truth about God and self yet neglect other essential elements? Will people admit the ways in which they receive that which they are willing to reveal before God and conceal the rest? It's a question that made one audience mad enough to attack Jesus (John 8:42–59).

I developed some idea of why Jesus took that risk when my wife, Donna and I were copastors of a West Hollywood congregation in the 1980s. We wanted to build a theological and psychological support structure for single adults, who were most evident in the worship services.

The scene cried out for decisive action. People clung to the church as a refuge from incestuous families, manipulative spouses, promiscuous roommates, or incessant loneliness in a rented room. Sunday worship and Thursday prayer services were their feeding places after extractive relations in the day and haunting nighttime memories of rejection during childhood (if we could call their early years childhood). Their desire was for a succession of extraordinary signs to shore up their massive insecurity with absolute certainties and to provide invulnerability to pain, indecision, and anxiety.

In the midst of their chronic uncertainties and crippling habits, Donna and I stressed mediation in worship, with teachings from the Scriptures and discussions of the ways in which each member had an impact on the life of another member. We kept relating the content of theology to the way in which we receive and respond to God's message as individuals—influenced by many delayed messages from the past—in a particular fellowship.[5]

It was a disaster. As one member said, "You feed us from the Word and give me thoughts to control the garbage in my mind. But it's not enough. I need to feel that white light in my soul every Sunday; it's like a laser that cuts through the accumulation of crud that I keep going back to during the week. I don't get that healing sensation in our services anymore."

Another said, "You quote Scripture to sneak in some psychology— and we learn from that—but where's the Spirit? The Spirit leads me directly. Where's your authority? What signs do you show us? I *know* what God intends for me because I hear him directly. I don't need any *man* between me and God."

Is that member right? Yes and no. The knowledge of God came directly to prophets (Isa. 6) and apostles (Acts 2:1-4; 9:3-6; 11:9-21). They had direct, authoritative knowledge of God. But "not all are apostles or prophets or teachers" (1 Cor. 12:29). There are variations in the sense of immediacy among gifts and no one is to raise one gift above another because it has more instantaneous impact upon an audience (1 Cor. 13:1-3, 8-10). The apostle Paul warns against "anyone who claims to be superior because of special visions" (Col. 2:18).

Paul's answer to questions of theological communication was to demonstrate love—the highest gift—in honest, intelligible messages which bring as much sensible conviction to those who hear as to the one who speaks (1 Cor. 12:31-14:26). This is mediated revelation, not only because of the way in which theology is made known between people, but also because of a belief about the way in which the will of God should consistently be known to any person— through faith, hope, and love (1 Cor. 13:13).[6]

"The message you heard from the very beginning is this: we must love one another" (1 John 3:11). It is the message of Christ, the mediator between God and his creation (1 Tim. 2:5; Heb. 8:6; 9:15; 12:24), which guides our lives through the mediation of the Holy Spirit. This is how we receive the truth of God. Those who bypass this inspired witness, and proclaim independent knowledge of God without human fellowship are liars (1 John 2:20-23).

Love reconciles directly with mediated revelation through this insistence: "No one has ever seen God, but if we love one another, God lives in union with us, and his love is made perfect in us" (1 John 4:12). The perfect answer for human imperfection and un-certainty is neither in faithful recitation of logical teaching from the patriarchs, nor in hope that today we'll experience all they received in a special revelation.

Perfect knowledge of God is the direct assurance through our conscience that we love as he first loved us. And how do we know how to love? Through the mediated testimony of those who wrote about what they heard and saw in God's Son (1 John 1:1-7; 5:1-3), confirmed by the present testimony of the Spirit in us.[7]

Divine and Human Testimony

When we interlock the knowledge of self and God, theology is a source for discernment and commitment despite potential deception and misinterpretation (James 1:22-27; 1 John 2:9-11).[8] For example, in chapter 7 we will see how an irate husband wants to concentrate upon the sin of adultery. His wife wants to talk about his beating her. The pastor asks if they have considered the way in which God has forgiven each of them and the way in which they are to forgive each other. She is willing to consider this major doctrine of the faith, but he is not. He is "selectively inattentive," returning again and again to the question of control over his wife that would come through condemning her for adultery. For the pastor, the doctrine of forgiveness and the numerous divine-human encounters of Scripture on forgiveness are vital checkpoints to the husband's selective inattention. As the pastor asks more and more about this emphasis upon adultery, he finds that the husband had been shaken by the surprise knowledge of his mother's adultery when he was a child. He had devoted his life to the prevention of such a shock in his own marriage. This was an area of the self that he had not explored or offered to God for a renewal of trust and faith in himself and others.

Any distortion of mediated revelation is an alarm bell, warning of inner deceit or conceit. An example is presented in chapter 9, where Helen claims to have complete discernment of good and evil thoughts in her husband. But this attributing of a godly characteristic to herself is not matched by any dependence upon the Word of God. All that Helen does is by her own strength. She uses characteristics of spirituality to hide her uncertainty about herself and her desire to dominate and control her husband. If she were more willing to know herself, she would have more accurate knowledge of God.

In the case of Helen, the pastor referred repeatedly to the historical revelation of God in Christ as presented in the Scriptures. He "tested the spirits" to see if the characteristics mentioned by Helen were those that the Scriptures attribute to any human person. He did not find what she affirmed. In this he was loyal to the theological objective of a knowledge of self, which is to know more about God at the same time that we know more about self. The incarnation of God in Christ was his point of reference for any discussion of spirituality in the life of Helen, and the gateway to any true knowledge of herself.

The Nature of Theological Statements

But how do we and our counselees know whether we are talking about the power of God or the power of a human sentiment? Since we need to grow in knowledge of ourselves and God, we cannot neglect either set of terms. Despite our best intentions, we find that it is often difficult to clarify the terms with which we seek to show the correlation of divine and human power. In fact, the understanding that we have of statements about psychological or theological power will often reveal our unspoken preference for one or the other.[9]

In *Thinking About God*, Professor John Macquarrie of Oxford University provides some specific criteria for any statements that we would call "theological."[10] I would adapt these for purposes of Christian counsel.

(1) Confession of faith in God by counselor, and often by the counselee.

(2) Characteristics of the counselor's attitudes and language that are congruent with counselor's and the counselee's understanding of what the Church confesses to be Christian faith.

(3) An experience by the counselor of communion with God as the companion of those who surrender their lives to Him, and the expectation of this companionship for the counselee.

(4) A comparison of experienced faith with other convictions and experiences of life that might be shared by the counselor and the counselee.

(5) A confession that God has presented himself concretely in revelatory events and persons which culminate in the Incarnation of God in Jesus Christ, as recorded in the Scriptures and apprehended in the work of the Spirit among us.

(6) A conceptual presentation of the mystery and transcendence of God by the counselor, who confesses that the Divine Being is not a subject to be grasped by the mind of humans.

These characteristics enable us to answer some questions about theology in counseling: How do we identify divine and human power in the solution of personal problems, and what are the areas of life in which a person will permit the knowledge of God to make a difference?[11]

This sounds very analytical, rational. To guard against the preoccupation of traditional systematic theology with "left brain" definitions, we must remember that the essence of theology is an intuitive awareness of something beyond ourselves. This is "spiritual theology," an ancient term that Kenneth Leach defines as the "search for a transforming knowledge of God" in his excellent study of *Experiencing God* (San Francisco: Harper and Row, 1985).

The Personal Hiding Place

The varied impressions and definitions of love (or its absence) will help us recognize the areas in which we reveal or conceal ourselves whenever we think of spirituality or theology. This is the direction in which wisdom would lead us as we try to explain God and ourselves. Such wisdom is "like good medicine, healing your wounds and easing your pains" (Prov. 3:8).

Why this emphasis upon "heal our wounds and ease our pains" through a theological system? Wisdom reminds us of a continual tendency to hide a wounded or unacceptable self. Some persons use intellectualism as a defense against unacceptable emotions. Others use supercharged emotions as a release from the tension of reflective thought. Neither would accept a third system, mediated theology, in which the Spirit of God guides the movement of love through both head and heart according to the record of the incarnation of God's love in Christ. Why? Because mediated theology opens the self to the self, mind to heart, and one person to another. There's no hiding place, not even in our thoughts of God, for this system insists that the knowledge of self and the knowledge of God grow together.

We must admit that fear and defensiveness may lead us to organize God's love through the security of a propositional system of theology which leaves people obedient, but unhealed of their blindness.[12] We may think logically about truth, beauty, and justice and still retain the presuppositions of thought that prevent us from seeing like Jesus, because our theology does not challenge the way we see ourselves and others (John 9:30–41).

The second system—or non-system—appears in periods when hurt seems beyond endurance. In such a time, anxious, anonymous individuals in a group will view an overpowering sensation of acceptance as "spirituality." The danger amid these sudden delights is an unthinking enthusiasm which leads to an exaggeration of direct revelation by discarding the biblical balance of communication with content. We saw this in people who just came to church because they wanted to feel good and experience a "white light" that would "clean them up" for the week, instead of dealing with the problems of their daily lives and their own ineffective ways of problem-solving.

The distortion occurs when there is no discernment of human response. There is such relief from former deprivation and such fascination with "signs and wonders" that the self is obliterated. One pastor told me, "Forget all that self-analysis. Paul commanded us to cast down all human imagination. Look only to Jesus. He's all power and we're nothing." Later I thought, I wonder if he has read James's warning against self-deception. Maybe he looked into the mirror of the self one time and didn't like what he saw (James 1:22–25). It is a tragedy to observe a theology that perpetuates human deceit. But it's understandable. The promises of power, known through sensations, bring instant relief and weekly reassurance. The secret compulsions of the self are not revealed; addictive thinking is hidden under repression and a special language that allows for emotional release without convicting confessions. The communication system is full of final answers and conversation-stoppers, such as: This is God's sign to me. I don't question. I am obedient.

To what is the person obedient? In a mediated theology, both the will of God and the will of his servants must be investigated. This is the foundation for wise counsel that seeks reconciliation of both human and divine disclosures:

> True and substantial wisdom principally consists of two parts, the knowledge of God, and the knowledge of ourselves. But while these two branches of knowledge are so intimately connected, which of them proceeds and produces the other is not easy to discover . . . no man can take a survey of himself but he must immediately turn to the contemplation of God, in whom he "lives and moves."[13]

NOTES

1. The complementary interaction of intuition and intellect in theology has been enthusiastically presented by James B. Ashbrook, *The Brain and Belief* (Bristol: I. N. Windham Hall Press, 1988). Professor Ashbrook's emphasis is upon research on left and right brain influences upon belief and behavior.
2. In the American tradition, propositional theology is commonly associated with the writings of B. B. Warfield or Cornelius VanTil. The "presuppositional"

counseling that follows this theology will rely upon a series of biblical proof-texts to guide decisions, as in the writings of Jay Adams, *Competent to Counsel* (Grand Rapids: Baker Book House, 1970). See James A. Oakland *et al.*, "An Analysis and Critique of Jay Adams's Theory of Counseling," *Journal of the American Scientific Affiliation*, September, 1976, pp. 101–109; John D. Carter, "Adams's Theory of Nouthetic Counseling," *Journal of Psychology and Theology*, 1975, 3, 143–55.

3. The sensationalists (or "enthusiasts" as Luther called them) rely heavily upon claims of "signs and wonders" to "empower" believers, as in the writings of John Wimber, *Power Evangelism* (San Francisco: Harper, 1986) and Peter Wagner, *How To have a Healing Ministry Without Making Your Church Sick* (Ventura, CA: Regal, 1988). For study of a similar emphasis in seventeenth and eighteenth century English and French Quakers, Methodists, Jansenists, and Quietists, plus some hard-earned lessons about the need for historical faith to be a guide for personal experience, see Ronald A. Knox, *Enthusiasm* (New York: Oxford University Press, 1961).

4. The most insightful writer on psychological definitions (and reduction) of theology may have been the Methodist, John Cobb, *Theology and Pastoral Care*. In writings from the psychology-of-religion point of view, Jungian analysis presents religious symbols as clues to unconscious processes.

5. The classic example of mediated revelation is the conversion of Saul. It is partially direct—Jesus speaks to him and Paul ever after, based his apostleship on this immediate apprehension of the risen Lord—but it is mediated through his experiences with others. The content of the revelation testifies to the impact of events as preparation in Saul's conscience for this confrontation: "Saul, Saul, Why do you persecute me?" (Acts 9:4–5). Saul's consent to the murder of Stephen sets the stage for revelation (Acts 8:1) and the visit to Ananias completes it (Acts 9:10–19). Again, the content of the revelation includes human action and relationships: "But get up and go into the city, where you will be told what you must do" (Acts 9:6).

The immediate sensation was powerful enough to knock Paul to the ground, but that was not identified in scripture as filling by the Spirit. He had to be obedient to the directions of the vision and become dependent upon the ministry of another disciple before he was healed and strengthened by the Spirit of Jesus (Acts 9:17–19). This is mediated revelation.

Mediated theology is expressed in worship, which is a "doxological" system of theology. Doxology is adoration of God on the basis of his revelation in mighty works and inspired persons. Wolfhart Pannenberg explains doxological as a mediated knowledge of God. It is indirect knowledge of the Creator through his works. To this extent, God is hidden and mysterious. No system of human thought or words can fully reveal who he is. Any words by which we seek to explain him must be surrendered to a higher purpose, which is his praise. See Wolfhart Pannenberg, *Basic Questions in Theology* (London: SCM Press, 1970), vol. 1, chap. 7, esp. pp. 215–34.

6. J. Christiaan Becker describes the sources of mediation in the writings of the apostle Paul as a continual search for "internal coherence" and "contingency

interpretation." *Paul the Apostle* (Philadelphia: Fortress Press, 1984), pp. 11–108. An example in American theology would be Jonathan Edwards, *Religious Affections* (1746).

7. Relevant passages from the Calvin's *Institutes* on the authority of Scripture and the internal testimony of the Holy Spirit are condensed by Hugh Thomas Kerr, *A Compend of the Institutes of the Christian Religion by John Calvin* (Philadelphia: Presbyterian Board of Christian Education, 1939), pp. 13–19.

8. John Calvin expressed the dependence of human knowledge upon divine knowledge thusly: "The knowledge of ourselves is not only an incitement to seek after God, but likewise a considerable assistance toward finding Him. On the other hand, it is plain that no man can arrive at the true knowledge of himself, without having first contemplated the divine character, and then descended to the consideration of his own." (John Calvin, *Institutes of the Christian Religion* (Philadelphia: Presbyterian Board of Education, 1936), vol. 1, p. 48).

9. Theologians often construct a theological system that is unknowingly shaped by their own psychological dynamics. This is the thesis of Oscar Pfister, *Christianity and Fear* (London: George Allen and Unwin, 1948).

10. John Macquarrie, *Thinking about God* (New York: Harper and Row, 1975), pp. 7–17.

11. A caution: no organization of theological propositions is to be identified as the power of God. He is not confined to any system we devise. As Søren Kierkegaard declared: "an existential system is impossible. Existence itself is a system—for God; but it cannot be a system for any existing spirit." Søren Kierkegaard, *A Kierkegaard Anthology*, ed. Robert Bretall (Princeton: Princeton University Press, 1951), p. 201. Martin Buber used a conversation between two God-fearers to present the problem of implicit versus explicit theological communication in *Eclipse of God* (New York: Harper and Brothers, 1952), chap. 1.

12. Two defenses are offered by some dogmaticians for the absence of reference to human response. One was found by Jacob Firet among Dutch Reformed theologians who thought that an emphasis upon the human condition was a "works righteousness." They maintained a doctrine of the Holy Spirit in which a person would be nurtured without any reference to human guidance. See Jacob Firet, *Dynamics in Pastoring*, pp. 102–107. The other defense would come from the academic followers of the early writings of Karl Barth, in which he maintains that any study of anthropology must be a study of the Christ alone. Consequently, Barth's anthropological writings contain only one reference to psychology, which is a statement about Wilhelm Wundt, the father of "brass instrument" psychology in the 1880s. Karl Barth, *Church Dogmatics* (Edinburgh: T. and T. Clark, 1960), vol. 3, pt. 2, pp. 286, 428.

13. Calvin, *Institutes*, vol. 1, p. 47. "The intimate connection between two branches of knowledge" in Calvin's writings would be called "correlation" in the writings of Paul Tillich. See Tillich's *Systematic Theology* (Chicago: University of Chicago Press, 1957), vol. 1. The value of this system was weakened by the wide range of concepts that Tillich sought to correlate. Adrian

Thatcher faults Tillich for the many inconsistencies. Ontological terms such as being, power being, dynamics, nonbeing, essence, potentiality, existence, and actuality were defined in various contexts and functions in contradictory manners. Adrian Thatcher, *The Ontology of Paul Tillich* (Oxford: Oxford University Press, 1978).

The meaning of correlation in theology has been considered by others besides Tillich, such as Tracy and Browning. David Tracy, in *Blessed Rage for Order* (New York: Seabury Press, 1979), criticizes Tillich and asserts that secular answers as well as secular questions should be considered in any discussion of theological correlation (p. 46). In *Religious Ethics and Pastoral Care* (Philadelphia: Fortress Press, 1983), Don Browning relates correlation to pastoral care with the assertion that questions and answers derived from various interpretations of the central Christian witness may be correlated with questions and answers that are implicit in various interpretations of ordinary human experience.

Some theologians and biblical scholars have provided examples of the type of correlation that is defined by Browning, such as Shirley C. Guthrie's "Pastoral Counseling, Trinitarian Theology, and Christian Anthropology," *Interpretation*, April 1979, pp. 130–143, and Walter Brueggemann, "Covenanting as Human Vocation: A Discussion of the Relation of Bible and Pastoral Care," *Interpretation*, April, 1979, pp. 115–128.

2

The Trinity:
The Self-Revealing Fellowship

The doctrine of the Trinity is the beginning of a mediated theology. Content and communication are combined in the faith-assertion that we experience God in the intercommunication of Father, Son, Holy Spirit.[1]

Knowledge of the Trinity is also the model for our human reception of the Word. This was the affirmation of Augustine in section 14 of *On the Trinity*. Imagery, thought, and volition are the human channels through which persons develop a loving understanding of self in re-membering and understanding the loving relationships of the Trinity.[2] An awareness of our original creation as persons-in-relationship is prompted and guided by Jesus' statements that his relation to the Father will shape our relation to him and to each other.[3]

The trinitarian theme of persons-in-relationship is often repeated in Christian counsel. It was prominent in my counsel with a thirty-year-old artist, Michael. He came to his first interview with a question, "Do you think that I am manic?" After some inquiry about his episodes of grandiosity, I agreed with the diagnosis made by his psychiatrist and asked why he wanted to talk with a pastor. He replied, "Well, I really want to find out if I understand the way things really are. Should I have these feelings of wanting to help everybody? Am I just serving myself—building myself up—or do I really want to build up other people?"

Neither of us could answer that question in the first interview. But in our ten interviews we found continual conflict between Michael's desire for a comfortable life without responsibility versus his desire to be kind to people and his desire for self-actualization. Our conversation generated two insights that came out of my trinitarian belief.

(1) Responsible fellowship is more important than personal introspection.

(2) A sense of awe before the mystery of the Trinity and our creation in the image of God is more appropriate for limited human beings than the pursuit (usually psychological) of total knowledge of self or fascination with personal religious experience.[4]

The Responsible Fellowship

One of Michael's continuing concerns during our fourth interview was self-love versus service to others. His questions led me continually to the "oneness" theme of John 17:11-12, 20-26: we know and fulfill ourselves in self-giving that is empowered by the unity of Father and Son. The Trinity is model and motivator of our lives.

I was fascinated by the frequent references to self-love versus service in biblical references to Father, Son, and Holy Spirit. Jesus is revealed to be the Son through God's voice at his baptism (Mark 1:11) and by the spirit power given him to do mighty works (John 5:19-22, 36; 10:31-38). The Son reveals the Father (John 14:1-11; Matt. 11:27), who grants him those who will come to the Son for salvation (John 1:12; 6:65; 10:27-30; 17:2, 6-13). To love the Father is to love the Son who is begotten of him (John 8:42; 14:20-24; 15:23; 16:25-28). It is through the Son that we learn to pray to the Father as "our Father" (Matt. 6:9; Luke 11:2). In this harmony of relationships, Jesus proclaimed the kingdom of God (Mark 1:15). The character of the kingdom is known in the ministry of the Son (Matt. 11:4-6; Luke 7:22). Through his perfect obedience to the Father, the kingdom of the Father becomes the kingdom of his beloved Son (Phil. 2; Col. 1:13; Eph. 5:5).

The Holy Spirit empowers the Son's proclamation of the work of the Father's kingdom (Luke 4:18–21). This is the Spirit of God that leads the Son through his ministry (Matt. 3:16–4:1; 12:28), through "the eternal Spirit" the surrender through the Father of the Son takes place at the cross (Heb. 9:14). The death of the Son upon the cross is part of the eternal obedience which he has rendered to the Father through the Spirit whom he receives through the Father (Eph. 1). "The Father is crucifying love, the Son is crucified love, and the Holy Spirit is the unvanquishable power of the cross."[5]

The love that characterizes the Trinity is vulnerable, open, self-giving, and self-revealing (John 3:16–21; 5:20; 10:17; 15:9; 17:20–26; 1 John 4:16, Rom. 5). It is the model for our own openness to one another. Through this sharing we know ourselves as friends. Christian friendship is measured by faithfulness and self-disclosure (John 15:11–15).

From these Scriptures I conclude that the intimate disclosure of Jesus to his disciples is the basic content of Christian counsel. Jesus' sharing of his relation to the Father is a model for our communication with the Father and with others: the model prayer (Matt. 6:7–15; cf. Jesus' prayer to the Father in John 17) is of a son to the Father; the disciples are included in the fellowship of Jesus' prayer to the Father as he reveals the most intimate trial of his life, the temptation and the agony of the garden. Paul summarizes this Father-Son communication that includes the disciples in his affirmation that God has broken down both the barriers that separate us from Him and the barriers that separate us from one another (Eph. 2; John 15:12–17).

The realization of ourselves through sharing with others was a theme that came up in almost every interview with Michael. It appeared in our first and second interviews as he talked about the value of omnipotent fantasies.

Michael: My therapist says that I become manic whenever I want to get back at members of my family or retreat into irresponsibility. Do you really think that I am that sick?

Sam: The psychiatrist can tell you how sick you are. I can tell you that he is right in relating illness to a sense of responsibility.

Michael: Well, there are times when I feel very responsible for other people. I want to do a good job at work. I want to care for the women that I have loved. In fact, when I get sick that's all I want to do, provide the best for everybody in the world. I would like to make everybody happy.

Sam: This sounds like a very godly attribute.

Michael: That's just it! When I'm sick I think that I am Jesus. I can be stronger than Jesus because I can do things for people without having to die, but then I get all messed up and when I am better I know that I cannot do much for anybody.

Sam: Maybe if you saw how much you could do and how much others could do there would be greater satisfaction.

Michael: Yeah, I can't set any limits. I feel like I will do it all by myself. I want to get all the credit and be loved by everybody. Is that godly?

Sam: You have the right idea, but in the wrong place. You're taking God's place in distributing perfect love and happiness. From my point of view, we are only servants of God in trying to do this. This is the way in which I'm able to accept some of my limitations in doing good.

Michael: Well, so far I have difficulty in accepting mine when I get sick. When I'm not sick I think that I am so limited that I can't do anything.

Sam: That's a good summary of the way in which you are more than responsible some of the time and less than responsible the rest of the time.

In the fourth interview, after we had talked for about fifteen minutes, there was more to be said about responsibility.

Michael: You know what I've decided? What I really don't like about life is the realization that I can't be God. You seem to accept the idea that you're not God, but it really provokes me. I want to do everything without any restrictions and without any risk. I want people to worship me, but I don't want to be too close to them. Do you see what I mean?

17

Sam: Well, intellectually I get the point and it is an important one. My feelings have never been quite as grandiose as yours so I can't participate in all of that, but I
get the idea that you can't do what you want for people
because you think that it has to be a solo performance.

Michael: Well, I want people to admire me and all that. It's just
that I like to do it by myself. Why can't I?

Sam: Because we were not created that way. For one thing I
believe that we are created to be servants of God and
therefore we have to be in fellowship with him if we
are going to do anything good. Also I think that he
created us to be in fellowship with one another and no
one of us can do all the good for the rest.

Later, the sense of responsible fellowship began to appear in specific
issues, as demonstrated in our fifth interview.

Michael: I really think that I've had enough of my therapist.
She told me that romance could not be a part of our
therapy.

Sam: When did she say that?

Michael: Well that was months ago when I first began to see her.
I told her what a beautiful woman she was and how I
would like to have a date with her and she said that the
only way for me to see her was as a patient.

Sam: So what's wrong with this?

Michael: Well, I'm in group therapy also and last night one of
the women told the therapist that she thought that he
was very handsome and loving and she would like to
go to bed with him. And he didn't tell her that she was
just a patient. He said that sexual feelings are a part
of therapy and that he appreciated how she felt about
him, but that it was not appropriate for them to do
anything more than talk about it. So why can't my
therapist be like that?

Sam: Well, I don't know. Are you going to ask her? She can
tell you much better than I can.

Michael: Oh, that would hurt her. So I think that I will just
leave the therapy and invent a good reason for it, like

18

	the way that I am getting better now and don't have so many omnipotent fantasies.
Sam:	That doesn't sound so good to me. We've talked about the importance of responsibility and loving, and now it looks like you're going to reject your therapist because you think that she has rejected you. And you will not be telling her why.
Michael:	So why do you think I should tell her?
Sam:	Tell her because of what we have said about love for one another. If you draw back in isolation, you're not being responsible to another human being.
Michael:	Well I'll think about it. Then what about this idea of me getting out of therapy because I feel better?

At the end of the next interview there were more questions about responsible fellowship.

Michael:	Well, I didn't tell my therapist what I thought about her. I just decided to stay with her. After all, I guess I still have some problems. I don't like my mother and father. It's getting worse because they do things to help me like paying for my therapy and inviting me with the rest of the family to vacations in Hawaii. What am I supposed to say when they do things like that?
Sam:	Well, what have you said so far?
Michael:	Well, I did write a birthday card for my father after the Hawaii trip and I read it when the family was all together for his birthday and I told him how much I appreciated the trip and how much the rest of us appreciated it also. But that's obligation isn't it?
Sam:	Sure. I like the fact that you are showing some appreciation for things that they do for you. It seems to me that they would not have so much power over you if you would openly tell them how much you appreciate them.
Michael:	But am I not supposed to be an independent person? Isn't that responsibility?
Sam:	You're not God. You can only lead a satisfying and healthy life when you depend upon other people in

19

some ways and they depend upon you. That's human responsibility. We have limitations and we help each other
with those limitations. And we express appreciation for
the help that we get.

Michael: Yeah, but I spent many hours of therapy talking about
how much I depend like a child upon my parents. What
about that? Isn't that sick?

Sam: Sure, but I don't want you to get fixed on some circle of
introspection. That is, if you keep on thinking that any
expression of gratitude is a sign of dependency, you'll
never act in a responsible way with other people so that
they will be happy to have you around them.

In later interviews, there was a continuing shift in Michael's feelings
toward awareness of the way that he did appreciate other people and
liked for them to appreciate him without his "being God." Although
I did not mention the Trinity as a doctrine in those parts of our
conversation, the Trinity was basic in my affirmation that we are
made for responsible dependency upon one another. I think that
Michael saw some connection between what I was saying and theology because of a comment that he made toward the end of the
second interview: "You seem to have this all together in your own
mind. You think that everything is OK for you because you see
yourself as a servant of Jesus. It's OK to be a servant because you
believe that God created us to be that way. So you don't have to be
omnipotent in order to help other people. Right?"[6]

The Mysterious Human

Michael's statement that "you don't have to be omnipotent" was a
statement of reconciliation to the limits in his own self-knowledge.
He didn't have to know everything that he wanted to know about
himself in order to have a workable purpose in life and contribute
to the welfare of others. As he said this, I thought, "Well, this is like
our knowledge of God. We don't have to know everything about
him to serve him with satisfaction. And just as there's some mystery
in him—like the Trinity—so he's created us with some mystery
about ourselves."

This conclusion seemed consistent with what I found in Scripture about "wisdom." The term is not a glorification of self-awareness. To have wisdom is to have enough knowledge of ourselves and God to take action—in our own lives and in our relations with others. This wisdom is the answer to the "knowledge for what" question that came up often in my conversations with Michael.

For example, in the first interview Michael describes what he thinks about when he is in a manic state and what he thinks about himself when he is not. My response was: "Maybe if you saw how much you could do and how much others could do there would be greater satisfaction." This is a summary statement, an attempt to point toward conclusions and action.

In the fourth interview, Michael asked a question about action that he should take.

Michael: Well, I want people to admire me and all that. It's just that I like to do it by myself. Why can't I?
Sam: Because we were not created that way . . .

I suggest a theory about life that will allow him to fit what he knows about himself into some plan. From this plan he will be able to settle into some kind of action.

The plan of action appears in the fifth interview when Michael says that he has a new knowledge about his therapist and that this will lead him to drop out of therapy. Instead, I suggest that he should use this knowledge as an opportunity to be more responsible and loving. This same emphasis appears later in the same interview as he talks about his mother and father. I praise him for writing a birthday card to his father and fit obligation and responsibility into the philosophy of life that should be important for him.

Michael answers the question "Knowledge for what?" at the beginning of the sixth interview by stating that his desire for unconditional love and total acceptance is an impossible search. He will have to come to some conclusions about life, such as the Christian conclusions, if he is going to move ahead with responsible decisions about life.

Now I would admit that it is easier to pursue this question "Knowledge for what?" with Michael than with a person who had not begun the process of exploring feelings and relating feelings to motivations and explanations for what we think or do. Many interviews with Michael would have included an emphasis upon his feelings if he had not previously been in therapy for a period of time or if he had not had the ability to quickly see the relationship of his feelings to action and motivation.

My emphasis is similar to that of Thomas Oden in *After Therapy What?*[7] Thomas Oden challenges Christian therapists to discuss Christian goals and objectives with their patients, to think about purposes of life that go beyond insight and acceptance of feelings.

My assumption behind this approach to counseling is that a sense of awe before God is more important than a sense of certainty in knowledge of ourselves.[8] Christian counsel is more concerned with the creation of spiritual conditions under which persons may learn to think about themselves as God thinks about them, than it is about the creation of comfortable conditions under which persons may ruminate about their own feelings. The latter is only significant as a phase of movement toward the former. In Christian counsel, an insightful self becomes a responsible self, responsible to God, to others, and to oneself.

NOTES

1. Because the Trinity reveals the content of God himself in revelation to us, the doctrine is considered primary by many theologians. Eberhard Jungel, *The Doctrine of the Trinity* (Grand Rapids: William B. Eerdmans, 1976), p. 3, considers the Trinity first in theology because it shows us the God who reveals himself in revelation. Until we know who is revealed, we cannot understand how and why the revelation comes to us.

2. Edmund Fortman considers this search for traces of the mystery of the Trinity in the world of creatures to be the most original of Augustine's contributions to the theology of the Trinity. (See Fortman's *The Triune God* [Philadelphia: Westminster Press, 1972], p. 148). The Augustinian tradition is traced in the modern theology formulations of Ebner, Moltmann, Bracken, Mühlen, and Von Balthasar in John O'Donnell, S. J., "The Trinity as Divine Community," *Gregorianum* 69/1 (1988) 5-34.

3. Fellowship is foundational for a theological interpretation of the Trinity, for the Trinity is God existing in a relationship where each Person finds existence and joy in the other Person. See Jürgen Moltmann, *The Trinity and the Kingdom* (San Francisco: Harper and Row, 1981), pp. 171-74.

4. When religious experience becomes an obsession, as Thomas Smail found among English charismatics, the Holy Spirit is an exclusive theological emphasis in which God as creator is forgotten. To remedy this, Smail wrote *The Forgotten Father* (Grand Rapids: William B. Eerdmans, 1980).

The Trinity: The Self-Revealing Fellowship

Who before *how* will distinguish Christian counsel from studies in the psychology of religion by psychologists and other studies of religion in the behavioral sciences. Christian counsel is based upon a belief that God *is*, and that the fact of his being precedes any inquiry concerning the way that he is known in the human soul. Because God is, his movement toward us will precede our awareness of him. He is the creator and we are the creature. He is the giver of life and knowledge, we are the grateful responders to his grace.

In contrast, psychological studies of the consciousness of God begin in personal awareness and proceed toward that which the subject calls God. As a scientist, the psychologist makes no judgment concerning the reality of God, but makes observations *as if* a worshiper is correct in his statements about the reality of the Deity. In the absence of any faith assumptions concerning the existence of God, the psychology of religion concentrates upon the process by which persons worship and the psychological state that conditions the type of theology to which they respond. The work is very valuable in these areas for Christian counselors, but it should not precede and certainly not replace a belief that God is, and that he has revealed himself through patriarchs, prophets, Christ, and the apostles.

One of the pioneers in pastoral psychology, Anton Boisen, was committed to the psychology of religion approach. In a criticism of Reinhold Niebuhr's *Human Nature and Destiny*, Boisen wrote: "I confess to difficulty in following professor Niebuhr's reasoning and in accepting the Christian religion as an authoritative revelation. For me, the primary sources of authority in religion are the living human documents, and I accept Christianity because its central insights seem to me to correspond with verifiable present day experience." (*The Chicago Theological Seminary Register*, January 1962, p. 32.)

A consistent emphasis upon trinitarian doctrine, especially the power of the Spirit, has been made by Wayne Oates in *Christ and Selfhood* (New York: Association Press, 1961); *Protestant Pastoral Counseling* (Philadelphia: Westminster Press, 1962); *The Holy Spirit in Five Worlds* (New York: Association Press, 1968).

5. Moltmann, *The Trinity and the Kingdom*, p. 83.

6. For a discussion of God's movement toward us see Jungel, *Doctrine of the Trinity*, p. 52.

7. Thomas Oden, *After Therapy What?* (Springfield, Illinois: Charles C. Thomas Co., 1974).

8. Oden refers to the pursuit of self-knowledge as "addictive accommodation" and presents the positive contribution of patristic theologians as an effort to recover the Christian balance between psychology and religion. Thomas C. Oden, *Agenda for Theology* (San Francisco: Harper and Row, 1979), pp. 22, 164ff.

3

The Incarnation
Divine Attitudes in Human Actions

In the previous chapter I reported attempts to bring insight and fellowship together in my conversations with Michael. We learned from each other in those sessions, but I'm not sure that the consistency of Michael's character was strengthened. We missed an effective element in wisdom, the power to move righteous attitudes into consistent actions.

In Christian counsel, the integrity of awareness leading to activity is centered in Christ, the wisdom and power of God. He embodies knowledge and obedience to God's will. Mediating theology is built upon the indivisible union of human and divine nature in his being.

How does the doctrine of the Incarnation move us from deception and procrastination to authentic actions that flow from loving attitudes?

The combination of authentic action with loving attitude is a major goal of counseling. In fact, it is the reason for many appointments with a counselor in the first place. People are troubled because they do not understand why they feel one thing and do another, or they report that actions are mechanical and that feelings are dead.

Where do we find the kind of power that enables us to combine attitude and action? In Christian counsel, empowering depends upon a basic doctrine of faith, the Incarnation.[1] Christ as the Word made flesh is the power for our personal unity in love (1 Cor. 2:10–16; 2 Cor. 5:16–21; 1 John; Gal. 5:22–26). The apostle Paul writes that God was in Christ reconciling the world to himself (2 Cor. 5:19). This was both an attitude of Father and Son to destine us in love to be his own (Eph. 1:5), and also an action by which Christ "emptied himself, taking the form of a servant, being born in the likeness of humanity" (Phil. 2:7 RSV). The action of obedience, even to dying on a cross, proclaimed the attitudes of love, humility, and obedience to God which glorified Son and Father (Phil. 2:8–11).

It is impossible to read any passage of Scripture about the Incarnation without a proclamation that attitude and action are combined. This should be enough to make the Incarnation central in any form of human counsel because the problem of attitude/action is so troublesome. But of greater importance is the unique way in which Christian faith combines attitude and action in a person—Christ Jesus. His life, death, and Resurrection combine attitude/action by combining divinity with humanity.

In this chapter we will combine attitude/action as a part of the Incarnation through three statements about the Spirit of Christ:

"The Word made flesh" is the *direct presence of God in human history* through his Son. Through the affirmation of his fully human life we believe that the Spirit of God will work in our own history as well. Doctrinally, we concentrate upon the historical details of the life of Christ in order that we may know how God works perfectly in a human being. Pastorally, we pay attention to all that we do and say so that we may know how the Spirit can duplicate in our lives the power displayed in the earthly existence of our Lord. The Incarnation is encouragement to see and state all that we are, for Jesus was completely like us, yet without sin (Heb. 4:14–16).

Attention to our history leads toward salvation because a power greater than ourselves is at work within us. We are not that power and we do not have the power to save ourselves. The motivation is from God. As Christ was obedient with unswerving faith to the Father in heaven, so we are to find salvation through the surrender of our mortal being to the eternal will of God. In the Incarnation we find both *model and motivator*.

Obedience is possible through the guidance of the Spirit, which

25

brings every thought into the obedience of Christ. The Spirit teaches us how attitudes and actions combine our human gifts with God's grace. This is the meaning of a *continuing incarnation*.

When these three statements are manifest in our counsel, then the Incarnation is recapitulated in the history of an individual. But the Incarnation will not provide power simply because we verbalize some of these statements. To believe that God was in Christ is to live as though his Spirit is primary in human empowerment (1 Thess. 1:4-7). Attitudes change and actions become authentic because the power that works in us is also working in a troubled person who believes that we can help (1 Thess. 1:6-10).

Divinity in Human Details

"Without the contingent details of Jesus' earthly life, God does not communicate himself."[2] Through the obedience of Christ to limitations of human life and death, every significant moral and spiritual option of life is made an occasion for the development of communion and obedience to the immortal God. The saving activity of God is known first in the human life of his Son and then in the recapitulation of his life in our own.

This development of the self toward salvation and sanctification was called "recapitulation" by an early father of the church, Irenaeus.[3] Recapitulation is the process by which a person identifies the deadness of self—in which attitude and actions are not united—and accepts Christ's life as the power and model for the union of attitudes and actions within self.

Recapitulation includes details of the life of Jesus and our own, but I do not consider this to be a mechanical attempt to live physically like Jesus—a celibate itinerant teacher with one pair of sandals. I mean a concern for the way in which the Gospel narratives remind us of how we all develop as human beings before God.

The process of recapitulation may be described in stages, each of which I will identify from a pastor's conversations with Mac. Mac, a handsome man in his early thirties, had come to see a pastor who "knew something about suicide." His wife, whom the pastor had already seen, had attempted suicide because she felt that he had neglected her. Now he told the pastor of his many good intentions, but of his difficulty putting them into action.

Pastor: It seems that you always want to do the right thing, but something is always getting in the way.

Mac: Yes, I guess that's so. In my business you have to spend a lot of social time with customers. That's what happens to my evenings.

Pastor: Would you say that the money you make is one of the things that you really live for?

Mac: Who wouldn't say that? All the sales meetings that I go to are built around that. But it wouldn't be fair to say that's all that I want. I also want to be promoted. I'd like to be president of the company some day.

Pastor: From what I know about you that seems to be the consuming goal of your life.

Mac: Well, you can't have everything and I've decided that once I have the money and the position I can then do some of the things that I want. The problem is, I can't make my wife happy while I am getting to the place where I could make her happy, if you see what I mean.

Pastor: You think that if you make the money and have the position, you would then have some time and interest in her?

Mac: Something like that. I really do love her and want her to be happy, but I just forget about some of the things that I ought to do for her. We don't have any big fights or anything, I just don't pay attention to her when she talks to me sometimes. Then she sits in the corner and looks sad. But I don't do anything about it.

Pastor: Why not?

Mac: Well, it's just one of those things.

Pastor: Ah, but it is more than that. It is probably the big issue that I keep talking about in sermons, but I can't always get the results that I want when I am talking with individuals like you.

Mac: What do you mean?

Pastor: We are up against the question of a man's contribution to life. What does he really live for? If he lives for what he can get out of life, which is the way I see you right now, then some people are going to be hurt if they depend on him. On the other hand, if he lives for what he

27

can contribute to life, then he can see the necessity of caring for those who love him and he will make time for that. We invest ourselves in that which means the most to us.

Mac: Yeah, that makes sense. So you think that I'm more interested in getting than giving?

Pastor: That puts it well.

Mac: So what do you think should happen?

Pastor: I think that my talk will not cause anything to happen so long as you are satisfied with the way things are going. I really think that I lack the power to do more than raise some questions. Some power from God has to make a change in you. When you get the idea that you are created to love and devote yourself to others, then you will begin to take some steps in that direction. But right now you look at the picture without any particular concern, other than for the general convenience of your wife—so long as that does not require much expenditure of energy on your part over a long period of time.

Mac: Well, that's quite a speech but I think that you've hit the nail on the head. I do get scared and pay attention to her for a few days or weeks, but then I get back to what I have to do.

Pastor: Yes, that phrase "what I have to do" is a sign of why I cannot change you myself.

Mac: Well, I do appreciate what you do for Sandra and me. She always feels better after she's talked with you, and you make good sense to me.

Pastor: Well, I'm glad to hear that. Perhaps we can talk again and I can find out more of why you've come to the conclusions you have about what you are going to get out of life. Would next week at this same time be OK?

In what ways does this interchange demonstrate recapitulation of Adam and Christ in us?

The pastor is trying to get to the *first stage of recapitulation* with Mac. That is, we want him to review his history as "Adam," the human in the flesh who has failed because of the temptations that are common to all humanity. But the pastor cannot lead him *to identify emotionally with his failures* in the way that Paul identifies with his failures in Romans 5–7.

Mac will not identify emotionally with what has happened to him. Emotional identification should be the *second step in our recapitulation* of the history of Jesus in our own lives. It is *the congruence of Jesus with our deepest feelings*, proclaimed in Hebrews 4:14–16 and 5:7–8. With "cries and groanings," the author of Hebrews describes the prayer of Jesus to the Father in the Garden of Gethsemane. All that any human person could experience in suffering and temptation has been emotionally experienced by our Lord in the days of his flesh.

This step in recapitulation is similar to the passion narratives, which do not present Jesus as a socratic figure who looks upon death philosophically, but as a person with the full range of human emotions, which included grief, love, anger, and anguish—yet without sin.

Mac is emotionally blocked from admitting his anguish. In a later interview the pastor noted his indifference to feelings, his own and those of others.

Pastor: So, how did you grow up to be so indifferent to other people and, as I see it, indifferent to yourself?

Mac: Well, I don't see that I am indifferent to myself. I dress well and I try to do the things that will impress others. Isn't that supposed to be one of my problems?

Pastor: Yes. What I mean is that you think well of yourself on the outside, and hope to get things done for yourself, but you don't act like someone who has been well cared for.

Mac: What do you mean?

Pastor: I mean that you are very anxious for the things that you can get and not anxious about the deepest relationships that would count for most people. Most people consider love and loyalty important because it has been important to them since childhood. But these things don't seem to be especially important to you, so I assume that they were not much in the picture of your life in the past.

Mac: Well, you might have something there. My father made lots of money when he was sober, and I always hoped that I could get as good commissions as he would get from sales. But he never had any time for me or my mother. I guess he loved me in his way, but I never thought about

29

him loving me. Sometimes I thought about my mother caring for me, but it was more a matter of polishing my shoes and brushing my teeth than anything else.

Pastor: So, unless something happens, you will probably go the same way as your father?

Mac: Yeah, and I guess that sometimes that does scare me. He was a very lonely person. He had lots of things, but he was unhappy. He was a big man for a while, but he was not much of a man around the house. Do you think I could be different from him?

Pastor: Well, that depends on several things. Do you have any examples of a more loving kind of relationship than you saw in your own family?

Mac: Oh yes. John and Alice, a couple that we visit from time to time, are just what I would like to be. He's our district manager and he really has it all together. He loves his wife and you can see that she loves him. The kids are happy to be at home. He makes money and knows what to do with it. Yeah, that's what I would like to be.

Pastor: So now that we have a model we need to think about the power that would mold you in that direction.

Mac: Yeah, well, I would like to be that way.

The father was distant from Mac and Mac is distant from himself and everyone else. Perhaps in his contacts with loving people he may see how much he has missed in life and begin to admit the pain and loneliness of growing up without love. But so far, judging from the pastor's verbatim, he will not do this. There are no "cries and groanings" that he is willing to utter from the depths of his history as a human being.

In the earthly life of Jesus there were "loud cries and groanings" (Heb. 5:7), which continually draw us to compare ourselves with him (Heb. 4:14–16). When we study *his life as an answer to temptation* we have entered a *third stage in recapitulation*.

There is no rejection or loneliness experienced by Mac that has not been met in the Gospel account of Jesus' life or the meditations of the Epistles upon his suffering. Mark 14:32–42 describes the shattering horror of anticipated suffering in the soul of Jesus. The language of distress is so strong that James Dunn notes the softening of Mark's

30

stark language into the lighter "sad, distress, grave" of Matthew's account (Matt. 26:37).[4]

Mac, who lacks the courage to openly admit his pain, could take courage from the Master Healer who restored function to the hand of a man who stood amid sullen religious leaders who condemned one who did good on the Sabbath (Mark 3:1–6).

If Mac is like many other men with a similar history, there is unexpressed grief because the child in him has died. Would he be able to weep as Jesus wept for the death of one whom he loved? (John 11:35) Would he ever be able to feel pity for the father who could not love him, as Jesus loved a widow who wearily followed the coffin of her only son? (Luke 7:13) If Mac could open his heart in this way, then he might be able to receive the love of his wife even as Jesus tenderly received the caresses of children who were like the first fruits of the kingdom of God to him (Mark 10:16). This might penetrate his "hardness of heart" (Mark 3:5).

Some of these comparisons could have made a difference for Mac when, in a later interview, he raised a question about his relationship with Sandra.

Mac: Well, why couldn't we live together without making any demands on each other? She wants to know what time I will come home for supper, or what I will do with her on the weekends, or whether or not we will buy a house. How can I answer those questions and get ahead in my business? And besides, I want to be my own man. If she would just let me love her when I want to, then we could get along much better. But when she makes demands on me, I don't have any use for her. She ought to understand that and let me alone at those times.

Pastor: I hope that she is learning to do that. But that just reduces the tension, it doesn't cause any growth in you.

Mac: Well, I guess that's right. But then I don't want any particular growth in that way. I mean, why couldn't people care about each other just when they want to?

Pastor: Because God didn't make us that way. He made us for lasting relationships in which we are willing to sacrifice some of our own time and convenience for the sake of

31

	those who depend upon us. You have a hang-up about this business of somebody depending on you.
Mac:	That's right, I never had to depend on my father and he never depended on anybody.
Pastor:	Well, as long as you are willing to see things his way, you won't see any reason to change that pattern. But you do see that there are some difficulties with a marriage in which you don't invest yourself. It really frustrates other people.
Mac:	Yes, I recognize this and I wish that Sandra would be more independent.
Pastor:	I think that she is becoming more this way. What worries me is your conclusion that this will make things right between you. It won't. You still are a person who will not grow the way that God intends you to be. Life just doesn't make sense when we live without lasting commitments. And those commitments mean that you cannot take off and do as you want to do anytime that you want to, even though you try to be nice about it and are not intentionally seeking to hurt anyone.
Mac:	I don't see that this has much to do with whether I am growing or not.
Pastor:	Well, I guess I said that because I think of you as a young adolescent. Psychologically you are about thirteen years old. You are asking the kinds of questions that thirteen-year-olds would ask. You are much more successful at getting along in life than a thirteen-year-old, but you see things the way a boy does when he first decides that he can be on his own. The big question is why don't people let me do what I want to do when I want to do it?
Mac:	Yeah, I guess that's about it. I was on my own at thirteen and I have been that way ever since.
Pastor:	Was there anybody who might have made a difference at that age? A friend? An uncle, or somebody else?
Mac:	No, not that I can think of. I did have some good friendships and I still have one from those days. Well, I say that he is a friend. I see him once in a while. But he has his interests and I have mine.

Pastor: I really wish that there were some lasting relationships for you. This would be one way for you to see the satisfaction that comes from investing yourself in other people.

We have identified a central problem of dependence versus independence in the life of Mac but we have not found any motivation for him to depend on others or receive their love into his own life. Any talk of dependence reminds him of the vulnerability of his adolescence and threatens the defenses that he has developed against rejection.

How could Jesus have been presented to him as a man for others, one who gave himself despite the rejection that he foretold? The pastor might have reflected with Mac about the way in which Jesus felt rejection, knew that he must go to the cross alone, and yet delighted in those who stayed with him until his last hour of trial (Luke 22:15; John 13:1; 15:14–16). Could Mac think of himself again as a lonely boy of thirteen who was determined to make his own way in life? Would he identify with the loneliness of Jesus who reached out in love to his disciples and found them squabbling among themselves as to who was to be the greatest? (Mark 9:33–35; Luke 22:24).

The purpose of a study of Jesus' longings in relation to our own is to bring us to a *final stage in recapitulation when we accept his success over temptation as a viable alternative in our lives.* In Pauline terms, the old Adam, with whom we identify, was tempted and yielded. Jesus as the new Adam was tempted and endured in obedience. Christ has transformed the Adamic failure into a renewed possibility for us to share in the divine life. We are like Christ when we live by his endurance and obedience. Every significant moral or spiritual decision becomes an occasion for the development of communion and obedience with God.

The second chapter of Philippians describes Christ's obedience to the will of God, in spite of human limitations, as the cause of his exaltation by the Father. This is the saving alternative that is available to Mac and to every other human being. We can achieve an attitude of obedience by God's grace and the power of Christ in the midst of the frustrations and disillusions of our humanity.

Mac's spiritual problem is an unwillingness to accept the conditioned character of human life. The childhood experiences that mark all of us are repressed by Mac with the illusion of invulnerability he

33

maintains. The pressures of the business world that increase Mac's competitiveness and further distance him from others and from his own inner feelings are only a fact of life to him. He thinks that he can achieve his goals without regard for the power of historical and social conditions upon his own life.

If Mac were to embrace the saving alternative offered in the archetype of human achievement, which is Jesus as the new Adam, his interests would center upon a new attitude rather than upon more achievement. The attitude of trust and faith would guard him against the self-deception and distancing from others that now destroys him. He would lay down his heroic ideal of individual accomplishment, for he would understand that God does not ask for heroes but for lovers.[5]

Mac admitted his desire for achievement as he described a conversation with the president of his company during a game of golf.

Pastor: So what did the president have to say?

Mac: Well, I had told him that I would like to know from him how I could become president of the company and he said that I was nuts. He said: "I've just come back from a lonely week in Bermuda. All I have to show for it is a sun tan. I'm sixty-two years of age and I have nothing to look forward to except spending money—and staying healthy. I've had one heart attack, and ten years ago I thought I would die because of all the antacids I was taking. I dislike my children and they dislike me because of the way I treated their mother. They don't want to see me and I don't want to see them. If my first wife had lived, it might have been different, but when she was gone I married a woman who expected more from me than I had time to give her. So we went our separate ways, and I married again. Now I am paying for *two* divorces. How come you want to become like me?"

Pastor: So, what did you learn from that?

Mac: That I may not be able to get everything that I want out of life, but at least I can get the money if I work right for it.

Pastor: And you will cut off any possibility of growing as a person because of that.

Mac: What do you mean?

Pastor: I mean that you will invest everything in getting ahead in the business and end up like the president. You are a nice guy on the outside, but there's not much on the inside. So you have trouble being loyal to people and the business of long-term relationships, such as marriage, just don't grow with you.

The pastor has contrasted the outer achievement with the inner shallowness of Mac. It was a theme to which he returned later in the same interview.

Pastor: But I'm really interested in what happens to you because you are a classic case of the "hollow man." Everything you want is outside yourself and you don't see yourself as making any contribution because you don't see much in there that could come out and make a contribution. Is this too severe?

Mac: No, I think that says it the way it is. And so you want to fill me up with something?

Pastor: Right. What I keep looking for is the right opening, the opportunity to suggest some thought or action that would open your life to a power beyond yourself. It's really frustrating to me. I know that God can do something in your life that is not going to be done by anyone else, but I don't know how to make it attractive enough for you to feel the need that way.

Mac: Well, that is a real problem. I think that I ought to do the right thing and I certainly believe in God, but I don't mind telling you that I don't think of myself as any great sinner or feel like praying or anything like that. When some problem comes up I try to solve it the best way I can.

Pastor: Well, that's what bothers me. The solutions that you are seeking are not lasting. You show a little more attention to your wife for a week or two because she has had such serious difficulties, but then you are as complacent with yourself as ever. That's what I would like to shake.

Mac: I know, I know. You seem to be doing what you can and I appreciate it.

35

Pastor: Thanks. These conversations are making me more religious, even if they don't have the same effect upon you.

Mac: Oh, how's that?

Pastor: Well, I know from my experience that we can have a nice conversation that will be interesting to both of us, but nothing will change unless you begin to think of what people require from you as a person and where you are going to get the power to be that kind of person.

Mac: Yes, I guess that is it. Well, I'm going to be out of town for a few weeks. So, I'll give you a ring when I can come in again.

I wonder what would have happened if there had been more conversation about the power that Mac needs to be the kind of person who can respond with love to others. If the power of God had moved through the pastor into the life of Mac at that point, Mac would have been transformed from empty hero to lively lover. Instead of solving problems in the best way that he could, he would have confessed the futility of trying to solve any problem with his present attitude of defensiveness and emotional withdrawal. The defeating attitudes of the old Adam would be overcome in the new Adam, Christ formed in him.

Mac would have learned this saving humility through a connection of the details of his own life with similar details in the life of the Lord Jesus. It is this recapitulation of the particulars of the life of Jesus in our own life that is one saving ingredient of the Incarnation. Just as God entered the consciousness of humanity through the earthly life of his Son, so he enters our lives through attention to the particulars of our existence. So long as the pastor can lead Mac to look at his own history and the devastating effects of early and late events upon his capacity for love, just so long will doors be open for Mac to connect his own specific history with the historical Jesus. The conviction of sin that will lead to salvation is always possible when we move through the steps of recapitulation: (1) reviewing our history as Paul did that of Adam, (2) identifying emotionally with the consequences of our conditioned existence, (3) studying the life of Jesus as the only adequate answer to the temptations of our existence, and (4) accepting the power of obedience to the Father as a viable alternative to our own vanity and despair.

The Incarnation: Divine Attitudes in Human Actions

This is the process by which attitudes and actions come together in the life of a person as the details of our history are compared with the human life of our Lord.

Model and Motivator

Will Mac become an authentic person whenever he relates the historical details of Jesus' earthly life to his own? I doubt it, even though his life would certainly be different if Jesus were his model.

Mac needs more than a model. He needs a motivator. The pastor sensed this in the conclusion of his last interview with Mac:

Mac: I know, I know. You seem to be doing what you can and I appreciate it.

Pastor: Thanks. These conversations are making me more religious, even if they don't have the same effect upon you.

Mac: Oh, how's that?

Pastor: Well, I know from my experience that we can have a nice conversation that will be interesting to both of us, but nothing will change unless you begin to think of what people require from you as a person and where you are going to get the power to be that kind of person.

Mac: Yes, I guess that is it. Well, I'm going to be out of town for a few weeks. So, I'll give you a ring when I can come in again.

Pastor: I will be very interested to see if something can begin to happen, beyond just what I can *say*. So, I look forward to seeing you some more and I'll be seeing Sandra several more times, I hope.

The pastor recognizes that Mac must not only know the kind of person that he must become but also receive some power to be that kind of person. Insight by itself will not save him. Even if Mac knew the attitudes that are required for him to be a loving husband, he is clearly unwilling to take the necessary actions to put them into practice.

The apostle Paul wrote in the first chapter of Romans that no one is going to change in the right direction just because he or she has knowledge. As Gunther Bornkamm interprets that passage, the

THEOLOGY AND THERAPY

ungodly world already has some knowledge of God. We know a great deal in the natural order of things about ourselves and God, but the knowledge is distorted toward the worship of ourselves. So, for Paul, the question is the personal application of knowledge (Rom. 1:28). Does the truth of God remain as a true recognition of the way that the world is made and do we acknowledge his power as Creator (Rom. 1:18-25)? Unless we praise and thank God for what we know about ourselves, we remain in the darkness of our senseless hearts (Rom. 1:21).[6]

God's answer to these inevitable human distortions is the Incarnation. Both the truth of God and the power to live by that truth are brought to us in Christ Jesus. Through his power we no longer regard ourselves from a human point of view but become new in our way of thinking: we begin to think and act with the mind of Christ. Attitude and actions are one when the reconciling work of Christ becomes our work of reconciliation to the world (2 Cor. 5:16-21).

In a passage that would specifically apply to the problems of Mac, Paul wrote "have this mind among yourselves which you have in Christ Jesus" (Phil. 2:5). Jesus did not seek power for himself, but humbled himself to all the limitations of life in order that the divine power of the Father might be known to him. The obedience of Christ is so great that no one can see him only as a model. If we truly understand what he has done, we will worship him and confess that he is our divine Lord (Phil. 2:9-11).

The Incarnation combines model and motivator because Christ is both human and divine. When we know the details of his earthly life, we know how much he became like us, but we also feel the power of his love enabling us to become as he is. It is this combination of human example and divine power that transforms Christian counsel.

In Christian counsel the need for a motivator appears whenever we recognize the restrictions of our own history. The pastor recognized this with Mac when he said in an earlier interview: "Most people consider love and loyalty important because it has been important to them since childhood. But these things do not seem to be especially important to you, so I assume that they were not much in the picture of your life in the past." The pastor is saying that Mac has neither model nor motivation for love and loyalty, which is badly needed in his present marriage.

38

Mac agrees with this, "My father made lots of money when he was sober, and I always hoped that I could get as good commissions as he would get from sales. But he never had any time for me or my mother. I guess he loved me in his way, but I never thought about him loving me."

"So," replied the pastor, "unless something happens, you will probably go the same way as your father?" Mac replies that this is so and that sometimes he is scared because he thinks about his father as a very lonely person.

In secular counseling, Mac's fear would be answered by "unconditional positive self-regard" from the counselor and from others. Christian counsel would go beyond this to incarnate God's love in the counselor and also proclaim the Incarnation to Mac. At some time the pastor would say: "You can stop being a hollow man if you're willing for that void in your life to be filled by God's love from Christ. He has the power to do in your life that which cannot be done because you did not experience love from mother, father, and others." Of course, the Incarnation means much more than God filling in the gaps in our human development, but this would be a relevant place for the pastor to begin. We often love God for our own sakes before we can love him for himself.

However the pastor begins to make the Incarnation a part of his conversation with Mac, he will be proclaiming something unique about the Christian solution to the problem of attitudes and actions. He will be saying that the ultimate change in Mac's attitudes and the power to act through love will come from a source beyond human history. He will proclaim as the apostle Paul did that the uniting of all things comes through God's plan to enter human history through his Son (Eph. 1:3–14). The proclaimed power of this plan for us is the resurrection of Christ (1 Cor. 15:45).

To say this is to say more than some psychologists or theologians are ready to say. On the one hand, secular psychology would say nothing about the working of God's power through the Incarnation, nor would a Christian counselor who is client-centered make any mention in a therapeutic interview of the work of the Holy Spirit in the change of a counselee. Whatever happens in those psychological encounters is bounded by human experience alone. On the other hand, there are theologians who take similar viewpoints in their explanation of our understanding of ourselves and

God. The influential German theologian of the World War II era, Rudolf Bultmann, was interested only in those parts of the Gospels which confronted us with the question of how we are to interpret our own existence. From this viewpoint, he wrote with great insight of the way in which the New Testament speaks to modern people. But any supernatural references to Christ would be considered beyond our modern consciousness and therefore relevant only to the way that people thought in the first century. Bultmann "demythologized" the New Testament tradition to increase the relevance of that tradition to our own day, but in the process he portrayed Jesus as an appealing prophet who was not the divine savior proclaimed in Second Corinthians 5, Ephesians 1, or Philippians 2.[7]

The essential information of these passages is that God actually was in Jesus of Nazareth and that he continues to be in the risen Christ for the reconciliation of the world to him. It is a statement of what is, much more than a statement of any human experience. To be a new person in Christ is to come into a new reality as well as a new way of thinking. In fact, the new way of thinking is an inevitable result of our awareness of more than ourselves in our human existence. There is so much more than ourselves in the Incarnation that Paul writes about working out our salvation "with fear and trembling" (Phil. 2:12–16). We are aware of an awesome power in us that can break the reign of sin in our lives (Rom. 6).

This proclamation of our personal awareness of God's power through Christ might be called theological objectivity. It is an affirmation of God as the source of all being who does not lie at the disposal of our human consciousness. There is an absolute primacy of God that conditions any thoughts about ourselves, our world, or him.[8]

Did the pastor believe in the theological objectivity of God? Could he affirm that a power beyond his own or Mac's understanding could work in both their lives? His last comments would encourage me to believe this, for he said his talks with Mac had made him more religious. He was aware that Mac must come in contact with some power beyond himself in order to change and that Mac would not receive this power just because of what he might say. What we do not know is the way in which the pastor experienced God in his own life and the way that he prayed for a power beyond himself to come upon counselor and counselee.

The Continuing Incarnation

Christian counsel is an awareness that the Spirit of Jesus continues to be incarnate in human flesh, both in the thoughts of the pastor as he talks to Mac and in Mac whenever he is ready to submit to a love beyond anything that he has ever known.

We realize the Incarnation in our counsel when we empty ourselves of fantasies about power, even as the Lord Jesus emptied himself of any desire to count equality with God as a thing to be grasped (Phil. 2:6–7; cf. 1 Cor. 1:26–31). When we accept the humility of the servant role of Christ, then his Spirit can continue to empower us. We literally become his ambassadors, representatives of saving power beyond ourselves.[9]

It would seem that this work of the Holy Spirit would come easily to Christian counselors because we face frustrations like that of the pastor with Mac. How often must we admit that people will not really change because of what we say?

But there are forces within ourselves, often shaped by our training as counselors, which inhibit the work of the Spirit. Sometimes there are fantasies of rescuing another person through our wisdom and love. On other occasions there is the tendency to interpret any stirring of God's Spirit as a neurotic fantasy. That is, we assume that the counselee is in despair and gives up on himself by projecting his dependency upon God. Or we may assume from our training that we are abandoning the counselee if we begin to think that some divine power must do what we cannot do.

These tendencies are overcome when there are several spiritual expectations in counsel.

First, there must be a continuous surrender of our own strivings for power, desire to save, and tendencies to reject others. This surrender takes the form of inner questioning of ourselves: What would the Spirit of Jesus do in the life of this person that is beyond what I can do? How open am I to the possibility of God's doing the unexpected work of grace in the life of this person? Why am I so frustrated about my own progress in this case when I am supposed to depend upon a power beyond myself? What can happen in the life of this person after our conversation? Do I really believe that prayer can be answered apart from my talking with this individual? What signs of God's working can I really look for in this person and in myself as we are together?

The last of these questions is the second way in which we become more aware of God's Spirit in counseling. This is the expectation that we will actually see something different in ourselves or the other person. We look for the fruit of the Spirit (Gal. 5). Whenever God's Spirit is at work, there will be something more than a pious attitude. There will also be powerful action.

In part, this action will take place because of the tremendous activity of the Spirit as witnessed in the New Testament. The work of the risen Christ is to bring reconciliation (Col. 1:21-23), to give us a new sense of identity as sons of God (Gal. 4:4-7), to receive life (John 6), and to experience liberation from all wickedness (Gal. 1:4).

In part, this relation of attitude and action will be seen in the character of the Spirit's work, which is to produce results. We will become ambassadors of Christ (2 Cor. 5:20), we will speak with the authority of Christ himself (1 Thess. 4:2), we will introduce others into the life of Christ (1 Cor. 4:14-17). Barriers will be broken down between us and other people, just as they have been broken down between ourselves and God (Eph. 2). Mind, heart, and will, will be transformed into spiritual service (Rom. 12:1-2).

We magnify the presence of the Spirit when we continually ask ourselves and our counselees about the fruit of the Spirit. In this way, we go beyond the subjectivism that has characterized so much counseling which emphasized the roots of problems. Instead, we investigate the root only when we do not see the fruit of Christian love in our own lives or in others. Therefore, whenever a person speaks about spirituality, I talk not only about surrender to God but also about a life of unselfishness. I ask counselees how others would know by their lives that they actually are living by the Spirit. That is, how do they incarnate the living God?[10]

The power of the Incarnate Christ to unite attitude and action is manifest (1) in the replication through our lives of the humanity of Christ, (2) as supernatural power fills our human motivation, (3) to produce the fruit of the Spirit in our character.

In these statements, there is an assumption that we must examine: Are we made to live incarnationally? If the history of Jesus is to become our history, what kind of persons are we to be? How can we actually participate in his divine power and at the same time confess our humanity? These are the questions to be addressed next, in an examination of the phrase "made in the image of God."

1. The human nature of the God-Man became the source of a debate in the early church that gave us the term "personality." The question was, how can divinity participate fully in humanity? The controversy over the "nature" of Christ's personhood was central in the first four councils of the church, culminating in the statement of the Council of Chalcedon that "our Lord, Jesus Christ, is both God and Man." For a summary of the debate, see William Temple, *Christus Veritas* (London: Macmillan, 1954), Chap. 8.

   The debate continued into the twentieth century, with Karl Barth's decision to discuss Christology only as anthropology, and Paul Tillich's reluctance to see any human details of the life of Jesus as significant in his definition of Jesus as the Christ. He wrote "the historical Jesus, namely, the Jesus behind the symbols of his reception as the Christ, not only did not appear but receded farther and farther with every step." Paul Tillich, *Systematic Theology* (Chicago: University of Chicago Press, 1957), vol. 2, pp. 98–102.

   A most sweeping rejection of any historical evidence for the life of Jesus is to be found in Rudolf Bultmann, *Kerygma and Myth*. This viewpoint is strongly attacked by other theologians, as in the analysis of the use of myth in the ancient world by Wolfhart Pannenberg. Professor Pannenberg notes a central defect in the argument of Bultmann: "The idea of the Incarnation of the Son of God, regarded as a myth, contains an extremely odd and disturbing element. For it does not merely state that God *appeared* in human form, but that He became *identical* with a human being who actually lived, He is a historical person, and even suffered and died as that person. . . . Hellenism had legends which told of epiphanies of heavenly beings in human or other forms, but never to the point of indissoluble identity with the form they took on." Wolfhart Pannenberg, *The Idea of God and Human Freedom* (Philadelphia: Westminster Press, 1973), p. 71. The presentation of Jesus as the Christ in the Gospels and the Epistles is contrary to the very nature of myth itself as understood in the age when the Bible was written. Pannenberg extends his argument concerning the crucial nature of historical details for an understanding of the revelation of God in Christ through his larger work, *Jesus: God and Man*.

   The impact of Jesus as the Christ upon the interpretation of human history is examined by Jaroslav Pelikan in *The Finality of Jesus Christ in an Age of Universal History: A Dilemma of the Third Century* (Richmond: John Knox Press, 1966).

2. Rowan Williams, *Christian Spirituality: A Theological History from the New Testament to Luther and Saint John of the Cross* (Atlanta: John Knox Press, 1979), p. 30.

3. Irenaeus wrote in *Against Heresies*: "He came to save all through himself . . . Therefore he passed through every stage of life . . . that he might be a perfect master for all, not solely in regard to the revelation of the truth, but also in respect of each stage of life." Henry Bettenson, ed., *Documents of the Christian Church*, Second Edition (London: Longmans, Green and Co., 1950), p. 43.

4. James D. G. Dunn, *Jesus and the Spirit* (Philadelphia: Westminster Press, 1975), p. 17.

5. For a discussion of this theme in the writings of Saint Augustine, see Rowan Williams, *Christian Spirituality*, pp. 81–89.

6. See Gunther Bornkamm, *Early Christian Experience* (New York: Harper and Row, 1969), pp. 54–59.

7. See especially Rudolf Bultmann, *Jesus and the Word* and the excellent evaluation of his contribution by Graham Stanton, "Rudolf Bultmann: Jesus and the Word" *Expository Times*, August 1979, pp. 324–27. In continental theology, the transcendence of God's revelation over our experience is a key emphasis in Karl Barth's writings, as in his *Evangelical Theology, An Introduction* (New York: Holt, Rinehart, and Winston, 1963), pp. 6ff.

8. In American theology, this emphasis has been strongest in the writings of Jonathan Edwards as in *Treatise on True Virtue* and *Dissertation Concerning the End for Which God Created the World*. For a discussion of this emphasis, see Clyde Holbrook, *The Ethics of Jonathan Edwards* (Ann Arbor: University of Michigan Press, 1973), pp. 1–9.

9. For other interpretations of Christ above self-understanding, see Wolfhart Pannenberg, *Basic Questions in Theology*, (Philadelphia: Fortress Press, 1970), vol. 1 pp. 39ff., 107–49; and his *Jesus: God and Man*.

10. Jonathan Edwards considered these questions in his examination of the signs of spiritual awakening during the first American revival in the 1740s. See his *Religious Affections*, available with full introduction by Paul Ramsey from Yale University Press or in an abridged edition from Multnomah Press.

4

The Image of God

When we are considering the relation of attitude to action, an inevitable question is: What is the structure of a person in whom attitudes and actions coalesce?

The question also is raised when we assert that God's actions are to power the actions of humans. How is a human being created to receive this power and put the will of God into effect upon earth?

These are questions about the image of God in man[1], questions which principally concern (1) issues of identity as human beings and (2) our mission among others consistent with this identity.

Identity and mission are central concerns of wisdom. Wise counsel in these areas depends upon knowledge of the structure of a person in relation to self, God, and others. This knowledge follows the biblical concepts of persons-in-relationships and is illuminated by modern studies of personality. Thus we increase the accuracy of insight, authentic response to God, and honest relations with others required in this proverb of wisdom:

A person's thoughts are like water in a deep well,
But someone with insight can draw them out.   (Prov. 20:5)

It would be difficult to justify some of the aggressive assertions of the pastor who spoke with Mac unless the pastor could back up his statements with some definite belief system.[2] In the previous chapter we examined one theological support structure, the Incarnation. In this chapter we will look at a related doctrine in the pastor-Mac interchange, the image of God in man.

Some doctrine of the image of God must be (or should be) underlying a final question of the pastor: "Is there anything that God could do in your life that would transform that satisfaction with self into service to others?" The intent is obvious, to connect self-identity with a sense of mission. Does the pastor have theological justification for this aggressive assertion about the way that Mac should think and act?

The first biblical reference to the image of God requires this combination of identity and mission. Gen. 1:26 might be paraphrased: "Let us make human beings as our dwelling place upon earth so that they may exercise authority there on our behalf." To be identified with the image of God is to initiate and maintain his work in the world.[3]

In this chapter we will discuss several aspects of the image of God: (1) the explicit combination of identity with mission, (2) the essential relationship of body to spirit in God's service, (3) the necessity of "I-thou" encounters, (4) the distortion and recreation of the image, (5) man as male and female.

Identity and Mission

To be in the image of God is to have the mission of acting for God. Image implies responsible service, identification as the representative of the creator. Our creation in the image of God prompts the question: "What does life require of us?"

Biblical bases for identity-in-mission begin with an exegesis of the Old Testament phrase "let us make man *in* our image." D. J. A. Clines concluded that the phrase should have the meaning of "in the capacity of." This would be similar to Exodus 6:3 "I appeared *as* El Shaddai," that is, in the capacity, nature of God Almighty.[4] Capacity is ability to fulfill a purpose, and the purpose is godly activity. The living God revealed himself to his people as God who acts, and his created beings are also to act on his behalf in the created order.

Identity-in-action goes beyond the popular psychological identification of self-understanding with insight.[5] To know oneself in biblical terms is more than introspection or self-knowledge; it is knowledge of purpose for living and a knowledge of self through the activities and attitudes that fulfill our created purpose. This is wisdom.

The Old Testament understanding of image is consistent with "being a person" or "becoming a person," a life of responsible service in relation to a higher power.[6] This interpretation is strengthened by ancient references in the Near East to the function of a king's image, which often stood at the boundaries of his land. The image represented one who was spiritually present although physically absent. A summary of the king's law was often engraved on the statue to signify that all who saw this image were to act in a certain way.[7]

This presentation of God's image as God's action may be basic to the insistent question of the pastor to Mac: "Is there anything that God could do in your life that would transform that satisfaction with self into service to others?" With this question the pastor distinguishes godly mission from the common complaint of unfulfilled persons: "Why haven't I been able to get more out of life?" It is a question that arises for many people like Mac, who have not received much love and security in the past and are now insisting upon as much as they can get in the present. The question about responsible mission is a gateway to the area of identity for a broken self.

Although the pastor appreciates the genesis of Mac's insistent complaint, he seeks to move beneath an extractive approach to life which endlessly repeats and entrenches a defective view of the self. An extractive approach would degenerate counseling into a chronic introspection of the psyche, fascination with structure of the personality, endless rumination about whether or not the individual is emotionally prepared to make responsible decisions. When people become this self-centered, they perpetuate a chronic emotional sickness.

The image of God challenges this preoccupation with a combination of identification and mission. On the one hand, a troubled person is encouraged to know as much about self as is necessary to get at the root of difficulties. But at the same time a Christian counselor is always asking, "Knowledge for what?" Will the knowledge of injustice in the past lead a person to a forgiveness of others in the present and a resolution to be just in dealings for the present and future? From a Christian perspective, self-realization is the threshold of self-giving.[8]

Body and Soul

In wise counsel, it is realistic to require insight and responsibility because biblical theology unites body and soul. All of the person is accountable to God. No part of the self is exempt from commitment to a godly mission (1 Thess. 5:23).

Mac had an opportunity to see this unity of body and soul in the remarks of the company president on a fishing trip. The president had now recognized the connection between his spirit of avarice and the miserable condition of his body and his past marriages. The president's fear of another heart attack and his testimony about his failed relationships were reminders of what could happen to Mac if he continued living by his current priorities.

Mac might also have learned something about the connection of mind and body from the alcoholism of his father, but so far he sees "no problem." He does not think of himself as any "great sinner" and when a problem comes up he "will try to solve it in the best way" that he can.

The biblical challenge to Mac's myopia is the statement in Gen. 2:7 that man is made from the dust of the earth. It is a statement repeated in other ways throughout the Psalms (Ps. 90:3; 103:14; 104:29; 146:46), in Isa. 29:16 and Job 4:19. Man is man because of the unity of his existence (Gen. 2:8), because of the commission to work (Gen. 2:15), the necessity of community (Gen. 2:18-24), the opportunity for communication (Gen. 2:19, 23), and —over all this— personal relation to God as a representative in God's world.

To read that man is dust of the earth into which God breathes his spirit is to know that each of us is created as a unity of body and spirit in God's service.[9] The subconscious part of Mac "knows" this unity. Just under the surface of consciousness is a restlessness, a vague dissatisfaction. This contradicts Mac's surface pretenses, his nonchalant dissociation of behavior and beliefs from feelings and relationships.

The inner connections cannot always be hidden. On one occasion, Mac's wife told the pastor that she often felt crushed at night by Mac's "fierce embrace just before and after he fell asleep." He made no attempt to romance her. Instead, he clung to her with a desperation that puzzled and panicked her.

In comments concerning his father, Mac begins to come close to the reason for the separation of body and spirit in himself. There was no integrated love from the father for the son. Mac "guesses" that his father loved him. There were no actions to go with the assumptions that a father loved a son.

Because Mac has never seen or experienced this interdependence, he cannot understand the vivid comment about mind-body relationships from his company president. He sees no relationship between the pursuit of money and the loss of health and family love. Since he cannot see this relationship, he opts for that which is most important to him, the money. The pastor then attacks this way of thinking by accusing him of being a "hollow man." In this sense he is close to Hebrew thinking, in which a person who did not integrate feeling and action, body and spirit was considered to be "false." To be a healthy person in Old Testament thought was to be a complete person. This completeness was considered necessary to do the work of God and to please him. To be in the image of God was to be a person committed in all parts to his service.[10] Such service began in a contrite heart and was openly displayed in all attitudes and actions.

The Flesh and the Spirit

The pastor is so committed to the unity of "body" and "soul" that he does not fall into a dichotomy that is often found in pastoral interviews, the separation of "flesh" and "spirit." A less biblically-oriented pastor might have identified Mac's materialism with "flesh," and preached a "spiritual" repentance in which Mac would forsake money, liquor, and late hours. The appeal would be to the will, followed by a repression of all "bodily" or personal desires.

Neither the writers of the Old or New Testaments had any concept of a "spiritual person" in which emotions obliterated will, reason fought against faith, or spiritual exercises took precedence over bodily functions. H. Wheeler Robinson described the Hebrew idea of personality as an animated body, not an incarnated soul. The person does not *have* a body, he or she *is* a body.[11]

This same unity continues into the New Testament (John 1:14), but has sometimes been misunderstood by the English translation of "flesh" for the Greek equivalent *sarx*. The misunderstanding arises from the Greek influence in Christianity by which the physical body was despised. But in the thought of the apostle Paul the flesh or the "needs of the body" (Rom. 8:13) represent rebellious human beings against God. For example, the wisdom that is "fleshly" (2 Cor. 1:12; 1 Cor. 1:26) is simply the wisdom of human beings apart from God (1 Cor. 2:5, 13).

Of course the flesh stands for that which is mortal (2 Cor. 4:11; 1 Cor. 15:53-54). But to speak of the flesh as mortality is to say no more than what Paul says, which is that we must all "abide in the flesh" (Phil. 1:24). We are to recognize our mortality, not reject it. The mortality is only a problem when it becomes a source of all pleasure, a god for the person (Rom. 8:7). This is Mac's manifest problem, an inability to subordinate personal desires to the higher goals of responsible relationships and enduring purpose in life.

If Mac could accept—and integrate—his total personality through dedication to God, the "flesh" would then be recognized as his natural and God-given form of earthly existence (Gal. 2:20). Every Christian is to "walk *in* the flesh," but not to walk *according* to the flesh, as though this life were everything and the created thing was to be worshiped rather than the creator (Rom. 1:18-32). The conflict of the flesh is not—as in Greek ethics—between our reasons and our passions, but a denial of our dependence upon God (2 Cor. 3:5-6) or, in Mac's case, a denial of dependence upon anyone, including God. Our godly dependence is imitation of Christ, who was perfectly obedient to the Father (Phil. 2). He lived in the world as "the Word made flesh" (John 1:14 KJV).

When the flesh is surrendered to God, it is in harmony with the other word for "the body" (or soul) which is *soma* in Greek. *Soma* stands for the solidarity of our creation as we are made to serve God (1 Cor. 6:13-20; Rom. 12:1; Phil. 1:19-20; 2 Cor. 4:7-12).[12]

The pastor often sought to establish this wholistic concept in Mac. Mac would have been a more complete person if he could have recognized the basic biblical concept of an interrelationship among physical functions, unconscious emotions, conscious decisions, and spiritual requirements of the self. One sign of his need for wholeness was his indifference to the feelings of others. The pastor sought to connect his feelings about others with his feelings about himself. Mac saw the connection between his indifference to others and the indifference of his father toward himself. At times he was scared by the thought that he might end up as a lonely person like his father, but he did not have the courage to admit the pain of his early relationships, nor the pain that he was now causing himself and others.

He could see no relationship between the need for identity as a fully integrated person and the mission in life that could bring him satisfaction.

The I-Thou Encounter

Mac's dissatisfaction with himself was matched by the dissatisfaction of his wife. She had dramatized her dissatisfaction with an attempted suicide, which prompted Mac to seek consultation with the pastor. But Mac could not see an intimate interpersonal relationship with his wife as a remedy for her dissatisfaction. His question was "Why couldn't we live together without making any demands on each other?" So far as he was concerned, marriage was a convenience and it was no longer tolerable if it meant inconvenience to him. So he asked the pastor, "Why couldn't people care about each other just when they want to?"

The pastor's answer demonstrated a third meaning of the image of God:

Because God didn't make us that way. He made us for lasting relationships in which we are willing to sacrifice some of our own time and convenience for the sake of those who depend upon us.

The theological basis for this assertion is to be found in the very being of God himself and in the creation of humankind as a repetition of this divine form of life.[13] The Christian doctrine of the Trinity reveals God as the source of harmonious self-encounter and self-discovery.

That which is true of God is also to be found in his creature in the encounter between God and humankind. Revelational content is combined with definitions of communication. Karl Barth has presented four aspects of "being in encounter": (1) reciprocal openness, (2) dialogue, (3) reciprocal assistance, and (4) doing the first three with gladness.[14]

These qualitative encounters are missing in Mac's relationships with his father, with his business associates, and with his wife. Especially in relation to his wife there is an absence of the I-thou

51

relationship which is considered by some theologians to be primary in our definition of humanity.[15] Without these qualitative encounters, Mac is handicapped in the performance of any genuinely human mission in life. He cannot perform as a husband, he does not understand the basic qualities of a manager, he does not know how to keep enduring relationships with friends or enjoy his father and mother.

The Misguided Mission

Distortions of the I-thou relationship have been debated since the patristic fathers, such as Irenaeus, posited an *Imago* in human nature which cannot be "lost" and *Similitado*, an original relation to God which has been lost since Adam.[16] The capacity for humanness remains, but the quality of intimate communication with God is missing.

The fathers of the church were grappling with an issue that was basic to the pastor's counsel with Mac. From the pastor's description, Mac was a handsome man in his early thirties who came to the pastor because he had a concern about the unhappiness of his wife. From the description and from the written dialogue it is clear that the pastor looks upon Mac as a human being, a person with capacities for loving and godly relationships. We could explain this in Ireneaus's terms by saying that Mac has natural endowments which identify him as a human being made in the *Imago* of God.[17]

The pastor treats Mac as a person made in the image of God, but does Mac treat himself the same way? No, something is missing in Mac's identification of himself and in his sense of mission in life. It is expressed early in the first interview when the pastor summarizes what he has heard from Mac.

It seems that you want to do the right thing, but something is always getting in the way.

Later in the first interview, Mac seems to recognize that there is something within him that is "getting in the way" when he asks,

So you think that I'm more interested in getting than giving?

The pastor continues this inquiry in the second interview when he asks about the "deepest relationships that would count for most people." Why have these relationships not been important to Mac? When Mac begins to admit there really are difficulties, then the pastor presents his concept of motivation.

I know that God can do something in your life that's not going to be done by anyone else, but I don't know how to make it attractive enough for you to feel the need that way.

Mac admits that this is a real problem. He believes in God, he doesn't think of himself as any great sinner, and he is going to solve problems "the best way I can." The pastor immediately admits that this is what bothers him about Mac. And why should he be so "bothered"? The pastor is admitting that human dialogue, empathy, confrontation, acceptance by others is not enough for Mac. Something must happen in his relationship to God for his self-identity and his sense of motivation to change.

Why is the pastor so insistent that God is the agent of change? When I asked this question of the pastor in a supervisory session he replied,

Well, there is a basic flaw in this guy. It's beyond me and I think it's beyond him. I mean, he doesn't know who he is. You can tell this by the way he uses words. He talks about "love," but he doesn't act like someone who loves his wife, and he certainly shows no awareness of what love could mean in himself.

The pastor is describing that which Irenaeus would refer to as the loss of *Similitado*, the original dialogue of a human being with God which defines and guides persons-in-relationship. Mac does not experience the quality of interpersonal communication that includes love, loyalty, compassion, justice, forgiveness.

The pastor identifies this loss as an inability to feel the emotional impact of words used by either the pastor or Mac. The more a word relates to sense of identity and mission, the more puzzled and opaque is the reaction of Mac.

Mac is lost in words. The words that he uses intellectually are not vital signs of affections that stir in his heart. There is no experience within him to stimulate the emotion that would go with "love," "loyalty," or other words for human affection.

Jonathan Edwards was the first American theologian to look carefully at this function of the affections. He identified the functional loss as a lack of harmony between head and heart, which leads to misidentification of words and lack of appropriate emotional and intellectual response.

Why? Edwards saw the image of God in his creation marred through the Fall. This was the time when chaos descended upon the created order. Light and regularity were obscured. The human being lacked integration of the total self with this environment, for persons after the Fall would admit no principle of motivation outside of the individual self. Humans now lived with the illusion of independent individuality. They no longer admitted God's presence in love.[18]

This dynamic explanation is consistent with the exegesis of the first four chapters of Genesis. In his exegesis of these chapters, Claus Westermann considers "the image of God" to be the statement about an event, a meeting of God with man and man with woman.[19] The special character of human existence is the I-thou before God. That is, we recognize ourselves in our mission, in interaction with others. As Westermann concludes, "Man is not yet man merely because he has been made." The creation story continues through a series of interactions between God and his creation. After the breath of life has been breathed into the living being that is man, the Garden of Eden is created as a place where man may fulfill his mission before God. The man is given a commission and a statement of his human limitations (Gen. 2:7–17). The capacity for intimacy and identification as male and female come through the creation of woman (vv. 18–25). The living being that began as dust-with-breath has become flesh in relationship. Through a succession of creative acts by God, the human created in God's image functions through feelings rather than through any physical structure. This is the meaning of I-thou relatedness.

When male and female transgress God's command, the I-thou relatedness is shattered. They have lost the freedom to respond to God according to the responsibilities that made them human. The third chapter of Genesis presents both the offense and the consequences in terms of humanity's loss of mission because humans no longer identified themselves as God's responsible representatives upon earth.

What remains in "humanity" after this offense? Westermann comments, "He still has one area of freedom: he can defend himself."[20] Humans retain the realization of their primal responsibility and the capacity of guilt.

The same theme is presented in the first chapter of Romans. Human beings can perceive their purpose in life both through what they see in God's creation and through the limitations of their lives in the creation. But although perception is possible, the continual curse of the fallen creature is an unwillingness to act on this knowledge through worship of the Creator. They will not "acknowledge God" (Rom. 1:28-32).

As a consequence of this rebellion, human beings are now incapable of returning to God on their own strength because they have lost the original perception of God as their maker and themselves as his representatives upon earth.

But does the resultant "inner depravity" of the creature mean that we have lost all knowledge of God and are unable to perform any part of the mission for which God created us?

The answer in the second chapter of Romans is more optimistic than some doctrines of total depravity would lead us to believe.[21] Paul's statements are an amplification of the creation narrative, in which, in pronouncing the curse that follows disobedience, the Lord God reinforces (Gen. 3:17-19) the commission to work that was already a part of the original creation (Gen. 2:15). Humans continue the work of God, they fulfill some of his mission, but they live a life of suffering because they no longer work for God. Instead, they seek to serve themselves.

In a dim and distorted way, fallen human beings continue their original mission from God because the "image of God" as *Imago* remains—as a capacity to hear and respond to God's saving grace. Both the Old and New Testaments assume that the image is never completely lost. Genesis 9 begins with a blessing to Noah and his sons that recapitulates the original commission to Adam and Eve. Psalm 8 speaks of human beings as the glory and honor of God through their work in the world. The apostle Paul uses the very phrase, "image and glory of God" to refer to humans in 1 Corinthians 11:7. The book of James states that we "are made after the similitude of God" (James 3:9, KJV).[22]

These conclusions about the distortion of God's image in his creation can be seen in the pastor's conversation with Mac. In their last meeting, the pastor has this comment:

> Well, I know from my experience that we can have a nice conversation that would be interesting to both of us, but nothing would change unless you begin to think of what people require from you as a person, and where you're going to get the power to be that kind of person.

The assumption of the pastor is that Mac's identity is incomplete and that only a power beyond himself can make him complete, restoring redeemed *Imago* and *Similitado* in the image of God.

The pastor does not think that Mac is so incomplete that he can have no knowledge of himself apart from divine grace. In the first interview the pastor assumes that Mac can see the value distinctions between money and the happiness of his wife. He presents a mini-sermon on what a person lives for. The assumption is that Mac can recognize the importance of this question in his own life.

But at the same time, the pastor does not think that Mac can really change his purpose in life apart from the power of God.

> I think I lack the power to do more than raise some questions. Some power from God has to make a change in you. When you get the idea that you are created to love and devote yourself to others, then you will begin to take some steps in that direction.

What does the image of God have to do with a change in Mac? The assumption of the pastor is that Mac's mission in life is marred because his identification is with self rather than with his Creator. Consequently, the pastor spends several interviews concentrating upon Mac's perception of himself and others. He delves into Mac's past relationships in an attempt to discover the reasons why Mac's self-perception is so distorted. What he finds is a person who continually hides from himself, even as Adam hid himself from God.

56

The Purpose of Male and Female

Why did Adam hide? He hid himself because he was naked (Gen. 3:10). This was the sign of his disobedience. The innocence of intimacy had been destroyed.

The capacity for intimacy came with the creation of the woman and the sign of their trusting openness with one another was nakedness without shame. When Adam violated God's trust, he destroyed intimacy. Nakedness was vulnerability that he could not tolerate apart from the confident presence of his Maker.

The return of innocent openness is the purpose of "one flesh" (Gen. 2:24–25). As Jesus discussed the disruption of trust through divorce, he pointed to hardness of heart as the cause and reminded the Pharisees that the original purpose of male and female was to live more closely with each other than with father or mother (Mark 10:2–9; Matt. 19:3–9).

How does the relation of male and female as one flesh become a sign of our original creation in the image of God? And how does this doctrine help us to understand and redeem distortions in the image?

Since the biblical doctrine of the image of God centers on events and responsibilities, we can discuss the meaning of male and female in terms of fulfillment or nonfulfillment of mission in life, clarity and distortion of self-image in relation to that mission.

These terms relate to intimacy in the context of gender. The distinct and complementary character of male and female is a primary channel for intimacy, the I-thou encounter which is modeled after the original innocence of human conversation with God, restored through Christ (Eph. 5:21–33).

The purpose of the distinctiveness of male and female is the modeling and fulfillment of open communication between distinct people through mutual trust and responsibility. The fulfillment of this relationship in the Genesis story is to be seen in companionship and procreation.[23]

In the Christian faith, identity and mission as male and female have been kept in continual and complementary tension. Jesus was unique as a teacher in his response to the question of his Jewish disciples about the necessity of marriage (Matt. 19:10–12). He considered the varied circumstances of people—some of whom found their identity as male or female without any urge toward marriage or sexual activity, some of whom were distorted by early events in the family to recognize that their capacity for intimacy in marriage was minimal, and some who found that their identity as male or female led to a mission in which circumstances would not permit a satisfying marital relationship.

In all of these instances, Jesus was working toward one surprising conclusion, that the primary mission of male and female was to serve the kingdom of God. Any reference to celibacy or marriage was of secondary importance. Although the first model for intimacy was the recognition by the man and the woman that they were made for companionship and procreation, this model did not determine the mission of all persons in the kingdom of God. In fact, Jesus warned against those who placed any kind of family relationship on a par with or above the mission of the kingdom. He declared that those who did his will would often have to be against their own household (Matt. 10). The new bonding in the body of Christ was presented by our Lord in his last lovefeast with the disciples: "I call you friends" (John 15:12–17).

This bold declaration to the family-oriented people of the first century would have seemed "unnatural." Or, if his statement had been read with understanding in the Middle Ages, it might have seemed to be perversion of "natural law."

How do we harmonize the teachings of Jesus with the common observations of our society that seem to be based upon the creative order of God? When we consider these questions, we have taken up the relationship between general revelation and special revelation, which will be the subject of the following chapter.

NOTES

1. "Man" is used in the generic sense of human being as distinguished from God. Man is also defined specifically as male and female. See Paul Jewett, *Man as Male and Female* (Grand Rapids: William B. Eerdmans, 1975), pp. 13–14.

2. In the second section of the book, on friendship, there will be some questions about the strengths and weaknesses of the pastor's boldness. For the sake of clarity, these methodological issues are reserved for later discussion.

3. To begin a discussion of the image of God with Genesis 1 is to correlate anthropology with the doctrine of creation. D. S. Cairns has made this the

standpoint of his criticisms and corrections of the restrictive doctrine of the image of God to be found in the writings of Karl Barth. Barth defines the image of God only in those who have made a responsible decision before Jesus Christ. (D. S. Cairns, *The Image of God in Man* [New York: Philosophical Library, 1953], pp. 180–84.)

To begin with the Genesis account of the image of God is to consider all humans in the image and likeness of God as descendents of Adam (Gen. 5:1–3). This correlation of the doctrine of creation with anthropology is amplified in the New Testament, where the image of God is correlated with soteriology, the study of salvation. The New Testament doctrine pictures the image as a likeness to Christ. This is a likeness that God has planned for our being, but which has been lost by sin. The likeness is restored by the grace of God in Christ. (See Cairns, pp. 28–30ff.).

G. C. Berkouwer connects anthropology with the sovereignty of God. He considers the central problem to be the possibility that fallen persons can still be human, in the sense that they still retain the image of God. Berkouwer maintains that the nature of persons after the Fall is still the work of God. *Man: The Image of God* (Grand Rapids: William B. Eerdmans, 1962), p. 133. But humans are still held accountable to God and preserved by his providence (pp. 178–187). This is in agreement with Calvin's writings about "general grace," the reason and understanding that is maintained in all persons because of God's mercy (p. 152).

4. D. J. A. Clines, "The Image of God in Man," *Tyndale Bulletin*, vol. 19 (1968), pp. 75–76.

5. The definition and distortion of insight has been explored by Bernard Lonergan, *Insight: A Study of Human Understanding* (London: Longmans, 1957). His position is summarized in David Tracy's *Blessed Rage For Order* (New York: Seabury Press, 1979), pp. 96ff.

6. This emphasis is especially strong in Berkouwer's *Man: The Image of God*, pp. 34ff. Some of the Scriptures cited by Berkouwer are Amos 9:1–4; Psalm 139:7; Jer. 17:9–10; 10:23.

7. Clines, "Image of God." This identity-in-action does not exalt works and minimize faith. That would be a precarious balance of false dichotomies. In both Old and New Testaments, identity and mission are bound together. The capacity of the creature is for both faith and works. Only the destruction of this unity through sin has made possible the over-emphasis of faith or works as separate categories of response to God.

In the case of Mac, there is an additional question: "Is a person human apart from fellowship with God?" From the viewpoint of general revelation, which we consider in the following chapter, the answer is: "Yes, but fatally flawed." The capacity to act as God's representative is still a possibility in Mac, but his ability to comprehend and follow the divine command has been fragmented. He does not see or act as though faith and works were related, whether he speaks of himself, his wife, his parents, or God. There is no unity of perception, feelings, relationships, and actions. As we will see in this chapter, the pastor is consistently concerned for the broken image of God in

Mac, his inability to act in the capacity of God's representative in love, faith, hope, and works.

8. For a psychoanalytic emphasis upon the same forces, see Erik Erikson, *Insight and Responsibility* (New York: W. W. Norton, 1964). The theme is presented in Reformed theology by G. Ernest Wright, *The God Who Acts* (Chicago: Henry Regnery, 1952).

9. Claus Westermann, *Creation* (Philadelphia: Fortress Press, 1974), p. 79.

10. Johannes Pedersen, *Israel: Its Life and Culture*, vol. 1, p. 411ff. This moral emphasis in the Old Testament upon bodily actions is open to misunderstanding, such as a tendency to determine a person's worth by careful behavior or acceptance of conventional mores. The apostle Paul is definite in Rom. 14 and Col. 2 that he is not counseling conformity to this world. There is no moral value in observing social regulations that make us look good in the sight of others. Instead, his argument in 1 Cor. 6 is that there are some physical actions that have definite moral consequences because the physical action is connected with our basic state of being, our opinion about others, and our sense of servanthood before God.

   The unity of spiritual-emotional-physical components of personality is demonstrated in Paul's insistence upon the resurrection of the body (1 Cor. 15:12–28). This unity is so important that he looks forward to the integration of the corporal self and a new corporality in the coming eternal life. The body is worth waiting for!

   Furthermore, the emphasis upon the bodily resurrection is connected with the resurrection of Christ from the dead. His bodily resurrection was a visible sign of triumph over the fear of physical death, hell, and sin. All these powers which affect our mortal body are broken in the triumphal resurrection of our Lord. See John A. T. Robinson, *The Body: A Study in Pauline Theology* (Chicago: Henry Regnery Company, 1952).

   The Hebrew use of physical organs to describe an emotional state is discussed in Hans Walter Wolff, *Anthropology of the Old Testament*, (SCM Press, 1984).

11. Quoted in Robinson, *The Body: A Study in Pauline Theology*, p. 14.

12. See James D. G. Dunn, *Jesus and the Spirit*, pp. 308ff. For more discussion on the equality and interrelationship of body and soul, see Robert Gundry, *Soma in Biblical Theology* (Cambridge University Press, 1976), pp. 199f.

13. Karl Barth, *Church Dogmatics* (Edinburgh: T. and T. Clark, 1960), vol. 3, pt. 2, pp. 184–85.

14. Barth, *Church Dogmatics*, pp. 247–85. In a realistic assessment of these existential endowments, Cairns writes: "The objection may be raised that this surely cannot be a humanity active and universal among men, for if it were, we would be very nearly in Paradise" (*The Image of God in Man*, p. 195).

15. Barth, *Church Dogmatics*, pp. 285–90.

16. See the discussion in Emil Brunner, *Man in Revolt* (Philadelphia: Westminster Press, 1947), pp. 93ff., 504ff.; G. C. Berkouwer, *Man: The Image of God*, pp. 38–48; Cairns, *The Image of God in Man*, pp. 73–86.

17. Just what are the "endowments"? Early and medieval explanations had elements of Greek dualism in them. For Ireneaus, the image of God in man was retained as the nature of a rational and pre-being. (Cairns, *The Image of God in Man*, p. 75). Later Catholic theologians, such as Augustine and Aquinas, regarded the image in the same way as a power of reason.

    The more existential theologians of the twentieth century have considered the image primarily in terms of confrontation between persons and capacity for mutual responsibility (Cairns, p. 191). Berkouwer grants the existential interest of man as the creature of God in historical relationships with God and other persons. This quality is never independent of God, who through a providence has maintained this image of himself in his creation. The relationship with God is also made central in Berkouwer's definition of *Similitado* as the bond of love that we have in imitation of God (p. 59, 101).

18. For a summary of Edwards's thought on the subject see Douglas J. Elwood, *The Philosophical Theology of Jonathan Edwards* (New York: Columbia University Press, 1960), pp. 65ff., 117ff.

19. Westermann, *Creation*, p. 56.

20. The key word in the sentence is "self." This is the organizing center of consciousness by which experience is systematized around that which the self defines as "good." Self is considered essential, in this definition, for an appreciation of values in life (morality) and awareness of need for God's fellowship (salvation). See William Temple, *Christus Veritas* (London: Macmillan, 1974), pp. 65–73, 214–15.

21. In *Adam, Eve and the Serpent* (Random House, 1988), Elaine Pagels develops the thesis that in the century following the conversion of Constantine, Christian teaching underwent a revolutionary change, from a doctrine that celebrated freedom to one that emphasized the universal bondage of original sin. The teaching of Augustine was a peculiarity of the fourth century and not representative of Christian attitudes that had prevailed for more than three hundred years.

22. Westermann maintains that the doctrine of complete corruption because of the Fall was first introduced in the apocryphal work of Esdras 7:118 and reached full development in the theology of Augustine. Westermann, *Creation*, p. 108.

23. Of these two purposes, companionship is primary in the teachings of Jesus (Matt. 19:1–6). Christian marriage is defined by the bonding of man and woman, not by the presence or absence of children. In fact, Jesus proclaimed that the preaching of the kingdom of God would separate parents from children (Matt. 10:21).

    This teaching does not devalue the importance of earlier bonding as a primary element in the formation of trust and identity in a child. Gender is established or distorted in the family. Some Christian counselors trace one root of homosexuality to problems of same sex bonding (e.g. father/son) and defensive detachment from the violence of male/female relations in the family. In confusion, the child may associate femaleness and maleness with the distorted reactions between parents. The deprived child may then seek a homosexual activity as a substitute for innocent friendship which was absent in the past.

For additional reading on homosexuality in relation to the Christian faith, see David Atkinson, *Homosexuals in the Christian Fellowship* (Grand Rapids: William B. Eerdmans, 1981); Richard Lovelace, *Homosexuality, What Should Christians Do About It?* (Old Tappan: Fleming H. Revell, 1984); Elizabeth Moberly, *Homosexuality: A New Christian Ethic* (Greenwood: Attic Press, 1983); Leanne Payne, *The Broken Image* (Westchester: Crossways, 1981). Moberly and Payne deal with the therapeutic issues that have been addressed in this chapter. In addition, it is important to read the correctives that have been provided by Christian scholars to the many errors in interpretation and omission of material in the well-publicized book of John Boswell, *Christianity, Social Tolerance and Homosexuality* (Chicago: University of Chicago Press, 1980). The most exacting corrections to the misinterpretations of Boswell have been published by David Wright, a senior lecturer in the Department of Ecclesiastical History, University of Edinburgh: "Homosexuals or Prostitutes?" in *Vigiliae Christianae* 38 (1984), pp. 124–153, available from Leiden, Belgium: E. J. Brill. A Roman Catholic criticism is in *Communio*, by G. W. Olsen, 1981. Ramsey MacMullen of Yale provided an evaluation as a part of "Roman attitudes to Greek love," in *Historia*, 1982, pp. 484–502. A long critical review of Boswell was given by J. Robert Wright of the General Theological Seminary (Episcopalian) in the *Anglican Theological Review*, 66:1 (January 1984). A short monograph by David F. Wright on early Christian attitudes toward homosexuality, which offers a positive correction to Boswell, is in press with the *Scottish Journal of Theology*.

5

General Revelation

The previous chapter has argued for a vestigial awareness of God's righteousness through our *Imago*. But of what are we aware? Can we only respond to the special revelation of God in Christ? Or is there also a general revelation of God in the world? Has God, by his prevenient grace, continued to make himself known in the things he has created, even when we misidentify and misuse them?

These questions introduce the possibility of and the balance between the finality of God's saving grace in Christ and a continuation of his grace through the world through which we become aware of ourselves, others, and our Creator.

The continuation of grace through personality is a key issue in mediated theologies. Respect for ourselves and our world is the basis for hopeful explorations of the self and of growth that combines self-knowledge with spiritual motivation for maturity.[1] Without this balance, the self may be repressed within the confines of propositional theology, like a dangerous beast chained by legalism, compressed by rigorism, and weakened by asceticism. Or the self may be unleashed through sensational theology and have delusions of limitless power ("I can do all things. . ."). God, rather than self, is now confined by the deprived person's belief that ecstatic experience requires divine favor ("If you pray in the name of Jesus, God has got to do what you ask. . .").

Can we find divine grace through human personality by embracing both head and heart as redeemable agents of reconciliation according to his original order of creation?

One assumption of the previous chapter was that the image of God forms a point of contact between God and human beings even when the creature remains in rebellion against the Creator.[2] Such an assumption raises questions about the way in which God makes his will known among us. Does God intend that we will continue to have some knowledge of him even when we are in a fallen state? Do points of contact remain in a variety of ways between humanity and Creator?

These questions have been debated for two thousand years under such categories as "general revelation" and "special revelation."[3]

General revelation is the understanding which God has given concerning himself to his creatures through the world in which we live (Job 37–41; Ps. 19:1–4; Matt. 5:44–45; Rom. 1:20). It is also the righteous law of the created order that is made known to human beings through the conscience (Rom. 2:1–2, 12–16).[4]

General revelation does not compete with the special, historical revelation of God in Christ, but is rather its presupposition. The apostle Paul declares to a mob at Lystra that God did not leave himself without witness, but does good things and gives the rains and the seasons that satisfy human beings (Acts 14:16–17). But Paul did not consider all these evidences of the general revelation of God to be enough for the people. He openly declared that the people had been misled into the worship of "vain things" rather than of the living God who had made heaven and earth (Acts 14:15–16).

The good news of God's *special revelation* is the correction of our distorted understanding of general revelation because of a perverse will. Wisdom now comes in completeness through Christ. He alone is the true light of God (John 1); the door to salvation (John 10:7, 9); the way, the truth, the life (John 14:6).

The connection between general and special revelation was an underlying theme of most of the pastor's conversations as reported in chapter 4. It is a basic doctrinal affirmation for Christian counsel. Evidence for this affirmation may be seen in my conversations with Michael (chap. 2). Our conversations were a continuing intersection of general and special revelation. As the interviews progressed, I kept asking: "What can I say or do that will move Michael toward the contact points between his fragmentary knowledge of what is right and the grand design for his life that can be revealed through an awareness of God's intentions for his life?

What answer is given to this question of correlation by systematic theologians? Sometimes the answer is: Nothing! There can be no relationship between the knowledge of God in the created order and the revelation of God in Jesus Christ.[5] This is a central affirmation of Karl Barth, as presented in his *Church Dogmatics* (vol. 1, sec. 2). On the other extreme are the writers Paul Tillich and John Cobb, who have influenced many pastoral counselors in the post-World War II period. Special revelation became a servant of general revelation in their writings. Tillich rejected any "supra naturalism," and redefined theological terms as myths which would help humans understand themselves and their world. A third answer came from Thomistic Catholic writers, such as Franz Boeckle. General revelation was considered in the special formulation of Thomistic theology as "natural law," an obligation from God which was implanted in human beings who could intellectually perceive the created order and respond correctly.[6]

Did any theologians believe in both general and special revelation? If so, did they seriously consider the relationship between these two as an aid to moral conduct and a source of divine salvation? Two theological traditions are helpful in an answer to these questions. The first is the Anglican tradition represented by such historical works as the lectures of Bishop Sanderson on conscience and the human law, the moral theology of K. E. Kirk and Lindsay Dewar, and the spiritual direction of Kenneth Leech.[7] The other helpful tradition has been that of Reformed theologians in Europe, principally Emil Brunner, *Revelation and Reason* (Philadelphia: Westminster Press, 1946) and G. C. Berkouwer, *General Revelation* (Grand Rapids: William B. Eerdmans, 1955).

Four guidelines came from these theologians as they agreed or disagreed about the relationship of general to special revelation:

(1)　There is both a general and a special revelation.
(2)　There is an inextractible relation between general and special revelation.

(3) The relation between general and special revelation has been distorted by sin.

(4) A fundamental objective of Christian counsel is to restore the relationship between general and special revelation in the hearts and minds of those who seek our counsel.

How did these principles of general and special revelation shape my counsel with Michael?[8]

Affirmation of General and Special Revelation

By the second interview with Michael I was affirming both general and special revelation. He asserted, "I always feel that I should work as hard" as powerful and loving people do. He thought that he should be as successful as they are in order to deserve what they get. I affirmed this fragmentary awareness of the way that God has made us with the statement: "Yes, I keep noticing this in you. The only way I can figure it out is to say that God has made us to be responsible and independent, along with our need to depend on others."

This was an affirmation of general revelation. It was followed by an affirmation of more than general revelation.

Michael: So, you think that when I just pursue my own easy way of life, I am denying something about the way that I am made and this is what keeps me dissatisfied?

Sam: Yes, that is the way I see it because that is my theological position. And in this case it is the only explanation that I can see for your continual discontent.

What was my "theological position"? It came up in our discussions about the attempt of Michael to be stronger than Jesus in doing good to other people.

You have the right idea, but in the wrong place. You're taking God's place in distributing perfect love and happiness. From my point of view we are only servants of God in trying to do this. This is the way in which I am able to accept some of my limitations in doing good.

The power behind this statement was my acceptance of the special revelation of God in Christ as revealed in the Scriptures, the church, and the work of the Spirit in my life. I did not make all of those sources immediately obvious to Michael, but they were very obvious in my own thinking. Even though I did not make specific references to special revelation, Michael discerned the connection between my belief in special revelation and my comments to him about general revelation. At least that is what I got out of one of his statements toward the end of the second interview.

You seem to have this all together in your own mind. You think that everything is OK for you because you see yourself as a servant of Jesus. It is OK to be a servant because you believe that God created us to be that way. So you don't have to be omnipotent in order to help other people. Right?

The Inextractible Relation of General and Special Revelation

The theological connection between general and special revelation is expressed by John Calvin.

For there are two different ways of working of the Son of God; the one, which becomes visible in the architecture of the world and in the natural order; the other, by means of which ruined nature is renewed and restored.[9]

It is this inextractible relationship that enhances the basic work of Christian counsel, which is to enable a person to know self and to know the will of God in relation to the self. The theological model for this operation in human understanding is the work of God in revealing himself both through that which he has created and that which he recreates through the special work of his Son and the divine guidance that was provided to patriarchs, prophets, and apostles. The culmination of this model is expressed theologically as the Incarnation. Christ combines the work of God in the first Adam with the work of God in the second Adam (Rom. 5–6).

Why would we say that this relationship is "inextractible"? The issue was addressed by Saint Augustine in section 14 of *On the Trinity*. Augustine described the way in which imagery, thought, and volition are the human channels through which persons move from knowledge and love of self to remembering and understanding and loving the triune God. We cannot investigate our own psyche without finding some traces of God's work. To explain what we find is to deal with God's general revelation, but always from the added viewpoint of special revelation. That is, the defect of our understanding caused by sin is corrected through the new understanding of ourselves in God through Jesus Christ. That which was fragmentary and distorted in the general revelation can become comprehensive and clear through the revelation of the very substance of God in his Son (Heb. 1).

From this viewpoint, the more deeply we delve into the knowledge of a person, the more we are compelled to explain that knowledge in the light of the revelation of God in Christ. Or, to move from Augustine's thought about this to modern existentialism, the more we know about the basic structure of the self, the more we must admit about the general revelation of God through that structure and the providence of God in recreating that structure through the special revelation of himself. This is the way in which insight becomes a part of our harmony with the way in which we have been made to serve our Maker.

How does this teaching work out in the practice of Christian counsel? Do we really find that the deeper questions about the self and the structure of the world will lead inevitably to understandings and explanations that come through supernatural revelation?

I faced one of these times in the fourth interview with Michael. He opened the interview with a statement that he could not be God. He noted that I accepted the idea of not being God. He, on the other hand, was really provoked by that admission. He wanted to do everything without any restrictions and without any risks. He wanted to be worshiped but he did not want to be close to people.

Sam: Well, intellectually I get the point and it is an important one. My feelings have never been quite as grandiose as yours so I can't participate in all of that, but I get the idea that you can't do what you want to for people because you think that it has to be a solo performance.

Michael: Well, I want people to admire me and all that. It's just that I like to do it by myself. Why can't I?

Sam: Because we were not created that way. For one thing, I believe that we are created to be servants of God and therefore we have to be in fellowship with him if we are going to do anything good. Also, I think that he created us to be in fellowship with one another and no one of us can do all the good for the rest.

That last statement "just popped out" of me. It was more a statement about myself and my own mission in life than it was about Michael and his particular circumstances. For the Christian counselor, the relationship between the knowledge of self and the knowledge of God is so inextractibly related, that any direct question about the way in which we function in the world will bring up something about God's revelation of how we are to function in the way that he has created us.

In the interviews with Michael, the inextractible relationship occurred most often when he gave an explanation for the way he was and the way he wanted to function. He would then ask me about this and I would respond by a comparison between his explanation and the explanation that I had from a theological point of view. Both in the interview from which we have just given a quotation and in the next interview, there were a number of questions about responsible fellowship.

Michael describes some ways in which he had shown some appreciation for his father and specified the way in which he was indebted to his father and the rest of the family for their care of him. But he was uneasy with this expression of gratitude.

Michael: But am I not supposed to be an independent person? Isn't that responsibility?

Sam: You're not God. You can only lead a satisfying and healthy life when you depend upon other people in some ways and they depend upon you. That's human responsibility. We have limitations and we help each other with those limitations. And we express appreciation for the help that we get.

Michael: Yes, but I spent many hours of therapy talking about how much I depend as a child upon my parents. What about that? Isn't that sick?

Sam: Sure, but I don't want you to get fixed on some circle of introspection. That is, if you keep on thinking that any expression of gratitude is a sign of dependency, you will never act in a responsible way with other people so that they will be happy to have you around them.

In this interchange we are demonstrating one of the functions of an inextractible relationship between general and special revelation, which is to clarify and deepen the explanations that people give for the way that they feel, think, and behave. Perhaps this is where I got the idea of Christian counsel rather than Christian counseling. I could not move with a person into deeper understanding of the reasons for behavior and attitudes without some theological answers to the questions that they raise about the most complete and harmonious explanations that could be given for attitudes and behaviors. This is what happened with Michael. We looked again and again at who he was in the light of the way he had been taught to explain himself and the way that he might explain himself if he accepted the revelation of God in Christ.[10]

The Relation of General and Special Revelation Distorted By Sin

Why do we have so much difficulty in recognizing who we are and what our relationship is to God who has made us? The biblical answer is: willful misjudgment of the reality of God's revelation (Isa. 1:3; Jer. 2:8; Rom. 1:21–23). The conclusion from this truth has been that the general revelation has been distorted in the minds of humans. Therefore the special revelation of God through patriarchs, prophets, priests—and finally in the complete revelation of Christ—was necessary to fulfill God's plan for the redemption of his creatures (John 3:16ff.; Eph. 1).

The particular question of Christian counsel in this teaching is: "Why was human knowledge of God blurred and what will be clarified about human knowledge after the cleansing effects of a new beginning in Christ?"

This question was central in the preaching and writing of the first

American theologian, Jonathan Edwards. The "Great Awakening" of the 1740s was a fruitful consequence of his explanation for our dreadful misjudgment of God's creation and the hope of a redeemed judgment through the Saviour.

Edwards considered the capacity for human reasoning to be deeply flawed. This flaw was seen in the effects of sin upon the unity of personality. Original sin broke the connection between head and heart. Consequently, people no longer had a complete understanding of what they heard, nor did they have full emotional commitment to the words that they spoke. Edwards described this as our "lost condition," in which we look at the signs of life, the great words of salvation and love, without an appropriate emotional response.

After identifying the symptom of original sin in the breakdown of head-heart communication, Edwards aimed first at the restoration of that unity. His preaching was designed to create the emotional conditions under which people could reasonably see the meaning of sin in salvation. When they could see the need for this connection to be made again by God, they were awakened to their condition and responsive to the gospel.[11]

To follow the thought of Edwards into modern terminology, we might say that the distortion of general revelation is an incapacity to recognize ourselves as the human beings who were made in the image of God. This incapacity is demonstrated in the split between affective and cognitive aspects of personality, between intuition and explanation, between rationality and the recognition of unconscious elements of our being.

So long as these splits continue within us, we cannot understand the unity of the world around us or respond to it by recognition that this is the work of our Creator.

Is this the way in which we see the defect of human understanding in our ministry of counsel? There were a number of remarks by Michael that demonstrated his ability to see and describe this difficulty in perception. In our seventh session he said,

You know what I have decided? I have been angry with God because he was God. I have tried to act like I was God myself. I mean, I felt that I could have whatever I wanted without having to work for it. And this is the way things ought to be. But I am just another human being like you. The world is not made like I want

71

it to be. Oh sure, I can go off into a manic flight to gain the satisfaction that I want without having to take any responsibility, but that doesn't seem so great anymore. I have got to think about gaining satisfaction from being a human being.

In this speech I detected two aspects of the question about distortion in general revelation and the relationship between general and special revelation.

Michael describes the distortion of general revelation as an inability to see himself as a limited human being. He has a grand design for himself and for his world. In manic flights he sees himself as God. When he recovers, he is angry because God is the real God and Michael is a god only in his fantasy life. This defect in perception has come about because of a separation between that which Michael feels about himself and that which is actually occurring in the world around him, and in himself. The dynamic reasons for this split go back into traumatic events of childhood. But an understanding of why he began to malfunction is only part of the problem. We must also explain why the malfunction persists. The split between head and heart maintains the misperception.

The second conclusion from Michael's speech is that the revelation of God as God is the ultimate corrective for the misperception that Michael has of himself. He implies that he will not gain satisfaction from being a human being until he has first accepted the corrective to his misinterpretation of life with a submission to the original order of life that has been offered to him by God.

Michael did make the connection between his misinterpretations of reality and the corrective revelation of God in the sixth interview.

Michael: Now, let me see if I have got something straight. My therapist keeps telling me that I am looking for an unconditional love and total acceptance. You are telling me that everybody has limitations and that this is an impossible search. Well, you did not put it in quite those words, but you have said that I will never be able to do everything that I fantasize; and I cannot expect my parents or anyone else to do everything for me that I want. So, it looks like I am going to have to

find somebody who is without limitations to give me
the acceptance that I want.

Sam: Yes.

Michael: So, this is where Jesus comes in. He is the one who
offers the kind of acceptance that I am not going to get
from anybody else. But I will not get that acceptance
when I feel like a manic and equal to him or above him.
I only have that kind of security that Christians talk
about when I give up trying to think that I can accept
everybody like God does or that I can hold my parents
responsible for accepting me like God should.

Sam: You've got it.

In this exchange, Michael is again showing the connection between the deprivation of love that led to the distortion of his
recognition of reality, and also the way in which the special revelation in Jesus will offer a continual restructuring and strengthening
of his realistic search for acceptance. This is the plan for his recov-
ery. First, there will be a basic change in his perception of himself
and his world and, second, there will be a continual interchange
between the new way that he sees himself and the qualities of God
in Christ that will maintain the responsible search for acceptance
and the expression of appreciation to those who aid him in this.

Restoring the Relation Between General and
Special Revelation

The model and motivation for an interrelationship of general
and special revelation is the mind of Christ. His way of thinking
about his earthly ministry is the model for our ways of thinking
about our godly mission in the world (Phil. 2:1–11; John 13:12–20,
34; 14:25–26; 15:18–27; 17:6–8, 17, 25–26). The Spirit of Christ
within us is the motivator for a comprehensive knowledge of love
for ourselves and others, a knowledge that goes beyond the general
revelation to include the "love of Christ which surpasses knowledge" (Eph. 3:14–19).

I tried to present this combination of general and special revelation
to Michael on the occasions when he was open about his conflicted
perception of himself.

Michael: If I don't carry my share of the load in the family, I feel bad about it. And then when I am out with some good-looking woman, I wonder why she spends time with me. I don't know. I would like to find some rich debutante who appreciates art and who appreciates me and who would take care of me for life. But then I get to feeling guilty about that.

Sam: You are one of the best arguments I have ever heard for the doctrine of the image of God.

Michael: *I'm* the image of God? I thought that identification with God was sick!

Sam: Well, yes, in the way you use it during a manic episode. But what I feel is a continual reminder in your emotions that you are made as a responsible human being. On the one hand, you were made for affection and appreciation from others. And on the other hand, you were made by God to be his servant in the vineyard, which is the world of his creation. And this includes your responsibility as a brother to your neighbor.

Michael: So, if I'm not treating the girl next door as my neighbor, then I should feel uneasy?

Is this *really* an example of the "breadth, and length, and depth, and height . . . to know the love of Christ, which passeth knowledge . . ." (Eph. 3:18, 19 KJV)? I doubt it, but it is all that I have to offer from that interview. At least, I was trying to combine general and special revelation in my own thoughts. That is, I sought to be as attentive as possible to myself and my client on the basis of the training I had received in counseling that leads toward general-special revelation. And I also hoped that I was open to the application of the Spirit to the particular feelings or thoughts that Michael and I had in our conversations.

Obstacles to Restoring this Relationship

But my hesitancy in presenting any definitive example of integration, general and special, has lead me to confess some difficulties in achieving this mature objective in Christian counsel.

First, I must admit that, as human beings, neither counselor nor client can speak with perfect knowledge.

There are so many flaws in our reasoning, so many surges of selfishness, anxiety and fear that reality is constantly distorted. Only through divine grace can we achieve the harmonious perception of self and the world that will give confidence to our decisions.[12] This perception is made possible by the indwelling power of the Holy Spirit, which creates a progressive unity between head and heart. The perception of and practice of love, for example, is still "through a glass, darkly" (1 Cor. 13:12). To relate general and special revelation is not only to confess that we are imperfect in our natural understanding, but also that our knowledge of the mind of Christ is incomplete (1 Cor. 13:9).

The sense of imperfection and incompleteness has characterized modern Protestant and Catholic discussions of personal moral decisions. John Macquarrie has taken the lead in formulating "natural law" in terms of general relationships rather than in a comprehensive and uncompromising system of specific laws and rules.[13] Charles Curran expresses the modern Catholic awareness of limitations when he qualifies the power of human reason by the word "some": "It is part of the Catholic theological tradition to uphold a basic goodness present in man, the power of human reason to arrive at some speculative and practical truths, and some continuity between man and grace."[14]

A sense of tentativeness is most appropriate in a discussion of human situations in which the created order, the world we observe, provides no definitive conclusions and the divine law provides no specific direction. So long as there is a sense of tentativeness in these areas, Christian counsel can be realistic in guidance toward decisions by individuals. The enemy of this humble concern is pride in the pastoral office and promotion of the church's authority.

The *second* confession is my *inability to fit difficult cases of conscience into a pre-set statement of church law or order.*

The problems created by an attempt to place organizational sanctions upon every tragedy of life is illustrated in the best of the post-World War I moral theologians, Bishop K. E. Kirk.

Kirk noted the dangers of pride and church authority in his discussion of the "nature and scope of moral theology."[15] He noted first that pastors sometimes consider their own authority as the final word in *doubtful* cases. This "blunted the discernment and narrowed the range of the individual conscience."[16] The second discrediting attitude was connected to "a probable opinion," that is, a course of action in which good or wise men see no sin or danger of sin, even though the counselee thinks that individual conscience or public opinion may be opposed. Bishop Kirk concluded that "probabilism" was a very real danger to the maintenance of a high ideal of conduct in the Christian community. He felt that the Church of England's loss of authority in the field of moral conduct was a direct result of its use of probabilism.

But in this statement were the seeds of discord between concern for troubled persons and security of an ecclesiastical organization. I learned from some students of Bishop Kirk that his desires to protect the reputation of the church in cases of divorce was a major cause of resentment against moral theology. One of the bishop's students, who later attained high office in the church, was incensed by the bishop's insistence that a godly missionary could have no place in the church when he returned as a divorced person from foreign service.

The bishop was acutely aware of the problems created by his injection of the reputation of an organization into the discussion of personal moral and spiritual problems. His biographer noted Kirk's attempt to reconcile church reputation and pastoral concern in divorce cases. Kirk decided that a divorced person could receive communion if the person were "invincibly ignorant." That is, the person knew the teachings of the church against divorce and yet believed that he or she was in fellowship with God, no matter what restrictions the organized church placed upon him or her. The bishop was willing for the "invincibly ignorant" to take communion so long as their divorce was not known in the place where they took communion, but he would not allow divorced persons to remarry in the church.[17] Thus the bishop placed public reputation above an acceptance for troubled people.

Some modern Roman Catholic scholars have sought to avoid the same danger by statements such as those of Charles Curran: "When Church pronouncements or statements concern specific issues, then the Church must realize that its statements cannot claim to have absolute certitude."[18] Bernard Häring notes the hundreds of restrictive laws of the church concerning the reception and administration of the sacraments and concludes that many priests then administer the sacraments with great anxiety and fear. His solution would be fewer restrictive laws and a reduction in the overpowering fear of the Church. Without this, he believes that love cannot be the primary consideration in the molding of the Christian life.[19]

Most Protestant theologians have accepted this spirit of tentativeness in relation to "natural cases of conscience."[20] But among fundamentalist Protestants there arose in the 1970s a teaching of absolute certainty concerning personal moral conduct that was equal in scope and certainty to any authoritarian statement by a Roman Catholic theologian. The difference was the fundamentalist's use of proof texts instead of Curia pronouncements about natural law. The most widely publicized writings by Jay Adams went beyond Roman Catholic moral teaching, extending a condemnation of suffering people to include those who are mentally ill.[21] The condemnation was supported by a reference to Psalm 58:3. The general assertion that condemnation of the mentally ill is the authoritative biblical approach seems to come more from his agnostic teacher, O. Hobart Mowrer, than from the Bible.[22]

The Mowrer-Adams condemnation of people in trouble was welcomed by some fundamentalists and evangelicals because they could not accept the client-centered emphasis of pastoral psychology in the post-World War II era. Many of these Christian counselors have not read the mainline denominational texts by Wayne Oates, William Hulme, or Paul Johnson. These authors followed the classical tradition of pastoral care in which there was a balance between judgment and acceptance.

This balance had first been broken in the 1950s through an overemphasis upon the client-centered method of Carl Rogers. Pastoral psychologists such as Seward Hiltner and Howard Clinebell pursued this emphasis to the point where no theological statements or ethical judgments were permitted in Christian counsel.[23]

The rejection of explicit theology in early writings by Hiltner and Clinebell seemed to be scientifically correct in the 1950s because of the acceptance of the unconscious among psychoanalytically-oriented therapists. In analytic theory, religious ideation was a conscious defense against unacceptable unconscious strivings. This defense system was to be discarded by the client before progress could be made in uncovering unconscious conflict.

Progress in Christian counsel has certainly been made through the insights of Rogers, Hiltner, Clinebell, and others. But it seems that with each new step in our knowledge of ourselves and God there is an over-balancing of emphasis toward general or special revelation. When we learn from psychology, the pendulum swings toward general revelation. Then there is a reaction against all general revelation in Mowrer-Adams. We seem to repeat the problems of the Reformation. The Reformers rejected "natural law" because of the Thomistic system of rational decisions that could be made apart from the special revelation of God in Christ.[24]

When we review the debates about general and special revelation from the days of Luther and Calvin to the days of Barth and Brunner, we can only conclude that this essential issue in Christian counsel cannot be institutionalized. No one system of thought can have the breadth, the depth, or the full knowledge of Christ in itself. All our solutions to human problems are partial and none of us can predict the exact way in which the Spirit will work in a particular case.

My *third* admission is that *no amount of natural ability, professional training, or spiritual devotion has given me more than brief clues concerning this question:* What is this counselee's motivation? Who can understand the depths of the self or the heights of inspiration from God? These statements of limitation come not only from the small amount of knowledge that I have of myself in relation to God, but also through a study of the theories of the unconscious that have come to us from Sigmund Freud and Carl Jung. My theological training was so set upon logical, conscious decision-making that I needed the corrective of theories on unconscious motivation. I am no longer comfortable with a rational process of decision which guides a troubled person toward logical conclusions which are in line with authoritative teaching.[25] There must always be some inquiry into the deeper way in which a person is able to accept theological teaching.[26] There is also a necessity for counselors to admit the force of unconscious motivation either through the basic structure of their character or through the mental mechanisms that condition their response to other persons.[27]

We are in a continual tension between intellect and "the affections."[28] Where is the balance? In the twentieth century, theories of the unconscious have often disregarded the intellect and deepened the concept of "affections." Consequently, counselors were trained to listen for deeper manifestations of emotions and inhibit any tendency toward advice-giving. The only "appeal to the will" was to be the creation of an accepting climate within which a person could express unacceptable emotions and resolve interpersonal difficulties through self-insight.

Both the theory of the unconscious and the methods of client-centered therapy were an advance over pious exhortations that were offered without any deeper knowledge of the self. "Natural law" could no longer be seen as an intellectual system of obvious precepts about the self. It must now be deepened to include strivings for good and evil that were below the conscious level and stress the unity of the self at all levels.

Although an awareness of the unconscious led to more tentative conclusions about the motivation for conduct, investigators of unconscious processes have increased the precision with which counselors can identify the elusive bases of motivation and the typical patterns of coping with expectations from self and others. Psychoanalytic studies of the unconscious led to descriptions of "coping mechanisms." These helped to explain why our rational decisions can be derailed by the unconscious mechanisms of repression, displacement, and projection. On the other hand, conscious decisions can be strengthened by the unconscious coping mechanisms of suppression, altruism, and humor.[29]

A further deepening of self-understanding as conscious and unconscious came through biblical studies of mind and body by H. Wheeler Robinson, Johannes Pedersen, D. R. G. Owens, John A. T. Robinson, and H. W. Wolff. Both the Old Testament and New Testament view of the image of God and the perception of self were now seen at much deeper levels than in the traditional emphasis upon the conscious, rational, reasoning self.

The biblical evidence is that human nature contains more than a psychological system which can be categorized, predicted, and controlled by experts in the natural sciences. Human beings are unified as body and soul, soul and spirit.

This is a transcendent anthropology, which requires a strong bond between the image of God, the created order, and the divine command.[30]

One center for the synthesis of these forces has been traditionally designated as "the conscience." This synthesizer of the human impulses and prohibitions received more explicit understanding—and limitations, as a result of studies in biblical anthropology and newer theories of the unconscious, as we will see in the following chapter.[31]

NOTES

1. John Oman, *Grace and Personality* (New York: Association Press, 1961).
2. Consider this quotation from John Calvin: "We lay it down as a position not to be controverted, that the human mind, even by natural instinct, possesses some sense of a Deity" (*Institutes*, V., x., 5).
3. The term "general revelation" is used instead of "natural theology" because of the identification of natural theology with a rational knowledge of God that is derived independently of the special revelation of God in Christ. Natural theology or natural law emphasizes rationality to a point where revelation seems unnecessary for an understanding of and creative activity by a person in this world. For a discussion of these two terms see G. C. Berkouwer, *General Revelation* (Grand Rapids: William B. Eerdmans, 1955), pp. 37–46.
4. For a review of various approaches to the knowledge of God in nature and in conscience, see L. Harold DeWolf, "The Theological Rejection of Natural Theology: An Evaluation," *The Journal of Religious Thought*, vol. 15:2 (Spring-Summer 1958), pp. 91–105.
5. This viewpoint is referred to as "christo-monism" by Berkouwer, *General Revelation*, pp. 112ff.
6. Franz Boeckle, *Law and Conscience*, tr. James Donnelly (New York: Sheed and Ward, 1966), pp. 82ff.
7. Christopher Wordsworth, *Bishop Sanderson's Lectures on Conscience and Human Law, Delivered in the Divinity School at Oxford* (Oxford: James Williamson, 1877); K. E. Kirk, *Some Principles of Moral Theology* (London: Longmans, Green and Company, 1921); Lindsay Dewar, *Moral Theology in the Modern World* (London: A. R. Mowbray, 1964); Kenneth Leech, *Soul Friend* (London: Sheldon Press, 1977).
8. The writings of K. E. Kirk and Emil Brunner were major resources to me at the time of counsel with Michael.
9. Quoted in Emil Brunner, *Revelation and Reason* (Philadelphia: Westminster Press, 1946), p. 62.
10. The importance of general and special revelation as an explanation of human nature is found in statements such as those of Bonhoeffer, "To be a Christian is to be a man." In quoting this statement, John Macquarrie adds that the natural law helps us to know the inner tendencies and interrelationships that make and keep human life human. John Macquarrie, *Three Issues in Ethics* (New York: Harper and Row, 1970), pp. 83ff.
11. Among the numerous works of Edwards published by Yale University Press and others, the most readable are his *Narrative of the Great Awakening* and *Religious Affections*. A discussion of Edwards' emphasis upon human capacity in the knowledge of God may be found in James Seller's *Theological Ethics*

(New York: Macmillan Company, 1966), p. 86, and in Douglas J. Elwood, *The Philosophical Theology of Jonathan Edwards* (New York: Columbia University Press, 1960), pp. 112–32.

12. The sense of harmony, defined as "beauty" was considered to be the comprehensive sign of salvation in the theology of Jonathan Edwards. See Elwood, *The Philosophical Theology of Jonathan Edwards.*

13. Macquarrie, *Three Issues in Ethics,* pp. 104ff.

14. Charles Curran, *New Perspectives in Moral Theology* (Notre Dame: Fides, 1974), p. 31.

15. Kirk, *Principles of Moral Theology,* pp. 13–15.

16. Ibid., p. 13.

17. Eric W. Kemp, *The Life and Letters of Kenneth Escott Kirk* (London: Hodden and Stoughton, 1959); K. E. Kirk, *Conscience and Its Problems* (London: Longmans, Green and Co., 1927), pp. 136–42.

18. Charles Curran, *New Perspectives in Moral Theology,* p. 155.

19. Quoted in L. Harold DeWolf, *Responsible Freedom* (New York: Harper and Row, 1971), p. 129.

20. See for example Lewis Smedes, *Mere Morality* (Grand Rapids: William B. Eerdmans, 1983).

21. Jay Adams, *Competent to Counsel,* pp. 29–40, 105.

22. Ibid., pp. 29–30, xvi.

23. Seward Hiltner, *The Counselor in Counseling* (Nashville: Abingdon Press, 1952), p. 136; and Hiltner's criticism of Clinebell as "devoid of any theological reference on connectedness," Seward Hiltner, "The Minister and the Care of Souls," *Union Seminary Quarterly Review* (Winter-Summer 1975) 30:2–4, p. 215. When I mentioned this quote to Clinebell, he smiled and said: "Perhaps the kettle is calling the frying-pan black."

24. For a discussion of the "natural theology of Rome," see Berkouwer, *General Revelation,* pp. 61–83. A defense of the system is found in Franz Boeckle, *Law and Conscience.*

25. The history of this "argumentative" method, and examples, are given by E. Brooks Holifield in chap. 2 of *A History of Pastoral Care in America* (Nashville: Abingdon Press, 1983).

26. Studies in biblical theology often redress our rational emphasis with the intuitive psychology of the Hebrew writers of the Old Testament. See Johannes Pedersen, *Israel,* I-II, esp. the discussion of dreams, vol. 1, pp. 134ff.

27. The effect of personality structure upon the shape of academic theology has been brilliantly presented by Oscar Pfister, *Christianity and Fear* (London: George Allen and Unwin, 1948).

28. For a summary of this development in the eighteenth and nineteenth centuries, see Holifield, *History of Pastoral Care.*

29. For the evidence from a study of Harvard graduates, see George Vaillant, *Adaptation to Life* (Boston: Little, Brown and Co., 1977), pp. 73–192.

30. See the arguments of John Macquarrie, who quotes with approval the opinions of Karl Rahner on "transcendent anthropology" in Macquarrie's *Three Issues in Ethics,* pp. 85ff.

31. This chapter has not discussed a related topic, the religious view of nature, or the doctrine of creation. For scientific and religious views of nature, see Leroy Rowner, ed., *On Nature* (Notre Dame, 1984). On the doctrine of creation, see Bernhard W. Anderson, *Creation in the Old Testament* (Philadelphia: Fortress Press, 1984).

Because of the personal emphasis of pastoral theology, the doctrine of creation has been subsumed under the doctrine of the image of God in this particular chapter. If I were writing a popular text on systematic theology, the doctrine of God would come first. This would be in keeping with the general response of Americans to the question: "When you think about God, how likely are each of these images to come to your mind?" The image chosen by 82 percent of the respondents was of God as Creator. Healer was chosen by 69 percent and Friend by 62 percent. *Psychology Today*, June 1985, p. 12.

6

Cases of Conscience

A common ground for discussion between all humans, regardless of their spiritual state, is the conscience. But is this a connecting link between human longing and divine command or just between humans? Should we receive the sensation of guilt as a storm warning of the soul or a side-effect of repressive culture? How do we know the difference, and what does human guilt have to do with sin as the distortion of our relationship to God?

Christian counsel has traditionally been associated with questions of conscience.[1] These questions were brought to a counselor because it was difficult for an individual to know how a particular set of circumstances could fit under some general rule of Christian character. In response to these inquiries from troubled parishioners, the medieval church developed a collection of precedents for conduct which would be very much like the case-study method of modern law. By asking questions about the nature of a moral dilemma, a priest would be able to find a precedent that would fit a particular case and state the general principle that applied to cases of that type.

The name for this type of counsel was "casuistry." Since most of the cases brought to the priest were perplexing, casuists did not offer absolute answers, but did advise that one course of action would probably be more moral than another.[2] Three procedures were used in casuistry. First, general principles were developed from a study of a variety of similar cases. These formed the precedents to be used in relation to a particular case. Second, there was the choice of a precedent that would be most applicable to a particular case. Third, the case was presented skillfully so that persons would find this answer applicable to their own circumstances.[3]

Casuistry was built upon a theory of the conscience that was systematized by Thomas Aquinas. Human beings were assumed by Aquinas to be rational persons who could decide between good and evil because God had provided general knowledge of himself in the world that he had created. Conscience was the application of the moral law of nature to particular actions.[4]

This application of conscience was seldom mentioned in Protestant works on pastoral counseling in the post-World War II period. The very term *casuistry* was looked upon with suspicion by Protestant pastoral counselors who had been trained to suspect that rational explanations were little more than a cover-up for forbidden unconscious processes. The rise of "dynamic psychology" was a fatal threat to the traditional mental exercises of casuistry.

There were some problems within casuistry itself. It contained an element of formalism that restricted the Spirit. There seemed to be so little openness to God's working in the inner life, more emphasis upon the security of always being right than commitment to faith and bold sacrifice.

In contrast to the caution of traditional casuistry, modern spiritual counsel is built on an adventuresome faith that God is faithful when we follow our deepest duty, whether we are "right" or "wrong" by the standards of conventional morality or made comfortable by rational deductions.

To place such emphasis upon an inner voice is to call for a clear definition of that which has been traditionally associated with inner response to the Spirit, or conscience.

Storm Warning of the Soul

How are we to define this all-encompassing, elusive term, *conscience*? Our answer to this question will determine the depths of spirituality in our counsel. Actually, we will be giving several answers, for people function at different levels of moral responsibility and each of these may be identified in some way with the conscience.

Conscience as Custom

First, conscience is often defined as an inner response to custom or to our way of making sense out of what we have been taught. Western philosophers have sometimes defined the conscience in this way, especially when they thought of it as an awareness of moral law. Kant thought of the conscience as direct intuition as tested by reason. Montaigne thought that the conscience proceeded from custom. In this he anticipated the Freudian emphasis upon the conscience as an unconscious censor that would bring us into conformity with the customary requirements of our civilization.

Definitions at this level of the conscience are often useful in counsel. The conscience is a necessary indicator of our awareness of the rights of others and our own. The necessity for conscience at this level has increased in the post-Vietnam era with its stress upon self-expression, decision making according to the situation of the moment, and an unconditional acceptance of almost anything but hypocrisy. The absence of moral instruction at this level of the conscience has caused a vague uneasiness in many young adults. They would like to have some moral basis for their decisions, but they have neither theoretical precepts nor personal examples of what is fitting. All they can do is "fit in." They endure all manner of personal injustice because they do not know how to define justice for themselves.[5]

Conscience as custom is also a key to understanding the injustice that middle-aged persons have heaped upon themselves and others. These are the cases that Freud described in which the conscience is an unconscious repressor of our basic desires, a parental voice of accusation from the past. This is the problem of the infantile conscience, the need to do whatever is approved by powerful people, the desire to do right without asking why.

Since this type of conscience is below the level of our self-awareness, we may find ourselves in the bewildering condition that was called "scrupulosity" by moral theologians of previous generations.[6] The condition was first described by priestly confessors who were continually sought out by exemplary individuals who wished to confess vague sins. No amount of penance or reassurance of forgiveness seemed to be sufficient. In the twentieth century, counselors observe the infantile conscience in those who have a vague sense of unworthiness whenever they violate a custom implanted since childhood. One of the most common examples is the turmoil of delayed adolescence, in which a young adult does not feel worthy to do anything beyond the approval of parents.

If we combine these *consequences of conscience as custom* we may avoid two errors in counsel. The *first* is to push the rational understanding of right and wrong without an awareness of unconscious motivation. This was a continual problem in the moral theology of the nineteenth century. The second mistake is more modern, an indifference to custom and the equation of impulse gratification with good mental health.

The first of these errors is avoided when we recognize the unconscious elements in all of our decisions. The *second* is avoided when we own what we have been since our childhood and recognize the necessity of naming "that which is just" to ourselves and others in the society of which we are a part.

What is the duty of a Christian counselor or a person who is conscientious at the level of customary morality? *We are to help people feel guilty about the right things and remove guilt about the wrong things.* The Lord Jesus denounced the Pharisees of his day for obsessive concerns about small issues, while they neglected the weightier matters of justice and mercy and faith (Matt. 23:13-24).[7] This is hypocrisy, an exclusion of love and a preoccupation with correct procedure as guarantees of righteousness.

The confrontation by Jesus is an opportunity to talk about a second level of conscience, at which we become aware of our unthinking assumptions of right and wrong. At this *second stage, conflict begins between what we have been taught and what God actually requires of us.* The Christian challenge is a transformation of the conscience (Rom. 12:1-2). This is the task of Christian counsel. We often begin our conversations with people who consult us because of some storm warning in their soul arising from the cultural conscience. With this as a beginning, we can move on to a deeper understanding of guilt and a surrender of ourselves to the Spirit of God who provides the conviction of sin for a godly repentance.

In the next three sections of this chapter I will describe the preliminary questions of conscience which shape guilt toward godly values. In the following chapter we will consider the answer to conviction of sin, which is found in repentance and the forgiveness of sins through the redeeming work of Christ.

Our first task is to relate the warnings of a cultural conscience to the deeper aspects of sin and guilt. A deacon and a pastor faced this challenge in their ministry to May Andrews, a forty-five-year-old mother of teenage children who was married to a businessman who occasionally attended church. The pastor first heard about May's problem through the deacon who said: "Mrs. Andrews has asked if my wife or I saw any tension between her and her husband at the church's Christmas party. I said that I thought it was OK, but she persisted in wanting to know if they might have given the wrong impression. She said that she was sometimes unhappy with her husband. I told her that if she had any problem about her marriage that she should come and talk to you, preacher."

The next week May consulted the pastor about the problem of a conventional husband who made all the decisions in their family. She had always tried to give in to him because she felt that he needed to feel that he was head of the house. Instinctively, she was sure that he was uncertain of himself and needed that cultural support. But now she was feeling that he had withdrawn more and more from her and that she had no one to turn to except a former sweetheart who had kept some social contacts with her ever since high school. From time to time the former sweetheart would call to say how he really cared for her and hoped that they could get together again as they did before she was married. She was frightened by her longings for this sweetheart from the past who seemed to offer all the affection that she was denied by her conventional husband. What should she do?

The pastor might have given the conventional response: "Let us pray that God will give you strength to resist temptation!" Instead of such an abrupt cutoff, the pastor took time to hear May's longings and *then* gave her some perspective on the way to resist adultery. In doing so, he avoided both the unfeeling sternness of traditional counseling and the nonchalant acceptance of any behavior which has characterized some counseling since World War II. The pastor recognizes the importance of family solidarity and self-respect to May and he will give some support to this part of her moral struggle.

But at the same time, he gives no support to the conventional wisdom of a dutiful and silent wife. He does not want her to feel guilty about speaking up to her husband, Alfred. In fact, his early responses to May are designed to make her feel anxious about a deeper moral problem, her lack of intimate conversation with her own husband.

May: God is not going to put up with me if I go on like this—thinking this way!

Pastor: Good point. If you commit adultery, he will be disappointed and so will I.

May: So what am I to do? My prayers at daybreak or at night are not answered!

Pastor: Well, since God doesn't answer us audibly, we have to look for signs of his power in our lives. One sign would be your willingness to let Alfred know that you really need him. It would show that you trusted enough in God's strength to admit your own weakness.

May: Oh yes. I hadn't thought of that as a part of prayer, but I did decide that I had to tell him something. I shouldn't break up the home without telling him something. So last night I woke him up and said that I couldn't stand things any more like they were at the ice cream social after church Sunday night. Other couples were laughing with each other, and I saw you put your arm around your wife. And I so much wanted him to do that to me! So I leaned over toward him, and he moved away. He moved away. And I felt all by myself. I told him it was just horrible!

Pastor: So you really told him how you felt, miserable and all that . . .

If this dialogue is successful, May will be helped because she will find a positive means of improving her marriage, namely the ability to speak openly with her husband about the deeper concerns of her life. This is the area of life in which elements of the moral law may grow: love and justice and mercy.[8]

Defeat through Self-Deceit

How is May going to manage the admission that she is a lonely, unloved person? This will get us deeper into the way that she sees herself and will avoid the common professional conclusion that her marriage will get better just because she tells Alfred of her loneliness. She might perpetuate a greedy desire for attention and an insatiable appetite for reassurance that would cause Alfred to close up even more as an act of self-preservation. The final state of her marriage would be worse than the first unless we can move her guilt and self-awareness to something deeper than the mere recitation of her emotional needs.

That deeper level was disclosed when May made some additional admissions in the first interview, namely that she had not been really close to anyone since the death of a beloved parent. Since then she had wanted to go back to the days when her children were little and she really felt that she was needed. Somehow the need for her former sweetheart had continually increased since the death of her parent. She'd not followed this temptation, but she continued to be worried.

Pastor: What did you do about this worry? How did it go away—if it did for a while?

May: I went to a counselor. He asked about my history and how close I was to my father. He helped me to see that I needed lots of love. That's why that man [the high school sweetheart] was so attractive. The counselor helped me to see that I couldn't go into an affair and feel right about my marriage. And I certainly couldn't tell Alfred about my thoughts, for he can't take something that upsets his masculine image. But I just wish I had someone to care for me.

Should May feel guilty because she has a desire for affection, a longing to be accepted and needed? No, but that need should be confessed, because guilt or self-approval appear in the way in which we acknowledge our needs and express them.

The problem of the conscience at this level is the issue of honesty and dishonesty, especially in relationship to self-love and pride. Saint Paul declared that in the process of self-glorification we change "the truth of God into a lie" (Rom. 1:25). We become vain in our imagination and our heart is darkened.[9] The Gospels record Jesus' recognition that people opposed him because they were blind to themselves (John 9). If the Pharisees had only admitted their moral blindness, they would have been healed by Christ. But since they stubbornly maintained that they saw all that they needed to see correctly, they remained in their sin.

The challenge of the Christian counselor at this stage of conscience is *to disclose the unconscious deceptions that keep us feeling vaguely guilty.*

If the counselee accepts this challenge, counsel will begin to include some elements of insight that have usually been defined as a part of psychotherapy. This would be especially so if the counselee has been unaware of the ways in which he or she has made needs known, both to self and to others. Unconscious processes will become partially conscious and this is one of the distinguishing marks of therapy.

Did May become aware of some of the unconscious deceptions that kept her feeling vaguely guilty? Late in the first interview, the pastor moved May toward a knowledge of herself that had been previously unknown. As they were talking about the "responsible citizen" who had been her sweetheart in high school, the pastor remarked that she must be looking for a secure, reliable man.

May: Yes. In many ways he's like the counselor. I fell in love with him. We talked about it. I love to be loved by someone I can just depend on.

Pastor: And for the moment you fantasize having that with the respectable citizen who will be your lover.

May: It's just that he is so considerate.

Pastor: Wait. That doesn't quite add up with the sense of judgment I see in you about your husband.

May: How's that?

Pastor: You size him up well and have no illusions about his good and bad points. But when you talk about the other man, you're a little girl again.

May: A what?

Pastor: When you talk about the man it's not with mature judgment, but with adolescent fantasy, like a fourteen-year-old who believes the line being fed her. Where's your realism?

May: About what?

Pastor: Well, for example, he knows what a time you had disengaging yourself emotionally from him in the past. Now, two months after the death of your mother, when you're very vulnerable because a major source of support is gone, he calls to offer support through an affair.

May: You make it sound like he's taking advantage of me!

Pastor: Well?

In this conversation the pastor identifies a fantasy of May's and also says that she acts like a little girl when she thinks about her high school sweetheart. She is living with adolescent fantasy. If May had been willing to talk more about her fantasy, then she might have discovered some of the ways in which she has deceived herself into thinking that she is still fourteen years old. In the first interview she did not do this, perhaps because the pastor then moved on to talk more about the dangers of putting her fourteen-year-old fantasy into action with her former sweetheart. He told me later that he wanted to be sure that she did not make matters worse by going to bed with another man, when he hoped to have additional conversations with her in which she would concentrate upon the ways that she had been handling her need for acceptance and affection.

Coping Mechanisms

It appears that May has handled her need for affection by *displacement*. That is, without being aware of it, she has placed her need for affection into relationships where it does not realistically belong. She thought that she was in love with her therapist and she might admit that she would like to be in love again with her high-school sweetheart. That which should belong in her relationship to her husband has been blocked and now finds expression in other ways.

Displacement is one of the three most self-defeating mechanisms by which we unconsciously cope with various stresses in life. This is the opinion of Dr. George Vaillant in his longitudinal research study of one hundred university graduates from adolescence to maturity.[10] The other two mechanisms are repression and projection. *Repression* is the conscious denial of needs that are strongly felt within ourselves. May, for example, may be repressing a strong desire for the dependence and security that she felt as a fourteen-year-old girl. (At least she is not repressing her need for affection. This much was recovered in her previous therapy.) The third common mechanism that often leads us to psychological defeat is *projection*. This is an attempt to read into the attitudes and actions of others a desire within ourself that is unacceptable. If May were not so aware of her need for affection, she might have projected upon her therapist and other men a desire to sexually possess her. In such a case, she would have denied any sexual urgings on her part, but would be continually worried about the way in which men sought to seduce her.

In cases where repression, displacement, and projection were identified as the principle unconscious means by which some Harvard graduates adapted to life, Dr. Vaillant found a concurrent failure in career, marriage, and maturity.

In contrast, other graduates developed favorable interpersonal relationships, business success, and personal maturity because they relied upon the unconscious mechanisms of suppression, humor, and altruism.

When we mention suppression, humor, and altruism we can see some hope for May. These unconscious mechanisms are just as powerful as the self-defeating ones but they lead to healthy coping with life. They are positive channels for moral influence, the ways by which love, justice, and integrity are gratefully expressed from the depths of our being.

For the present, May needs the workhorse of morality, suppression. *Suppression* is the ability to almost automatically postpone immediate gratification in favor of the long-term attainment of a desired goal in life. It is a concomitant of a positive and confident self-image, in which we know that we have the power to suppress some desires of the present time and that we will be rewarded by hard work and discipline and that the result will be a better enjoyment of that desire at some time in the future. Suppression is also possible because we are realistic in our estimates of what others will approve and disapprove from us. We know that some rewards are possible at the present time but that others are inappropriate. Furthermore, we have a realistic picture of who we are and how we will have to act in order to gain socially-approved desires in life.

In suppression, we do not deny a desire, as in repression, but figure out ways to fulfill that desire in appropriate ways, if possible. May has admitted her need for intimacy and now she must think of ways to satisfy that need. Can she develop enough self-respect to seek this appropriately with her husband, children, and associates? Or will the mechanism of displacement defeat this by continuing to fuel her adolescent fantasies with the feeling that she is in love with her former therapist or with a man who represents the idyllic love of a fourteen-year-old?

Perhaps the pastor can help by the introduction of another positive mechanism, *humor*. Humor is the ability to laugh at our startled or baneful look when we must suppress something. Or it is a smile at the way that others seek so frantically to achieve that which will come to them anyway if they would just continue to be sensible in their course of action. It is a cheerful recognition that minor checks to our ambition or the mixture of good and evil in every decision will only prove in the long run that we are lovable human beings. The pastor tried to move toward some humor after May said, "You make it sound like he's taking advantage of me!" The pastor replied, "Well?"

May:	(Pause) I hadn't thought of that. I admit that he just wants sex. But he is so considerate.
Pastor:	Considerate in what way?
May:	He treats me like a person.
Pastor:	Hmm.
May:	You doubt this?
Pastor:	Yep.
May:	Why?
Pastor:	First, he's not going to marry you. If he really knows you, he knows that children's love and social or community respect are very important to you.
May:	Yes. It's dreadful to think what the children would think of me . . .
Pastor:	And your considerate man would mess all that up (smile).
May:	You can be sarcastic. (Pause) Perhaps I need it. But why doesn't God take away my temptation?

May would have been healthier and more moral if she could have laughed at herself instead of referring again to God and her temptation. One of the ways in which God could deliver her from her temptation would be through a wider perspective. Could she rise above herself and look at the middle-aged woman who is pretending that she is a fourteen-year-old girl in love? That is slightly ridiculous. And since she has not yet yielded to the action that would follow such a fantasy, no great harm has been done. But she has suffered because of an unrealistic way of looking at herself, and if she could accept the unreality with good humor, she would not only feel some relief from tension but would also be able to talk with her former sweetheart as a mature, responsible woman.

The pastor said to me in a later conversation that he also wished that he could help May to feel more of Christ's self-giving love in her relationship to her husband and to other people. In this he would be strengthening the *altruism* which is another positive coping mechanism for mature living. Much more will be said about altruism in a later chapter on the Holy Spirit. But the pastor wondered how he could lead her to find satisfaction in her love for husband and children at the same time that she must admit her overwhelming need to be desired and held close. The pastor is actually seeking to reduce the strength of an unhealthy mechanism, displacement, and increase the strength of healthy mechanisms such as suppression, humor, and altruism.

In this pursuit of insight and honesty, the pastor strengthens the conscience as a monitor of our perception of ourselves and our interpretation of others. In this he parallels the preoccupation of the apostle Paul with inward honesty versus self-deception. The apostle appeals for "the mind of Christ" as a redeeming guide to a humble awareness of our human limitations and a confident belief that we can see the way in which we are to function redemptively in a social unit (see especially Phil. 2 and Rom. 12). In contrast, those who have "the mind of the flesh" are, by their cunning and underhanded ways, blinded from an awareness of the truth about themselves and about God (2 Cor. 4:1–6; Rom. 1:18–23). Spiritual death comes with the mind of the flesh because such persons cannot see that their basic problem is a failure to accurately perceive self and God. They do not understand their own actions and, even when they know what is right, there is no will within them to do it (Rom. 7:13–8:8).

When we have perceived guilt at this deeper level, we see more than isolated actions that transgress the mores of society. We see a total bondage of the self to unrealistic and unproductive assumptions about ourselves, unconscious pride in our condemnation of others, and inner frustration in our attempts to love and be loved.[11]

When we consider our conscience at this deeper level then we are ready for the transition from guilt to sin that is in the question of the apostle: "Wretched man that I am! Who will deliver me from this body of death?" (Rom. 7:24). We move from a concern for specific attitudes and acts over which we have some conscious control into the all-encompassing hold of unconscious processes upon our ways of thinking and acting. We are faced with the limitations of our human existence, which—apart from an act of surrender to the God who has originally made us—do not permit us to know ourselves as we truly are in the depths of our being. Only when we are willing to be remade in the image of his Son do we have the capacity to see how we were originally made to love others as we love ourselves (Eph. 2).[12]

Deadly and Redeeming Guilt

Why should we move so steadily in Christian counsel toward deeper levels of guilt? Are we not increasing morbid preoccupation with real and imaginary backslidings through this relentless process? No, for as I have already indicated, one purpose of Christian counsel is to reduce scrupulosity, the obsession with petty details that obscures the deeper issues of love and justice. But more important, an awareness of our deeper motivation may save us from unproductive forms of repentance. Only when people know how they feel guilty and why, can they distinguish between the "worldly grief that produces death" and the "godly grief that produces a repentance that leads to salvation and brings no regret" (2 Cor. 7:9–12).

"Worldly grief" is the common guilt of an individual who wishes to continue what is already being done so long as punishment can be avoided. Guilt for such a person is the substitute for punishment that will relieve the conscience of obligation to think more deeply about motives or relationships. In such a case, guilt is the product of preoccupation with the self and its pleasure. Such guilt is a warning that pain must be avoided by doing something to avoid punishment for the pleasure that one desires.

95

In contrast, *"godly grief"* is anguish over the hurt that we have *caused to another,* or the way in which love has been diminished toward us or others. It is a primary concern with relationships rather than with self-image and personal comfort. Because it is an outgoing concern for others, godly sorrow leads to repentance, a humble confession that the design of our life must be transformed into the image of God's Son (2 Cor. 15:18–20). Such repentance is self-giving (Mark 8:34ff; Matt. 16:24) and leads to action that increases our sense of life and love (John 10:10). To the contrary, a morbid remorse is anxiety and regret that produce nothing.

The pastor could have left May with some morbid remorse for her adolescent fantasies. He wants to talk more with her about these fantasies, but in the first interview he chose to move toward observations that would strengthen her concept of herself and stress actions that developed good relationships. If she is going to feel sorry about anything, she should feel sorrow for a lack of openness in communication with her husband and a desire to withdraw from adult responsibilities into the fantasies of adolescence. At least this is what the pastor told me that he was trying to do in the conclusion of his first conversation with May.

Pastor: Look at the way you're moving. First, you have told me that you woke up your husband several nights ago and told him what you were feeling and how things needed to change. You didn't back down from an expression of all that you felt that you needed in relationship to him. Isn't that different than getting in bed with the other man and being engulfed in all of those fantasies? You did face reality. That's a sign of strength.

May: Well, I guess so.

Pastor: Guess?

May: All right. I know that took some courage.

Pastor: Good. Congratulate yourself. You're not as weak as your fantasy leads you to believe.

May: But in some ways I am.

Pastor: I agree. You need time to get over this bereavement and feel strong in yourself again. You need time to see if your conversation with Alfred will make a difference. Your coming to me is a sign that you want to figure out what to

	do with your feelings that will conserve your strengths, and not give way to dependency in this time of weakness.
May:	I guess so.
Pastor:	Guess?
May:	(Smiles) Well I do want to do the right thing. Things may not improve with Alfred. But I don't want to lose what I have.
Pastor:	Right. Now where can you find friends who will fill in for what your mother was to you?

The pastor is stressing a third major objective of Christian counsel concerning the conscience, *to distinguish outgoing godly repentance from self-serving sorrow and defense against punishment.* Perhaps in another interview May will be ready to talk about the ways in which she has sought to manipulate her husband to do what she wanted done without an open discussion of her desires or a statement of what she thought was just and unjust. How much responsibility will she be willing to take for distortions in communication and for withdrawing from her husband into fantasy? When she accepts that responsibility and desires to change, she will be moving toward repentance and newness of life.

The Conviction of Sin

Will May be able to accept this responsibility by herself? Not yet, for the transition from anxiety about guilt to awareness of sin takes place when we recognize our moral blindness and inability to change ourselves by a conscious act of the will. If May comes to accept her tendencies toward withdrawing into adolescent fantasy, then she will be ready to surrender herself to a higher power who can deliver her from that moral regression.

If the result of counsel is to be repentance that leads to life, then the Christian counselor must accept *a final stage in the movement from a guilty conscience to a sinful soul, which is to surrender ourselves to the Counselor who convicts us of sin.*

Two questions need to be answered in relation to this assertion. Why is the Holy Spirit so closely connected with conviction of sin? And how do we view sin under the guidance of the Spirit of God?

First there is the question of the Spirit's relationship to sin. This relationship is presented by Jesus in his statement that the Counselor will convict the world of sin, righteousness, and judgment (John 16:7-11).

The Spirit is related to sin because this is the witness to God's love that contrasts God's order for life with our disorderly selfishness, rebellion, and hate. Apart from this divine standard of righteousness we would not be sure if our judgments of self and one another were conviction of sin or something else. In his first letter to the Corinthians, Paul makes a definite distinction between the judgment of "a human court" such as the Corinthian church and the light that comes from God to disclose the will or purposes that we have within us (1 Cor. 4:1-5). Later in that same letter he speaks of those who have a weak conscience which is easily defiled (1 Cor. 8:7-13). These are people who judge by outward appearances or jump to quick conclusions.

Whatever the deficiencies of the conscience may be, it can never be considered as a completely reliable guide to the knowledge of sin. Sin is a rebellion against God's love, a disregard of the purposes for which he has created us, and a lack of gratitude for our creation as his children. Only the Spirit of God can search out our hearts and convict us of that which is essentially a dishonoring of God, the rejection of his love.

In May's case we saw a woman who may be rebellious against God, but that has not yet been identified. What we did see was a wife who felt anxious and guilty because of her fantasies concerning other men. This was guilt and it was appropriate. The pastor did not condemn her as sinful because she was aware of her temptations and he did not condemn her for her fantasies. He observed the restraint that any of us should show in moving toward conviction of sin. Conviction is a work of the holiness of God conveyed through his Spirit and is not to be confused with the precondition of a sense of sin which would be the kind of guilty conscience that May displayed.

Conviction brings power into our lives when we are convinced that we have rejected God's love. By accepting the power of the Spirit to convict, we also obtain the Spirit's power to transform, to change, to make us more into the image of God in Christ than we might have thought possible—or even desired. In fact, I suspect that many people would prefer to stay guilty rather than to feel sinful, at least as I am using the word *sin*. For if we were to be "convicted" of sin, we would recognize the presence of an overpowering force that required righteousness of us and had the power to make this possible if we would surrender our wills to that of the Spirit. Faced with that awesome threat, many persons choose guilt because it does not really require that they change. In fact, a small amount of guilt after some willful transgression may relieve some persons of anxiety because they feel the punishment of conscience. Having punished self psychologically for some form of self-indulgence, the culturally-conditioned conscience may now relax while the person awaits another opportunity to enjoy pleasure with the minimum of pain that guilt causes.

The "conviction of sin" is a recognition that we are children of God who must live by his will rather than by our own. We are called to love him as our Father, and our neighbor as ourselves. When we admit this standard of judgment over us and our position as creatures in the presence of the Creator, then inevitably, changes take place in our lives. But when an individual recognizes that these changes may take place, the person may draw back from this awareness into the self-conceit and spiritual blindness that Paul describes in the first chapter of Romans. It is in this way that sin may often be seen as rebellion against God. We do not want to admit that he has the power to convict us as people who do not love as we ought to love. We do not want to accept the kind of love that he would give us, for it would reduce the fantasies that console us and the selfishness that causes us to hold on to what we are and refuse the faith that would impel us into a new life.

May has not yet come to an awareness of that choice or to the time of rebellion or submission. If she continues her conversations with the pastor this crisis will arise. Will she admit that the continuation of her fantasies about other men and her unwillingness to confront her husband is soon to be seen as a denial of love for him? This is the sin for which she would be convicted, an unwillingness to share herself as a loving human being with another human being whom she is pledged to love. Will she reject the knowledge that she has been created to love, and thereby rebel against God? Or will she be convicted of sin in the sense that she will ask God's forgiveness for her withdrawal from hope and love, and seek his strength to be a vulnerable and honest person with her husband? When she is willing to receive the Spirit as her guide in the expression of love and the admission of what she needs, then she will also be ready for the power of the Spirit to transform a conventional relationship into a righteous relationship in which there will be mutual submission and interdependence.[13]

The Holy Spirit prompts us to look beyond customary guilt and the deeper guilt of self-deception to the basic question of sin: Am I living authentically according to God's creation? In leading us to this question the Spirit also is serving as our teacher, our guide to truth (John 14:26; 15:26; 16:12–15). We need to know the truth about ourselves. How are we made and for what purpose?

Sin as Pride

When we see sin as a transgression of the way in which we were made before God, several possibilities appear to us. The first is that we might disregard the nature of our creation in an attempt to be more than human. This is a belief that we can live above the limitations of life, a refusal to accept the finiteness that Jesus accepted when he took upon himself the form of a man and became obedient even to the limitation of life that is represented by death (Phil. 2:1–11).

This is the sin of pride.[14] Sometimes it is a feeling that we are exempt from the problems of others because of our moral superiority, which is the warning given by the apostle Paul in the second chapter of Romans. Sometimes our pride is seen in our feeling that we ought to be above moral temptations and human limitations, which was the point of view presented by the devil to Jesus in his temptation (Matt. 4).

May would have been guilty of this type of sin if she had pretended that she were invulnerable to the temptations presented by her high school sweetheart. The pastor would have created this kind of sin in her if he had assured her that because she was a Christian she was above temptation. Fortunately, the pastor acknowledged the possibility that she could commit adultery and openly discussed with her the way in which the former sweetheart was planning to seduce her.

A realistic discussion of what might happen to us in our human condition will be our antidote to the sin of pride. With humility, May can admit that she could be drawn into adultery. Therefore, she listens to what the pastor says about the way in which the trap is being laid for her and will draw back because she recognizes the unhappy consequences of such a possibility.

Essentially, May and the pastor are admitting that all of us are made with limitations. So long as we live within those limitations we are free from the sin of pride. It is only human for May to long for more affection than she is receiving from her husband. She should freely admit this need and then seek courage to openly discuss this problem with her husband. If she falls into the deceit of assuming that she is above temptation, then she is already in a state of sin.

Since there seems to be no evidence that May will move in this direction, it may seem inappropriate for me to emphasize this type of sin. But I learned from Valerie Goldstein's article on sin from the feminine point of view that men need to continually be reminded of the sin of pride.[15] Out of her background in theology and psychology Goldstein observes the constant emphasis of Reinhold Niebuhr and others upon "hubris." Goldstein thinks that this is correct—about men (and perhaps especially about theological professors who author most of the books on the subject). To the contrary, Goldstein thinks that the major sin of women in the twentieth century has been depression rather than pride. Women have felt that they were inferior beings and that they were made to suffer in silence. They have disregarded their place as persons of equality with men, made in the image of God.

Sin as Depression

To think of depression as sin is to recognize the second way in which the Spirit of God instructs us. We were not made to be intrinsically inferior to anyone. Paul specifies in the third chapter of Galatians that in Jesus Christ there is neither male nor female, bond nor free. The first chapter of his first letter to the Corinthians is an encouragement for people who have been made to feel inferior by the world to recognize their strength of self in Christ.

This second possibility for sin, in which we see ourselves as less than human, is before May. She does lament her moral weakness, her longing for a childhood sweetheart, her fear that she may go to him and ruin all that she loves in her home and community. She is continually cast down with worry about her weak self.

The pastor recognizes her feelings without accepting her premise that she is a weak person. Instead he challenges this point of view by references to the courage she shows in openly discussing with her husband the difficulties of their marriage. She is not as weak as she might think herself to be. If the pastor can continue to challenge her depressive thoughts about herself with actual evidence of strength from God within her, then May will be saved from the typical sin of the middle class American housewife, which is to sink into moral weakness because this is how the culture has taught her to be.

Sin as Sensuality

In addition to sin as depression there is the danger of sin as sensuality in May. Reinhold Niebuhr in *The Nature and Destiny of Man* has equated sensuality with the second possibility of sin against humanity. Sensuality flourishes on the assumption that primeval impulses have such power over us that we cannot control them. We excuse ourselves during periods of unrestrained sensuality by saying that this is what any normal human being would do under similar circumstances. Using this thought pattern, May could have persuaded herself that her natural desire for affection should be met outside of marriage since she is not receiving tender love within marriage.

The pastor counters this temptation with the straightforward affirmation that adultery is sin. He observes with her the consequences of adultery in terms of her self-respect, her love for her children, and her desire to be respected by them and by people in the community. In this he is affirming that which is better in her than the sensuality that might consume her. It is an appeal for her to be fully human, to recognize that she can lead a life of fidelity, self-respect, and love despite unfulfilled longings.

Appropriateness and Completeness

Should every case of conscience move steadily from awareness of cultural conditioning to conviction of sin?[16] No. May is a textbook case which was chosen for teaching purposes because it illustrates many aspects of the conscience that we might see in a year of counsel. Other individuals will concentrate upon one facet of conscience and seem to have no trouble with the rest. So, for example, a woman of May's age might desire to work again after twenty years of homemaking. A traditional husband like Alfred might say that "people will raise questions. They'll think that I'm not a good provider." If May and Alfred are accustomed to "talking out things," they can negotiate some settlement of a culturally-conditioned expectation of what a "good wife" will be. If they are like most middle-aged couples I have known, she will happily work and he will make sophisticated excuses to his "family-oriented" friends.

The deeper sharing of May and Alfred is too disrupted for any quick and authentic settlement of differences. Time is needed to move through a variety of psychological and theological problems. But is it imperative that we follow the order of issues in this chapter? No. May's is a case of elective counsel where counselor and counselee have leisure to choose the appropriate time for a discussion of some new discovery in relationships, self-concept, cultural conditioning, philosophy of life, social roles, theological significance. The order will be explosively different in some crisis counsel, such as the case that begins the next chapter.

What we can conclude from cases of elective or crisis counseling is that timing and completeness are essential. Timing requires both alertness to opportunities for disclosure and awareness of deeper urges, in order to reflect on a counselee's mood or offer some confrontational classification. Confrontational classifications of sin and forgiveness will be dominant in the case of Robert and Linda Marsh.

Completeness is possible in the counsel for May. She is willing to review aspects of her problem that involve a restructuring of male-female roles, an awareness of her need for affection, and the necessity of open communication with Alfred.

But in the forthcoming case, Robert and Linda are not so open. Their conflicts preclude completeness.

What is "completeness" in cases of conscience? That is the central issue for our next discussion, on sin and atonement.

NOTES

1.   The implications of this statement are theological. One implication is that the conscience of an inquiring person is the focus of Christian counsel and that the answer of the counselor will deal with complicated questions from the perspective of the Christian faith. The other implication is that Christian counsel serves as a conscience for theology as a whole. Christian counsel

helps theology to shape its agenda and formulate its conclusions in conscious relation to the people who are served by the church. Communication must be considered in the formulation of content. A discussion of this latter function of Christian counsel in the thought of Karl Rahner may be found in Robert Kinast, "How Pastoral Theology Functions," *Theology Today* (January 1981), pp. 425–38.

2. Kirk, *Principles of Moral Theology*, pp. 13–15.

3. Eric W. Kemp, *The Life and Letters of Kenneth Escott Kirk, Bishop of Oxford 1873–1954* (London: Hodden and Stoughton, 1959), pp. 49–50.

4. Casuistry was always under suspicion from evangelical Protestants because of its reputation for double-dealing. This was especially noticeable in the doctrine of probabilism, wherein a precedent would be set by good and wise men who saw no sin or danger of sin in the action, but the person who was following the action knew that a contrary opinion would probably be more moral (Ibid., p. 13.). In the post-Freudian era, such manipulations of morality would be called rationalizations, and this would be enough to kill casuistry. It was already suspect even in the days of Bishop Kirk, when his wife complained: "Kenneth spends all his time inventing clever reasons for doing with a good conscience what we all know is wrong" (V. A. Dement, "Kenneth Kirk as Moral Theologian," *Church Quarterly Review* 158 [1957]:432). It might be said to the credit of Bishop Kirk that he warned against another deficiency of casuistry, which was the danger of formalism, the tendency to define what is right or wrong on the basis of natural law. The bishop noted that natural law is a code without sanctions, an appeal to what seems to work in our world rather than a duty by which we are to be disciplined (K. E. Kirk, *Ignorance, Faith and Conformity* [London: Longmans, Green and Co., 1925], p. 41).

The tendency to rationalize self-serving actions through casuistry was exposed with satire by a seventeenth century scientist and moral rigorist, Blaise Pascal; in *Penseés and Provincial Letters* (N.Y.: Modern Library, 1941), especially pp. 406, 407.

For a sympathetic approach to moral reason by an influential casuist of the Puritan period, see author W. Hopkinson, *About William Law* (London: SPCK, 1948), chap. 3, "The Moralists." An example of casuistry as taught to theological students is Charles Wordsworth's *Bishop Sanderson's Lectures on Conscience and Human Law, Delivered in the Divinity School at Oxford* (Lincoln: James Williamson, 1877). For an example of the modern Roman Catholic movement away from a concentration on laws to an emphasis upon the personal and communal aspects of sin, see Bernard Häring, *Sin in the Secular Age* (Slough, England: St. Paul Publications, 1974).

For a discussion of various theories of the conscience, including Aquinas, see Dale Moody, *The Word of Truth* (Grand Rapids: William B. Eerdmans, 1981), pp. 238–53; Donald E. Miller, *The Wing-Footed Wanderer: Conscience and Transcendence* (Nashville: Abingdon, 1977); Kirk, *Ignorance, Faith and Conformity*, pp. 1–41. A realistic approach to the application of moral principles guided by an informed conscience may be found in Edward Leroy Long, *Conscience and Compromise, An Appeal to Protestant Casuistry* (Philadelphia: Westminster Press, 1954).

5. In a report on gang rape at fraternity parties, investigators for the Project on the Status and Education of Women, Association of American Colleges, found that the rapes were often considered to be the victim's fault by the college males. Also, "other girls blamed the victim rather than supporting her." Rape victims often left school. The victims were very reluctant to tell anyone about the rape or to report it. In fact, several related studies of college students have found that a high number of girls report the experience of sexual coercion or violence without actually thinking of themselves as rape victims. Both male and female students seem to have developed an extraordinary tolerance for the idea of forced sex. The confusion about their own rights as a person was so widespread among women that the report concluded with a page of recommendations concerning the development of "honor codes," the prohibition of alcohol at campus parties, open discussion of the negative treatment of women as sex objects, support from the administration for rape prevention programs. A bibliography of the studies is also included. Julie K. Ehrahart and Bernice R. Sandler, "Campus Gang Rape: Party Games?" (Washington, D.C., Association of American Colleges, 1985).

6. John T. McNeill, "Guilt and Its Treatment Viewed Historically," *The Chicago Theological Seminary Register* (January 1962), pp. 22–26.

7. In this paragraph we have touched all too briefly upon the important issues of law and gospel in pastoral care, which have been explored by Rodney Hunter in *Journal of Pastoral Care* (September 1976), pp. 146–158. The issues have been of particular importance in Lutheran theology, as in the summary by Gerhard Forde, *Law-Gospel Debate* (Minneapolis: Augsburg Press, 1969) and in Roman Catholic theology, as presented by Franz Boeckle, *Law and Conscience.*

8. The inner relation of spontaneous grateful love with moral precepts is a continual theme in the works on the conscience. See C. Ellis Nelson, ed., *Conscience: Theological and Psychological Perspectives* (New York: Newman Press, 1973); Claude Pierce, *Conscience in the New Testament* (Naperville, Ill.: Allenson, 1955); John Macquarrie, *Three Issues in Ethics,* chap. on "Conscience, Sin and Grace"; James B. Nelson, *Moral Nexus* (Philadelphia: Westminster Press, 1971), pp. 15–39; K. E. Kirk, *Conscience and Its Problems* (London: Longmans, Green and Co., 1928); Carl D. Schneider, *Shame, Exposure and Privacy* (Boston: Beacon Press, 1977); O. Hobart Mowrer, "Some Constructive Features of the Concept of Sin and Guilt in Psychotherapy," *Journal of Counseling Psychology* 7, no. 3 (1960): pp. 185–201. Helmut Thielicke, *Theological Ethics* 1. 15–17.

9. See related passages such as Heb. 3:7–19; Rom. 7:14; Rev. 12:9; 2 Cor. 11:3; Gen. 3:13; John 8:39–47.

10. George E. Vaillant, *Adaptation to Life* (Boston: Little, Brown, and Company, 1977).

11. It is remarkable to note that popular religious moralists are continually condemning transgressions of community mores with quotations from the apostle Paul. Yet the apostle has only one sinful action to report about himself, that he

"persecuted the church of God" (1 Cor. 15:9). Otherwise, the apostle thought that he could boast about his exemplary life (2 Cor. 11:16–12:13). The concern of the apostle was with the spiritual blindness and lack of insight that seem to plague the popular religious moralists who always quote him.

12. For some of the distinguishing marks of guilt and sin, see Reinhold Niebuhr's chapter on "The Equality of Sin and the Inequality of Guilt," in *Nature and Destiny of Man*, (New York: Charles Scribner's Sons, 1949) vol. 1, pp. 219ff.

13. How will the Spirit actually work in her life to make this possible? This is a question that we will consider in relation to another case when we come to a separate chapter on the work of the Holy Spirit. We are also left without an answer to a question that will surface if Alfred remains adamant: "Should I stay married to a man who shows me no affection?"

14. For a summary of biblical and theological passages, see Niebuhr, *Nature and Destiny of Man*, vol. 1, pp. 186–203.

15. Valerie Goldstein, "The Human Situation: A Feminine Viewpoint," Simon Donager, ed., *The Nature of Man* (New York: Harper and Brothers, 1962), pp. 151–70.

16. The question is raised because of a continuing legalism in pastoral care and counsel. Seventeenth-century scholastic Lutheranism developed a rigorous order of Law and Gospel in progression from conviction of sin to reception of divine grace. Eighteenth-century Calvinistic revivalists depended upon the steps to salvation which were preached by Jonathan Edwards. (See John H. Gerstner, *Steps to Salvation* [Philadelphia: Westminster Press, 1959].)

Nineteenth- and twentieth-century pastors exaggerated the verbal aspects of steps to salvation with questions and answers codified as "four spiritual laws." The sequential method was given popularity in Norman Vincent Peale's ten steps to prosperity through positive thinking.

7

Sin and Atonement

What is essential in the counsel we offer to people with a troubled conscience? Are there some theological requirements which must be met for effective resolution of sin and/or guilt?

The psychological components of these questions revolve around our awareness of resistance. People do not wish to disclose the hidden processes by which they make decisions. They are much more content with minor adjustments in relationships which will pacify the cultural or family aspects of conscience.

The theological requirements of counsel must also face the questions of resistance. Does a counselor really have the power to persuade another human being to disclose the secrets of the heart, to define some mistakes and transgressions as rebellion against God, to dedicate the whole self to the Creator through repentance and newness of life at a deeper and higher level of experience? These questions heighten our dependence upon a Divine presence in any counsel that is measured by restoration of relations with God and others.

The essential elements of a redeemed conscience include confession of sin, experience of forgiveness, sense of justification by God's grace, reconciliation with God and others, hope and joy in the stability of a sanctified life.

These are interrelated consequences of the one great act of Christ, the Atonement. His sacrificial life for others is the central criteria for the process that moves from confession to sanctification: How completely is our life lived for others by the model and power of Jesus' life before his disciples?

Two questions of conscience come out of this focus upon the Atonement.

First, how deep is the gulf we have dug between our perceived selves and God/others/inner self? Is the conscience troubled because of some embarrassing episode in life, which may or may not lead to hurt and inconvenience to a narcissistic self? Or is the soul in grief over the rupture of friendship, the betrayal of love, a contempt for God's graciousness? Are we dealing with remorse (worldly sorrow that leads to death), or repentance and reconciliation (godly sorrow that leads to life)?

Second, will power from beyond the self be required to complete the restoration of relationships with self/God/others? Must the power of the Atonement be a part of this process, or is acceptance by counselor and self enough?

Repentance or Remorse?

The depth of disintegrating relationships will often be signaled by the outrage that one person expresses toward another in counseling. A theologically preoccupied counselor may see the outraged person as a victim and quickly suggest forgiveness as the essential step toward reconciliation.

But this prescription before diagnosis may be met by counselee resistance, either because the counselor has not accepted the extent to which a person has been shattered, or the extent to which a person will denounce others as a means of self-protection.

What is being protected? Whether the person is victim or victimizer, there is fixation upon the self. This is a defiance of the Atonement, in which injury was overcome by sacrifice for others rather than protection of the self.

But which aspect of the Atonement is most salient during outrage: forgiveness or repentance? Will not both be necessary at some time in the process of healing?

These questions steady us in crisis counseling when quick judgments are demanded by victim or victimizer (both of which may be embodied in one person). If the atoning work of Christ is to be complete, each person will need opportunity to reflect upon and experience more than one aspect of the move from conviction of sin/experience to forgiveness/justification/reconciliation/sanctification. Who can know the order or the emphasis of these elements of the Atonement without inquiry into the reasons for outrage?

The pastor of a suburban church needed this comprehensive view of the Atonement during some blazing moments between a couple whom he had never seen before. The case began when a member of the pastor's congregation, Mrs. Oles, called him on an October evening to ask that he talk with one of her friends, Linda Marsh. Linda had sought comfort from Mrs. Oles after being physically abused by her husband, Robert Marsh. The abuse came after Robert overheard Linda in conversation with her lover.

After some telephone negotiation, Robert and Linda came to see the pastor later in the evening.

Robert explained that he "beat the truth out of her." Linda replied that she was tired of her husband and attracted to the supervisor at work who was so kind to her. She maintained that sex with the supervisor had been only for a brief time and that for the last few months she just liked to talk with him.

Linda said that she was tired of her husband because he would drink on the weekends and often become physically abusive toward her and the children. Then, Robert became more animated.

Robert: My friends told me I should have killed you!
Pastor: Why didn't you take their advice?
Robert: Because I love her. But she can't do me like this. A man doesn't have anything if he does not have his honor. I'm the man who makes the decisions in the home. Not her. She wears tight dresses and lots of perfume, and I tell her to tone it down and she defies me.
Linda: I want to dress like other women in the office. I don't think it's provocative.

Robert: Well, to my likes of thinking, you are. And I don't like it.

Pastor: How long has this disagreement been?

Robert: Since we moved here. Back home she dressed to please me. We never had no trouble. I thought we had the right kind of marriage. We were sweethearts in high school. We got married and I worked while she went to college. Her folks paid for it. Then when I got transferred here a few years ago she began to change. A man has got to rule his own house.

Linda: He doesn't have to beat up people to get his way.

Pastor: Why not?

Linda: Well, because I love him.

Robert: Then why did you do what you did?

Linda: I don't know, but I'm sorry and I'll stay just with you and I want our marriage to work.

Robert: Well, Reverend, how do you make a marriage work when something like this happens?

Linda: Yes, how do you?

Pastor: I'd start with admitting hurt. Both of you have shown how much you can hurt each other and how dreadful each of you feels at the hand of the other. Now that you admit this, the next step is forgiveness of each other.

Robert: How do I forgive someone who does something like she did?

Pastor: By first asking God to forgive you for what you did.

Robert: I never did anything like *that*.

Linda: I guess everyone has some favorite—or something— sin. The one that you just think is the limit. Well, a man thinks adultery's it. For me, it's having my eye blacked or a tooth knocked loose or his storming at the kids. They're terrified. I understand; so am I.

Pastor: You frustrate him and he frightens you.

Robert: I'll tell you what I'm afraid of, that my marriage will go just like my parents'. My mother ran around on my father. He never did anything about it. I swore that would never happen to me. Now it has.

Pastor: So you've had a big fear for years . . .

Robert: Ever since I came home early from school and saw my

110

mother with another man. I never had seen anything like that before.

Pastor: It's still right there—before you . . .

Robert: Yes. I could hardly go to school the next day. And then when my parents divorced, I still got some feelings about what my mother did to my father and me.

Pastor: As a kid you found out how much injustice there is . . .

Robert: And I hate it. I hate it with a passion. Why me?

Pastor: I don't know, but you've asked the question that opens the door to some understanding. If you keep saying all through life that you've been done an injustice and never say, OK, that's just one of those things, and keep going, you'll be angry all the time.

Linda: He is. I wondered why, until I told him what I had done. He beat me and cried and told me what had happened when he was a boy.

Pastor: Yeah. Well, now we can see things more clearly. Today's hurt opened up the big hurt of years ago. All the hate from that date has been building up for this day.

Robert: I guess so. It's what I always feared. I feel like I'm not a man anymore.

Pastor: Well, you won't be if the feelings from twenty years ago rule your life today.

Robert: So what am I supposed to do? Forgive her?

Pastor: Let's start with something that God can do something about. Ask him to forgive you for hating your wife so much because of something that happened even before you knew her.

Robert: You think I've been unfair?

Pastor: In a way, yes. You have cause to be angry because of how she hurt you just now, but not because of what your mother did to you years ago.

Robert: But to forgive her for *that*?

Pastor: I know it makes a big difference to you, which sin to forgive. But it doesn't matter to God. In his sight, unjust angry feelings are just as sinful as adultery.

Robert: But how am I going to control her? If I forgive her, she'll have her way.

Pastor:	Good statement. Can you control her now anyway?
Robert:	It doesn't seem so.
Pastor:	So why not start with something that you can do something about—your own feelings.
Robert:	What do you mean?
Linda:	He means not blowing up about things and coming home drunk.
Robert:	Shouldn't a man get mad when his wife does these things and defies him?
Pastor:	Neither of you will help each other if you keep up this "I win, you lose" way of thinking. When both of you seek God's forgiveness, you can have power to control yourself. That's what I'm after, rather than your control of each other.
Robert:	I'd sure like to have that. But I pray and I'm still the same. And now this . . .
Linda:	This is over. I believe God will forgive me—but will you?
Pastor:	Let's start with each of you asking God to forgive you, OK? Do you ever pray together?
Linda:	We say the blessing every night.
Pastor:	What if I pray, and you pray for yourself?

(They nod.)

Eternal Father, heal the hurt in the hearts of your children. Take from them the misery of memories from the past. Grant them courage to believe that they can have self-control when they submit to your control over their lives. Forgive them for their own errors so they will believe they are good enough to be strong in controlling themselves.

(The couple are in tears. They stand, and both embrace the pastor. Linda puts her arm around Robert, but his arm is to his side. The pastor tells them to call in a day or two for another talk.)

During the rest of October and into November there were occasional conversations between the pastor and the couple. On some occasions one or the other would see him alone. Linda became more and more concerned about God's forgiveness of her sin. But it soon

112

became apparent that the sin was not just adultery. There was also a manipulation of her husband through her sexual seductiveness when she wanted her way and through statements about her superior education when he would not agree with her. He would then lose his temper and hit her.

Robert continued to be haunted by the thought that he was no longer a man because his wife had done to him the most terrible thing that he feared in life. He maintained that he must keep up his self-confidence by demanding that she give him the details of her adultery and obey him in the way that she would dress. He was willing to admit that he did not feel lovable and that this was a long-standing problem. But he could not feel that he would be a strong man if he forgave his wife.

At times the pastor was reflective of the couple's feelings; at other times he prayed with them or for them. He encouraged personal insight and he encouraged their appropriation of God's power through prayer and through fellowship with Christian people. But any progress by the couple was fragile.

In December the couple began to attend the pastor's church. But two difficulties emerged. First, the couple came early to the Christmas party of a Sunday school class and sat in their car while other members of the class arrived and went into the house. Robert observed that some of the women of the class were wearing fur coats. He concluded that he and his wife were not good enough to attend the party, and drove home. The other difficulty was Linda's feeling that members of the class knew about her adultery and were talking behind her back. Despite reassurances from the pastor and from Mrs. Oles, she continued to "feel unclean and they know why."

The Marsh family ceased to attend the church and responded with indifference to telephone calls from the pastor. But in an April telephone call Robert had something to say:

Reverend, I would like to see you, and all that, but not about your church. You see, we're back in our old church. They had a glorious revival last week. Linda and I rededicated our lives to the Lord. Pastor, you should come to hear our evangelist! All the people are so on fire, and they're so happy to have us back. It's just like heaven. You should come tonight and hear him. We've just found our place.

Atonement or Outrage?

What is the spiritual state of Robert in his "place"? So far as the pastor knows, Robert has not grown to the precondition of forgiveness that would be an acknowledgment of his sin, hardness of heart, and impulsiveness. He did acknowledge that a power beyond himself was necessary in order for him to change, but he did not have faith that God would redeem him if he admitted *why* he needed redemption.[1]

Why is the process of sin and forgiveness so incomplete in the lives of these conflicted people? We can see some of the psychological reasons in the reporting of the case: Robert perceives the infidelity of his wife as an outbreak of the basic threat to his security that came as a child with the knowledge that there was infidelity between his parents.

Robert is outraged by the recurrence of a childhood injustice. At least that is the way he sees it. All his actions toward his wife are justified by that perception.

Can outrage lead to atonement?[2] Not so long as Robert sees himself as a victim. In his present condition, he concentrates on how he has been wounded and rejects any human or divine reconciliation or repentance. To him, this would mean a loss of strength. He must keep up his defenses.

The apostle Paul may have a word for Robert regarding the separation of "worldly" from "godly" sorrow (2 Cor. 7:8-10). Worldly sorrow is a concentration upon the self and its protection against that which may increase woundedness and weakness. As Kierkegaard wrote, "morbid remorse" fixes too much attention upon the self.[3] In this fixation, there is no place for a change of mind and intention. Instead, there is only regret, a desire to do away with some hurtful relationship or undo some embarrassing episode. This is a never-ending spiral of defeat which, as the apostle writes, leads to death.

In contrast, godly sorrow leads to life. It has no regret. In distinction from the self preoccupation and defense that is often referred to by Paul as "the desires of the flesh," repentance is an acceptance of the mind of Christ (Eph. 2:3; 4:17; 1 Cor. 2:16; Rom. 12:2). The protection of the self is given over to God and all the sorrows of the self are borne away by the "man of sorrows."

In this process of "godly sorrow," hurts from the past are not forgotten but rather forgiven. The events that caused wounding are not changed, but our perspective toward them is given new meaning by our submission to a Christ who has accepted all our injuries and triumphed over them through the dedication of his sacrifice for all of us.

How can the pastor bring this awareness of atonement into the outrage that Robert and Linda Marsh feel for each other? For one thing, the pastor consistently seeks to connect God's love with the sense of outrage in both of these hurting people. He speaks about God's forgiveness when he questions Robert concerning the way in which he is going to forgive his wife. This is not immediately successful, for Robert does not understand the relationship. The pastor tries again to make a connection by stating that God can forgive Robert for hating his wife. Will he be willing to forgive his wife in the same way? Robert considers this to be an unfair request because of the sin that the wife has committed.

The pastor also seeks to lead the Marshes to a deeper level of God's judgment that would provide for them the depth of acceptance that will bring healing.

What is "depth of judgment" for the Marshes? It would be an acknowledgement of sin as fixation upon the self—a desire to protect that which is seen as essential for the self without regard for the needs of others. The rage and resentment of Robert and Linda are expressions of this sin. But they do not see that. Again, in Pauline terms, they are blinded by "the mind of the flesh," the feeling that they must protect themselves and cause remorse in anyone who hurts them.

The pastor has not yet called upon either of these confused people to "repent." He is working on the precondition of repentance which is "conviction of sin." This is a general term for the combination of hurt, regret, anger, fear of punishment, defensiveness, and self-pity that must be acknowledged. The dangers of worldly sorrow need to be openly faced before godly sorrow can be effective.[4]

Sin or Sins?

Robert and Linda would not move from a preoccupation with "sins" to the deeper level of "sin." The pastor seeks an opening through such comments as this:

If you keep saying all through life that you've been done an injustice and never say, OK, that's just one of those things, and keep going, you'll be angry all the time.

If Robert had opened the door to this understanding, he might have been led back to a discussion of "original sin." That is, he would have talked about the reasons for the preservation of his anger from childhood that has become entrenched as hate. He might have admitted that there was some basic attitude in his life that was warping all of his existence, and that he was powerless to overcome it by his own strength.

If he could come to this admission, the pastor could say: "Welcome to the club of original sinners, old boy." He might have talked about the way in which human desires and reactions are twisted into all pervasive forces of evil that do not let go of us. There is something in our very nature as human beings that tends toward the distortion of our identity as people made in the image of God, that destroys our mission to live for God in this world. Neither Robert nor Linda have yet comprehended the destructive effects of the warping of our will that we call original sin. They do not yet know why their self-perception is so distorted and why their defensiveness has produced such destruction. If the Spirit should prepare the way for that kind of understanding by the Marshes, they would then understand why the pastor is so insistent that they pray and compare their own forgiveness to the forgiveness that God provides. They would admit that they must be one with the rest of humanity in the acceptance of their tendency to distort the injustices of childhood into a lifelong pattern of resentment and hate. With this admission would go a commitment to the self-giving love exemplified in Christ, which provides the only eternal remedy for the evils that we experience and perpetuate in this life. Theologically, this is "justification," God's faithfulness to us despite our faithlessness before him (Col. 2:11–21; Rom. 1:16ff.; 3:21–4:25). This is the supernatural grace that can empower forgiveness and sustain any move toward self, God, and others.

Forgiveness Before Reconciliation?

Robert and Linda may not be interested in any conversation about justification as a theological process, because their primary concern is for "justification" as a psychological defense. They are preoccupied with the vindication of their own opinions and in getting some apologies from the partner. They do not desire change or newness of life. Their energies are fixed on a reinstatement of relationships as they were before a "blow-up." Anxious to reduce awareness of personal faults, they plead or threaten for "reconciliation"—on terms set down long before the appearance of fighting and adultery.[5]

If the pastor is realistic, he will counsel the couple to admit barriers and remove them as a part of reconciliation. One barrier is a focused victimization, a feeling by each that they have been hurt by the other. Another barrier is a sense of self-righteousness.

The remedy, which is modeled in the Atonement, is vulnerability. This laying aside of defensiveness begins when a person has a sense of strength through God's forgiveness that allows the individual to admit his or her oneness with all who sin against God and against us. The motivation for confession is gratitude that Christ has purchased our pardon.

Gratitude is the sign of inner change. God's forgiveness makes a difference in the way we love, as Christ loved us. The change of our self-perspective is referred to in biblical terms as a "change of heart" (Acts 2:37–38; 8:22; Luke 3:8; Mark 1:15; Rom. 4:7–8; Eph. 1:7; Col. 1:13–14; James 5:15; 1 John 1:9; 2:12). It is only after this change of heart that we can move to reconciliation.[6]

How can the Marshes move toward divine forgiveness in a way that will eventually lead to human reconciliation?

One part of this movement would be an acknowledgement of having betrayed the trust of another and of another having had their trust betrayed as well. *Repentance is an admission of the destructive behavior that we perpetuate upon others and that they inflict upon us.* With this admission of something radically wrong in our world, there is the possibility of looking toward God for an answer. What has he done about the hurt and anger that we now admit? This question is an opportunity for a discussion of the Atonement, the answer of God to the radical injustice of this world.[7]

Another part of forgiveness that leads toward reconciliation is an *admission of the way in which injustice has been internalized as injury.* We have turned against ourselves and others; often there is a turning away from God as well. Are we willing to pay this price to maintain the hurt? This is a vital question for both Robert and Linda. So far

Robert can only say: "I never did anything like *that!*" He continually feels humiliated.

If there is to be either forgiveness or reconciliation, Robert must move from humiliation to humility. That is, he must admit some of his own imperfections, vulnerabilities, and tendencies toward selfishness and insensitivity. This is one of the reasons for the pastor's questions about the difference between violence and humility. Who can make such distinctions? If Robert were to admit that he is just as sinful as his wife, then some humility might come into his life as he relaxed his self-righteousness. Without some relaxation of that defensive attitude there is little possibility of openness toward the spouse, much less understanding and compassion.

Linda seems to be more open toward an admission of imperfection. She may be ready for another stage in the movement from forgiveness to reconciliation, *which is mutuality and negotiation*. At least she says that she would like to make some agreement with her husband so that he would not continue to threaten and beat her if she continues to be faithful to him. She seems to be more free than her partner from the need to accuse and to punish or seek revenge. There is more openness both toward herself and toward him. But her sense of being forgiven is very incomplete, for she must still believe that she is being looked down upon by the proper people in the Sunday school class that she and her husband attend.

If Linda could find some reciprocity in her negotiations with her husband, she might feel strong enough to move toward a fourth stage of forgiving which would be a redefining of her relationship to her husband and a new sense of worth in herself. She would then be in the change of life design that John Calvin called "a change of mind and intention."[8] She would have moved away from the morbid remorse that fixed attention upon the self and reduced her self-confidence. Instead, there would be a confidence in the forgiveness of God and in the restoration of relationship to a spouse.[9]

When we think of the movement from forgiveness to reconciliation, we recognize that this is always possible toward God but not always possible toward another person. Either Robert and/or Linda might hold out for "justice" even though they reject the basic source of justification, which is reconciliation with God. Because this justification is primary, the pastor has made his efforts more toward reconciliation with God than reconciliation with each other. His desire is for an inner peace in each spouse, a sense of grace of God that will bear fruit in humility, forgiveness, and reconciliation (Eph. 2:14, 22; Col. 1:21-23; Rom. 5-8).[10]

Atonement or Acceptance?

The perceptive reader will notice that the pastor has some awareness of the psychological wounding of Robert and Linda, and yet he persistently turns them toward God rather than toward self or each other. Why is this? Is he trying to avoid open discussion of difficulties because he is inhibited in the area of hate and hurt between humans? Or is he seeking to bring a reconciling power into their awareness so that they can receive strength to admit their own weaknesses and be vulnerable to each other?

If the second assumption is correct, he is more concerned about the Atonement that he is about human acceptance. From the case study, it does not seem that he ignores the process of human acceptance, but that he has turned his own acceptance of these people into an opportunity for them to accept the atoning work of Christ as model and motivator for forgiveness and reconciliation between themselves.

This open distinction between atonement and the resulting human acceptance is not compatible with much of the writing about acceptance and forgiveness in the popular days of pastoral psychology, 1950–1980. Atonement in that period was a subset of the psychological process of acceptance. This was a most helpful method for the correlation of client-centered doctrines to the need for counselees to feel forgiveness. So long as the theological doctrine of the Atonement was compatible with a psychotherapeutic requirement of unconditional love for a client, a counselor could feel at ease with Christian convictions and therapeutic practice. But if there was any "contamination" of the therapy by a systematic biblical review of the process of atonement by Christ, theology was rejected.[11]

Just as we have seen incompleteness through the misperception of forgiveness in the attempted reconciliation of Robert and Linda, so there is incompleteness in a subsuming of atonement under psychological theories of acceptance. The therapeutic incompleteness results from an elimination of the model for forgiveness and reconciliation—which is Christ, and the absence of his power as the preeminent motivator for a change of heart in counselees.

A biblical emphasis upon the Atonement will differ from psychological theories of acceptance in several ways.

First, psychological theories of acceptance are limited to the study of conflicts within the self and with other persons. The reconciliation of these conflicts comes in psychotherapy through the power of unconditional acceptance. This is considered enough to remove the damaging effects of socially imposed images, so that intrapsychic conflict may be settled in favor of deeper awareness of and reconciliation with all aspects of the self.[12]

The biblical doctrine of atonement would certainly include this reconciliation within the self and with others (Eph. 2:11–22). But the power for that reconciliation will come from the God whom we have rejected.[13] When we are willing to accept Jesus Christ as the mediator between us and God, the gulf is bridged both between hostility among humans and hostility toward God. In the biblical order, a preoccupation with self-conflicts is unproductive unless there is surrender to a power beyond the self.

The second distinction of the Atonement from acceptance is the supernaturalism that saturates all biblical teaching concerning reconciliation through Christ. The "redemption through his blood, the forgiveness of our trespasses," is a sign of Christ's "immeasurable greatness." He is "far above all rule in authority and power and dominion and above every name that is named . . ." (Eph. 1:7, 20–23). It is this supernatural force that reconciles us in all ways to God and others. This is also the force that casts down the Evil One, who constantly seeks to disrupt our relationships with God, with others, and with ourselves.[14]

In the biblical meaning of atonement there is a depth of acceptance that is matched by a depth of judgment. The human tension of intrapsychic conflict is heightened by the divine-human tension between the original order of creation and the defiance of this order by the creature. Both the heights of God's acceptance and the depth of his judgment are portrayed in the biblical emphasis upon divine judgment as opposed to the limited acceptance and judgment of humans for each other (Gal. 5:4–6; Rom. 2:13; 5:19; 8:33; 1 Cor. 4:4).

An early psychologist, William James, was sensitive to the range of acceptance that is available through an emphasis upon divine judgment. In his examination of the "religion of healthy-mindedness" versus "the sick soul," James concluded that the "completest religions" would be those in which the "pessimistic elements" were best developed. He found in Christianity (and in Buddhism) a willingness to include sorrow, pain, and death as elements of religious experience. These "religions of deliverance" had a place for both the optimism of those who found strength in themselves and the pessimism of those who cried out to a supernatural Being for deliverance.[15]

NOTES

1. Linda seemed to have more sense of forgiveness for her sins and reconciliation with God, but there was no deeper understanding of her manipulative ways. She wanted relief from feelings of guilt, but she had not received godly justification, for this would require submission of all her ways to God and an acknowledgement that righteousness came through His forgiving love rather than through her education or seductiveness.

2. A central theme of John Patton's *Is Human Forgiveness Possible?* (Abingdon Press, 1985) is rage reinforced by self-righteousness. This lifelong method of defense is rooted in shame. Patton also distinguishes shame from guilt. Guilt relates more to acts, and shame relates more to a feeling of failure as a person.

3. Quoted in William D. Chamberlain, *The Meaning of Repentance* (Grand Rapids: William B. Eerdmans, 1954), p. 26.

4. The pastor's strategy would be in line with Patton's pastoral advice that forgiveness is something to be discovered rather than something to be accomplished. What we need to discover is our desire to remain powerful while insisting that we are virtuous.

5. The psychodynamics of this denial are presented by Karen Horney, *Our Inner Conflicts* (New York: W. W. Norton, 1945), pp. 131ff.

6. The distinction between forgiveness and reconciliation is important for us in an understanding of justification. We must distinguish the initial act of God, his forgiving love, from the perfect fruition of that love which is our act of reconciliation with him. The power that unites forgiveness and reconciliation is justification, the redeeming work in Christ that brings his righteous mind into our minds so that we can accept the communion that God intends for us. See Vincent Taylor, *Forgiveness and Reconciliation* (London: Macmillan, 1948), pp. 65ff.

   There is much more that could be said about the subject of sin and atonement. Bernard Häring has presented a liberating, personal, and growth-oriented concept of sin in *Sin and the Secular Age* (Slough, England: St. Paul Publications, 1974). The particular passages for his emphasis are Matt. 25:41–46; 1 Cor. 6:9–10; Gal. 5:19–21; Rom. 1:24–25, 13; 1 Pet. 4:3; 2 Pet. 2:12–22; Rev. 21:27; 22:15). A Barthian emphasis upon divine judgment in relation to sin comes through Edward Thurneysen, *Theology of Pastoral Care* (Richmond, Va.: John

Knox Press, 1962), pp. 138, 147, 187ff.). A very helpful distinction between the equality of sin and the inequality of guilt is made by Reinhold Niebuhr in *Nature and Destiny of Man*, vol. 1. A discussion of original sin as an answer to the question, What is my mission in life? may be found in Otto Weber's *Foundations of Dogmatics* (Grand Rapids: William B. Eerdmans, 1982), vol. 1, pp. 606–12. A plea for a return of therapeutic concern for sin and divine reconciliation is found in Karl Menninger, *Whatever Became of Sin?* (New York: Hawthorn Books, 1973). For a summary of New Testament thought, see Vincent Taylor, *The Atonement in New Testament Teaching* (London: Epworth Press, 1940).

There will be additional discussion of reconciliation in chap. 8 on the reconciliation between our will and the will of God, chap. 9 on the guidance of the Spirit toward sanctification, and chap. 10 on the fellowship with believers that is our human evidence of divine forgiveness and reconciliation.

7. *Radical* injustice is a theme that received little attention from writers of pastoral psychology before the 1980s. In part, the neglect may have arisen from a preoccupation with problems of the self and a suspicion of those who saw evil coming upon them from some external source (such as society, or cosmic, demonic forces).

Whatever the reasons, Christian counselors received (before Scott Peck's *People of the Lie* [New York: Simon and Schuster, 1983]) little training on courage and coping in the face of massive social evil and entrenched personal evil in spouse, parent, child, employer, or associate. This seems strange in the light of numerous articles on social injustice in the issues of *Pastoral Psychology* from 1950. Perhaps the movement was too restricted by the privatism of Freudianism, as John Huffman commented in his review of John Patton's *Is Human Forgiveness Possible?*; see *Pastoral Psychology*, vol. 35 (3) Spring, 1987: 229–31.

8. Calvin, *Institutes*, vol. 3, sec. 3, p. 5.

9. I have adapted these stages of forgiveness from the article by Bobby B. Cunningham, "The Will to Forgive: A Pastoral Theological View of Forgiving," *Journal of Pastoral Care*, June 1985, pp. 141–49. For a sensitive and instructive discussion of the steps to forgiveness, see Lewis B. Smedes, *Forgive and Forget* (San Francisco: Harper and Row, 1984).

10. The theological question of reconciliation from the divine and human points of view is discussed in chap. 3 of Taylor, *Forgiveness and Reconciliation*.

11. See for example, Reuel Howe, *Man's Need and God's Action* (Greenwich, Connecticut: Seabury Press, 1953), in which Howe excludes all substitutionary and satisfaction theories of the Atonement in his correlations with the clinical meaning of acceptance.

12. This serious defect in Christian counsel was addressed by Don Browning in *Atonement and Psychotherapy* (Philadelphia: Westminster Press, 1966). The merit of his study was a careful discussion of the most historically prominent theories of the Atonement. Following Gustav Aulen's grouping of these theories into classic, Latin, and moral types, Browning examined the works of Irenaeus, Anselm, and Horace Bushnell. In each study he gave special importance to the doctrine of God.

13. Acts 5:31; 26:18; Col. 1:13-14; Heb. 9:15-28; Rom. 4:7-8; 5:1-11; 1 John 1:5-10; Mark 1:4, 2:1-12.

14. The power of Christ over the Devil was a major theme of the earliest writer on the Atonement, Irenaeus. As Don Browning correctly notes, in Irenaeus the Devil is an objective power that holds the deeper growth forces of humans in bondage. But this reference to a supernatural force of evil that fights against reconciliation with God is unacceptable in modern psychotherapy. Browning sought to reduce this dissonance through the equation of the Devil with our interpersonal cultural environment. The supernatural "principalities and powers" mentioned by the apostle Paul would be considered as psychological explanations of threatening conditions to the self-worth of an individual. This is the explanation of Don Browning, *Atonement and Psychotherapy*, p. 216ff.

15. William James, *The Varieties of Religious Experience* (New York: Modern Library, 1902), p. 162.

8

The Will of God and Our Will

When we are reconciled to God, does this mean that Christ takes complete control of our character? Do we still make decisions—or just put into operation the predetermined will of the Father? Is all righteous power from God, or is our willpower also involved in the witness of God in this world?

These are questions of the relation between God's will and our will. Individual answers call for many qualities of wisdom, some of which depend upon the development of our character and some upon God's power and providential or miraculous movements into our history.

Will we always have an answer, and be led in the right direction? Theological answers vary. Fanaticism claims complete knowledge of God's will and the power to overrule all chance or choice that may threaten us. Fatalism denies chance and severely limits choices. All has been predetermined by God or natural forces. A mediated theology encourages a search for godly purposes and the development of maturity in choices—but always with an awareness of time and circumstances (including death) beyond our control.

Wisdom is the affirmation of life in the face of approaching death.[1] The affirmation is for freedom of God's will and our will to

124

be exercised in a world that has limits. The encompassing sign of human limitation is death.

How can we live with freedom when we know that death is inevitable and that disasters may overtake us? The biblical answer is power to act with wisdom because we believe that God acts, within our limitations, with guidance and strength.

These are faith affirmations of a mediated theology in which God's will is actualized through our will. Obedience to God and personal responsibility are harmonized. But the harmony is not perfect, for all of God's purposes are not immediately apparent to us. There is always an element of risk in our decisions. Not only are our interpretations and applications of the divine will imperfect, but also we must live with awareness that the best of our decisions can only postpone death.

Yet God continues to strengthen our will for choices that are within his will.[2] This is possible in a process of faithful confession that our will is not always to follow God's design for our lives. We have our own ideas about a good life—and this fetters our will. The bondage is so strong that counsel often fails when we begin to examine the hidden assumptions of life that cripple us. We refuse to recognize the limitations we impose upon ourselves.

At least this is the conclusion of the counselor for Robert and Linda. His evaluation of the case ended with this comment:

I felt that they were prisoners. They strove to come out of habits and attitudes that bound them so tightly that no human release was possible.

I asked him if there could have been a divine source of release. The pastor answered:

Yes—but—I tried through prayer and counsel to lead them to forgiveness. I remember one time when Robert came alone. After we had talked about the control of his temper and about his need for forgiveness, we went into the sanctuary and knelt before the altar. I prayed for his release from the terrors of childhood and from adult memories of betrayal. I asked him if he would like to pray and he said that he wouldn't. I put my arm around him and he was as tense and tight as a drum.

Robert and Linda are so unfree that they do not believe, or wish to believe, that anyone could free them—even God. So long as this attitude is perpetuated, they cannot "do the will of God." They will not allow God the freedom to work his will in their lives because their own will is still held captive by dark fears of hate, jealousy, and revenge.

The case of Robert and Linda indicates the inseparable connection and contrast of God's plan and human purposes. In the Scriptures, the will of God is equated with the content of the Christian life.[3] The connection is expressed in the wisdom literature.

A man's mind plans his way,
But the Lord directs his steps. (Prov. 16:9)

God's Plan and Human Limitations

God's freedom is the power to do what he wills with his own (Rom. 9:18-25). His will is that all of creation should live according to his purposes (Eph. 1). To accomplish this purpose in the presence of human rebellion, God sent his Son into the world to restore our original creation as servants of the Father who live for his glory (John 3:16-21).[4]

God's plan is made with the foreknowledge of human weakness, evil in the world, and deception by "principalities and powers" (Rom. 8:28-39). Despite these obstacles, he has predestined those who accept his purpose, as set forth in Christ, to be conformed to the image of the only begotten Son of God (Rom. 8:28-30; Eph. 1:3-10).[5]

All this is a part of God's freedom, which we are to experience as freedom rather than domination and blind obedience. His plan is not a detailed road map through life, by which we may avoid all natural evil and have the security of divine success in every undertaking. Knowledge of and obedience to God's will do not save us from the physical and emotional threats of tribulation, distress, persecution, famine, nakedness, peril, or sword. Instead, his will has the overall spiritual purpose of preserving our relationship to him, guiding us through the Spirit of his Son, and sustaining us in the midst of conscious and unconscious errors, natural and supernatural destructiveness (Rom. 8:35-39; cf. 2 Cor. 11:23-29).

An awareness of godly mission despite limitations is often called "our destiny." It is a sense of God's guidance in the midst of that which is unexpected and unknown, threatening and disabling. This is providence.

The great threat to providence-as-destiny is fate, the continual encroachment of limited conditions upon our existence (2 Cor. 4:8–9). It is the unalterable tragedies and uncertainties of life that would stand between us and God (Rom. 8:35). To those who are victimized by fate, evil (either natural or supernatural) is an assault upon the self, a threat of nothingness in the face of diminished productivity, the cessation of activities that give significance to life.[6]

Robert is vulnerable to this threat because he thinks that he is a victim. To counteract this fatalism with a renewing sense of destiny and purpose, the pastor prays with him. It was a prayer for faith in God's freedom despite the unfreedom of Robert and Linda. The emphasis is also seen in the pastor's statement that both Robert and Linda must begin with forgiveness from God, followed by forgiveness for themselves and each other. This is God's purpose, to reestablish his relationship to humankind and the relationships of one person to another in love.

But the Marshes will not accept the outworking of God's freedom because they are unwilling to be free in themselves. That which has been given by God as natural human emotion is twisted by selfishness and deceit into attitudes and actions that are destructive both to self and others (Rom. 1; Gal. 5). Such a condition of psychological civil war is described as "bondage" because the person is under the control of unconscious forces or conscious motives that are irresistible to the human will (Rom. 7). So, Robert wants his marriage to "work." He believes this will happen if he can rule his own house. But he cannot recognize changes in the relationship of power between himself and his wife, and he cannot control his temper when his wishes are not obeyed. He hates divorce and adultery, but he is unwilling to see himself as the kind of person who could receive the support and loyalty of his wife.

I suspect that Linda suffers a similar lack of freedom. She also wants "our marriage to work" and she wants to "stay just with him." To some extent she knows why she has been unfaithful to her husband, but she has no deeper insight into her coquettishness: that it is one of her ways of getting what she wants from her husband or from anyone else. Because of this bondage, Linda cannot really feel forgiven by God or by members of the church they begin to attend. She continues to "feel unclean." She thinks this is because of unacceptance by other persons, but I would suspect that it is also rooted in her own lack of freedom to acknowledge her manipulative use of sex and of her higher education as protection against the rigid demands of her husband or as opportunities for her to dominate him.

With so many restrictions upon the will through the "flesh," how can we speak of any human freedom for the Marshes or anyone else? Realistically, freedom is not described in the New Testament as a constant quality of human behavior, nor is it considered to be unlimited. Instead, it is a gift, the power to evaluate our past and to reappraise our future. It is freedom to see how we have been bound up in our own conflicting desires; freedom is reidentification of ourselves as children of God (Gal. 4:1-11). Surrender to God's power brings a new self, with new self-identification, self-acceptance, and self-correction.

But everything does not change immediately (Phil. 3:12-16). The power we receive from God does not overrule all our circumstances at once, or even empower us to change ourselves according to our own desires. In many ways we are still bound by our culture or remain the creatures of unexamined habits. Even though there may be an instantaneous realignment of the center of the self toward God, the subsequent growth in grace is a slow process and we are still much more of ourselves than we may wish to be as we try to do God's will (Rom. 7).

To be free is not so much a total liberation as it is a faithful acknowledgment that we are very limited. To accept God's freedom over us is to confess and accept the limitations of our freedom and to place no ultimate trust in our own decisions or the decisions of anyone around us. Freedom is a life of faith in God as the ultimate source of security, direction, and redemption. Faith is freedom to exercise our limited power of decision making as a part of God's will for our lives. It is Paul Tillich's "courage to be" with a knowledge that we are human beings who are given divine purpose by God.[7]

The pastor tries to introduce this kind of freedom to Robert when the latter is asking how he is going to control his wife. His argument is that until he can control her, he cannot risk forgiving her. But then the pastor asks a question: "Can you control her now anyway?" Robert admits that it does not seem that he is doing so. "So," replies the pastor, "Why not start with something that you can do something about—your own feelings?"

Here is a limited area within which Robert can actualize freedom of choice, but he cannot act even within that limited area because human freedom requires self-identity and actualization. That is, Robert must see himself as the kind of person who is worthy before God and others before he can exercise any realistic control over his own emotions. At the present time, he cannot tolerate delay in gratification. His tension must be immediately relieved through fighting or drinking because he doesn't believe he has enough strength within him to overcome present frustration. Furthermore, he probably has not been rewarded in the past for delaying gratification and did not learn how it might be accomplished. As a substitute for inner strength, Robert "dumps" his anxiety and frustrations through actions that do not require self-control, such as hitting his wife or getting drunk with his friends.

Human Plans for Superhuman Certainty

Robert can be less than free through impulsive adaptation to any frustration that overcomes him. Or he can be more than free through the assertion that he absolutely knows the will of God and makes no choices as a human. The pastor who wrote this case was persuaded that Robert and Linda went back to their old church because it was one in which there was no human freedom or choice. All decisions for their good were already known through obedience to sermons and confirmation in private prayer.

This sounds like fanaticism, a favorite religious escape from freedom. It is a favorite for deprived and depleted people because anxiety over choices is reduced to zero. The vagaries of self-knowledge and the possibility of chance disasters are obliterated. Absolute certainty comes through a dualistic world view in which every event in the life of a saint is dictated by God and defied by the Devil. As a colleague of mine stated in an earnest sermon:

This is spiritual warfare. God and Satan contend for our souls. We're puppets. Let God pull the strings!

Fanaticism substitutes human for divine certainty through a denial of self-insight, personal motivation, and interpersonal responsibility. It sounds very comforting and reassuring when we are faced with life-threatening situations, such as the one faced by Rachel.

I was active in a prayer group as well as in a local church that sponsored the prayer group. In the prayer group I shared the alarming warning of my physician that a biopsy of some lymph glands was necessary to determine if they were benign or malignant. I said that I had always been very afraid of hospitals and that I had thought since childhood that I might die at an early age. I had woven together a pattern of reassurance in prayer that God would protect me against illness if I faithfully served him. I had become completely convinced that godly service was a guarantee against illness.

What was I to do, now that the physician announced the possibility of a life-threatening disease? My prayer group had a variety of answers: "Have no fear! God will heal you." "We will pray for you. We will call you every day until you have finished the test."

Among other responses, I heard one person say: "I know this feeling. Since childhood I have felt that something dreadful was going to happen to me. It is a terrible dread, but God gives me certainty about his word so that I can always know that I am in his will. I always seek him and he always gives me the right answer."

I thought about this last response as the group was praying. It did not make sense that God would give the perfect understanding that this person proclaimed. I wondered if there was some deeper reason for this person's absolute certainty about godly things.

Several days later, I heard a Christian teacher discuss the difference between the "special vision" of those who are "puffed up by human ways of thinking" (Col. 2:18) and the humble vision of one who proclaims "Woe is me!" (Isa. 6:1–6). I said to myself, I have been having "special visions"! I have tried to control my fear with magical thought. I have thought that God is going to make an exception of me among all the women of the world. For a few moments I was downcast by this admission, but then I thought, Well, I would never have realized this if I had not begun to be honest with others about what I fear. I might as well admit the defense that I have used against fear in the past. Maybe I don't need that defense anymore, now that I have a group of faithful people who surround me in my time of fear. As I thought this, I had a feeling that God was looking at me in a different way from what I had thought of him before. He did not seem to be so stern, so judgmental of my weakness. Instead, I had the distinct impression that I was loved and cared for. I burst into tears and afterwards felt that I really was secure as a child held in the strong arms of my Creator.

Several days later, I began to think about the person who was always sure of God's commands. I thought, Why, there is another "special vision"! That person is also afraid of death and disguises the fear by pretending that there is no doubt about decisions. That person rises up with pride because of the need for that special vision. I wonder if that person has ever had an open discussion with anyone else about the fear of death? Maybe I could be that person.

Rachel is now dealing openly with a life of faith despite chances of death or serious illness. She took the action of openly declaring her fear in a prayer group and later made plans to introduce her finding about "special visions" to another member of the group. In this way, action becomes a part of any search for God's will.

This emphasis is of special importance to counselees from super-spiritual churches. These churches are in the "highways and hedges" of ruined humanity. They bind up the wounds of those who are broken in spirit and psyche. But they leave on the bandages and soon decorate them with scripture verses, pious shibboleths, and catchy phrases. The wounded are bound with the grave clothes of Lazarus. These broken people cannot take many large steps in the Christian pilgrimage. Their weakened egos do not allow bold decision making. In answer to this depleted condition of the self, the super-spiritual churches offer reassurance; God will make himself known in some visible, infallible way! Then the fearful persons will be relieved of any risk-taking in a decision. They will "put out the fleece" and God will provide some unmistakable sign of his leadership.

In this pseudo-therapeutic theology for the inadequate, the biblical emphasis upon discipleship as a pilgrimage is distorted.[8] Instead of a steady walk of faith, as recounted in Hebrews 11, damaged persons are presented with many cautions that are calculated to undermine self-confidence. Then there is a sudden prodding to leap a fantastic distance "by faith." But they are like Mark Twain's "celebrated frog of Calaveras County," which was secretly fed lead shot on the night before a crucial contest and could not jump. A heavy load of guilt has the same depleting effect upon deprived people in super-spiritual congregations. In counsel, they desperately talk about the will of God, but always from behind the veil of a deceived self. This is their protection against the terror of a miscalculated action. I vividly remember the lesson taught to me after ten sessions of counsel with a middle-aged woman who said: "I prayed and prayed that God would lead me, but it never happened because I would not go to the starting line. I kept pretending that I was something other than who I really am. God only finds you where you are, not where you think you are. When I finally let him come to me as I am, I experienced the forgiveness that is going to give me strength to lead an honest life."

Acting with Assurance

"Strength to lead an honest life" is a statement of wisdom to detect deceit and cope with chronic problems. In the case of this woman, it was the courage to admit the well-founded jealousy she had developed toward a more beautiful and favored sister. My counselee really had been rejected by her mother, but she had not admitted this. All she could say was, "I must do my best so I will find favor with God and man." This meant hours of pious work in church and community "with no thought of self. My will must completely submit to God's will."

Yet each Sunday she burned with envy as the pastor praised the good works of others and seldom mentioned her sacrifices. It was not until the sixth week of counsel that she blurted out: "I want to be noticed! I don't know why—or do I? It's been with me ever since Mother couldn't go to my junior high graduation because she didn't have a good dress. She had spent her money on a new dress for my sister, and explained that my sister was so pretty that she just had to have new clothes. Could that be why I want somebody to praise me?"

When we can ask those questions, we are ready to know God's will because we can admit our own motivation to ourselves and to him. This is the beginning of wisdom.

But the lady had never been in a church group which would have led her to develop honesty about her own will and the way she distorted God's will (her presented problem to me was: "How can I have more zeal in doing God's will in church work"). Like many other people, she had missed a major resource for the knowledge of human and divine will, described in Scripture as exhortation, counsel, comfort, edification, building-up. The resource is human mediation of divine grace:

> Let us be concerned for one another, to help one another to show love and to do good. Let us not give up the habit of meeting together, as some are doing. Instead, let us encourage one another all the more (Heb. 10:24–25)

This is one of the three great resources of faith during trial: (1) the witness of the Spirit through Scripture that God has entered a covenant of forgiveness and guidance with us (Heb. 10:15–17); (2) the witness of a purified conscience that we can freely receive guidance from God in times of weakness (Heb. 10:19–22; 4:14–16); (3) the witness to one another in exhortation during suffering that is a daily antidote for deception and isolation (Heb. 3:13; 10:24–25; 10:32–36; 12:1; 13:1–3).

Knowing and doing the will of God is a constant interaction of the divine and human will through prayer and meditation, biblical and theological study, Christian counsel and group guidance, which should result in intimate fellowship.[9]

All these elements of interaction are essential in Christian counsel. When the first two are missing (prayer and meditation, biblical and theological study) the inner life of a believer is not strengthened and over-dependence upon social or ecclesiastical judgments develops (Paul rejects such judgments in the first part of 1 Cor. 4). When the other two elements, Christian counsel and group guidance, are rejected, isolated individualism flourishes and Christian fellowship is reduced to warm, fuzzy interactions among people who carefully hide their inner thoughts.

Character in Community

We know and do the will of God through the harmonious interaction of the elements that have just been described. These are the acts that produce assurance of God's presence through the "fruit of the Spirit" (Gal. 5:22–26). The primary evidence of this Christian maturity is a willingness to bear one another's burdens with enough humility that the person who is "overbalanced" will become strong enough to balance the burden with self-respect. This kind of sharing is a guarantee against self-deception and hypocrisy (Gal. 6:1–10).

The guarantee is based upon the life and teachings of Jesus, who perfectly obeyed the will of God—even to death (Phil. 2:8). To the followers of John the Baptist he gave this assurance:[10]

Go back and tell John what you have seen and heard: the blind can see, the lame can walk, those who suffer from dreaded skin diseases are made clean, the deaf can hear, the dead are raised to life, and the Good News is preached to the poor. (Luke 7:22)

This evidence of God's will is both within us and in our relations to others. Both our attitudes and our actions must draw from this assurance.[11] Why? Because our actions may not produce changes in a threatening environment or prevent illness, misfortune, and death. Why should we continue to pray and assemble with other Christians for guidance and strength when loved ones grow physically weaker and the wicked continue to defraud us?

The Pauline answer to unaltered circumstances was the utilization of trouble as a proving ground for inner faith, a testing of endurance, God's approval, hope, heartfelt love.[12] This attitude in times of distress gives a sense of harmony with God (Rom. 5:1–5).

What is this inner harmony? It was first demonstrated on the American scene by Jonathan Edwards's case studies of conversion during the Great Awakening of the 1740s. In enumerating the signs of "religious affections," Edwards placed greatest stress upon the fifth sign, which was an inner sense of delight in the ways of God and a social reinforcement of this in association with God's people. The delight was felt not only in the emotions but also in the intellect, as people developed a sense of perspective in their view of the world and an awareness of the harmony with which God intended for people to

134

live with each other, with him, and with nature. Edwards thought of this as the apex of our sense of beauty in harmonious relationships that reflected the beatific vision of Christ himself.[13]

The emphasis upon inner harmony and the perception of beauty as a sign of God's will is especially needed for those who desperately call for God's freedom while they are unfree in themselves. One sign of disharmony in such persons is the demand for premature explanations of events in life or immature thinking about God's vengeance or special blessing. To redeem the thinking of these persons in conflict, we may ask them how a knowledge of God's will can make sense out of all their relationships, bring inner serenity and sensitivity to the needs of others.

But how can we talk about serenity and sensitivity when questions about God's will are often connected with tragedy and disaster? Who can make sense out of some of the evil that we see in this world? An answer to this question is found in the doctrine of providence, which is the confidence of God's presence in all circumstances. With this perspective, the catastrophes of life are judged less in terms of our own convenience than they are by the vividness of God's presence and the fulfillment of his promises to sustain those who turn to him in time of trial.[14]

Is God responsible for some of our circumstances, aside from the adverse circumstances brought on by our own evil desires, the selfish structures of society, or the snares of the devil? We cannot know the answer to that question immediately, for it takes some time for the fruits of an experience to be clear to us. But we can judge a circumstance to be a part of his leading if it creates opportunities for the types of service that are described by Christ in his conversation with the disciples of John or in his warnings to the crowds in Jerusalem (Matt. 25:31–46). Any action or event that increases the glory of God (which may include the altering of circumstances or attitudes) can be recognized as a sign of his prevenient grace.

The Mystery of Evil

In counsel we can often identify altered attitudes as signs of faith, but what evidence do we find of altered circumstances as signs of God's will? What about chance, accident, fate as alternative explanations?[15]

We are looking for signs of God's providence or prevenient grace. These terms encompass prophetic and messianic hopes, the Incarnation of the Word of God in Christ, and the indwelling of the Holy Spirit for the building up of the ideal community within which the will of God may be actualized.[16]

H. H. Farmer provides a more succinct definition of providence (1) as ultimate succor and (2) as sacred demand. In *The World and God*, Farmer demonstrates the relationship of these two terms as basic to our understanding of God and ourselves.[17]

Our usual preference is for conversation about "sacred demand." We find assurance of God's activity in character change or inner strength during adversity (cf. Rom. 8:31-39).

We are less sure of ourselves when clients ask about changes in circumstances, which may be proximate or ultimate succor. Their questions may be about explanations of evil ("Why do bad things happen to good people?") or identification of miraculous intervention.

Wisdom literature does not answer the metaphysical problem of evil. Why bother, asks the writer of Ecclesiastes,

In days to come we will all be forgotten. We must all die—wise and foolish alike. (2:16)

Then what is wisdom in the face of evil and death? The New Testament response is confidence that God suffers with us and strengthens us with his presence during adversity. Christ's death and resurrection is the sign that evil can only trouble us for a time, and within this time the movement of God is for our redemption (Col. 1:20-27; 2 Cor. 4-5; Gal. 1:4; Heb. 4; Luke 22:42-44). This is the wisdom that makes us mature in the midst of "toil and struggle" (Col. 1:28-29).[18]

Maturity that stands the test of toil results in inner courage and loving associations, based on understanding of ourselves and God's intentions for us. The relation of friendship—between God and Christ, Christ and us, and ourselves and others—is "the key that opens all the hidden treasures of God's wisdom and knowledge" (Col. 2:3; 1:20-22).

Paul promises nothing more, but some counselees ask for more. Does God alter circumstances as well as the human heart? Does he continue to send miracles of physical healing in addition to the forgiveness of sins and wisdom in the face of suffering?

The answer of many counselors is a demurring that sounds like fatalism. They explain that unalterable circumstances loom over us and we cannot tell the difference between chance and providence when we are delivered. So why not settle for some form of determinism and relegate God's unmistakable interventions to an earlier age?

This is premature closure of a complex question. Why not go the way of wisdom and admit the difficulties of full understanding, but keep open the possibility that God may move on our behalf through the timing of events and our awareness of their appropriateness.

> He has set the right time for everything. He has given us a desire to know the future, but never gives us the satisfaction of fully understanding what he does. (Eccles. 3:11)

The acts of the apostles demonstrate God's intervention through the ordering of events and a quickening of our mind to the way that events are related to his will. Saul is so stunned by a light and a voice that he waits for three days in Damascus. During that time, Ananias is called in a vision to restore Saul's sight and announce the coming of the Holy Spirit (Acts 9:7–19). Peter is shaken out of his ritualism by a vision in which he is commanded to eat unclean things, and while he wonders about this, Gentiles knock on his door with an invitation to enter the house of Cornelius (Acts 10:1–23).

When we are aware of his purposes for us, time offers an opportunity for us to follow God's power in human events. Jesus refused the invitation of his brothers to go at the appointed time to Jerusalem for a feast, with a reminder that his mission must be congruent with God's design: "The right time for me has not yet come. Any time is right for you" (John 7:6).

It is useful to know the difference between our convenient time and the fulfillment of God's eternal purposes when people request miracles.[19] These signs of God's providence are not ours to command, no matter how desperate our desire for healing.[20] All we can know about time in relation to miracle is the clustering of the miraculous around crises in Israel, first in deliverance from Egypt and establishment in Palestine, and second in the disintegration of the nation and the rise of a prophetic consciousness. The time of powerful signs from God culminates in the early days of the ministry of his Son (Matt. 4:23–25). There were occasional recordings of healing toward the close of his ministry (Luke 18:35–43), but after the confession of Simon Peter at Caesarea Philippi (Mark 8:27–30) and the similar confession of Martha at the graveside of Lazarus (John 11:27), the focus of Jesus' ministry was teaching about his approaching death (Mark 8:31–33).

The ebb and flow of the miraculous is also evident in the ministry of Paul. A miraculous event is recorded on two of his missionary journeys (Acts 14:8–17, 19:12), but Paul never announced these as sign of his apostleship or gave them prominence in his letters. When he is defending himself as an apostle against false apostles he confesses that he has asked for healing and not received it (2 Cor. 11:12–15, 12:7–10).[21]

If we admit that the timing of miracles is a mystery, do we abandon this sign of God's power upon the earth?[22] No, Paul's solution was to designate miraculous healing as one of the instrumental gifts for building up fellowship in Christ. Some can have this ministry. But all participate in love, the great gift of God that empowers us to do his will in a variety of ways (1 Cor. 12:4–26).[23]

But some counselees will feel abandoned by this teaching. They need power now. There must be some sign to heal and lift up the depressed, diseased, deprived. This is what people plead for and this is what some counselors promise them. This creates the hazard of fanaticism, in which we insist that human need will dictate God's timing and our concentration will generate divine healing (e.g. "My hands are getting warm; I know the Spirit is moving").

In the midst of this special emphasis we can open our hearts to the need for all of God's gifts to come upon those who suffer or stray, and seek a fellowship in which all are honored and available. Not everyone has the power to work miracles or to heal diseases. We are not commanded to set our hearts on any of these instrumental gifts. Instead, our ministry is to center upon the ordinary, daily, reliable work of love, supported by faith and hope (1 Cor. 12:29–13:13).

A variety of gifts requires a healing community. The body of Christ, which combines acceptance and frustration, consolation and judgment, is our resource against pride, deception and isolation that characterized some "gifted" persons in the Corinthian church.

The fellowship is our way toward wisdom in knowing the will of God. Those who interpret the will of God for the entire congregation are to be honored above those who sound very godly but only edify themselves (1 Cor. 14:1-4, 19).

This emphasis upon fellowship and sharing is troublesome to needy people who are absorbed in their individual conflicts. These persons may conform to the individualism of American culture, which excuses their secrecy and isolation.

The church has maintained that the Spirit is the power of God to draw fearful people into friendship, brotherhood, citizenship. How does the Spirit of God work in our privatized world among those who despair of intimacy and yet desire nearness to God? Are we to understand the Holy Spirit as individual gift or is there always a "fellowship of the Spirit"? Do we look for the signs of God's power in ourselves or among others? These are some of the questions about the Holy Spirit that we will consider in the following chapter.

NOTES

1. Erik Erikson, *Insight and Responsibility* (New York: W. W. Norton, 1964), p. 133; James L. Crenshaw, *Studies in Ancient Israelite Wisdom* (New York: KTAV Publishing, 1976), p. 193; and *Old Testament Wisdom* (Atlanta: John Knox Press, 1981).

2. The connection between the freedom of God and the freedom of humans is often discussed by theologians. Paul Ramsey, in his introduction to Jonathan Edwards's *Freedom of the Will*, notes that "Edwards is not as concerned about Arminian theories of self-motivation as he was about the advancement of human liberty over the freedom of God himself" (Paul Ramsey, ed., *Jonathan Edwards's Freedom of the Will* [New Haven: Yale University Press, 1957], p. 27). Edwards considered freedom of the will to be basic for uncompelled acts. He did not mean by this to say that there was no cause or determination of the acts that came from beyond the human will. In this he was one with Augustine and Luther in distinguishing moral necessity from physical necessity, which might also be defined as the difference between determinism and force or between causation and compulsion. See Ramsey's discussion of this in the introduction to Edwards' *Freedom of the Will*, especially p. 42.

3. Heb. 13:21; Rom. 12:1-2; Phil. 2:12ff; and D. Müller, "Will, Purpose," in Colin Brown, ed., *New International Dictionary of Testament Theology* (Grand Rapids: Zondervan, 1971) vol. 3, pp. 1015-1023; and G. Schrenk, *"thelema,"* in Gerhard Kittel, ed., *Theological Dictionary of the New Testament*, Geoffrey W. Bromiley, tr. and ed., (Grand Rapids: William B. Eerdmans, 1967), vol. 3, especially p. 58.

The importance of "will" in the connection of theism, value, and reality as experienced by the individual is presented in William Temple, *Christus Veritas* (London: Macmillan, 1954), pp. 7ff., 50.

4. See further discussion in Schrenk, *"Thelema."*

    In systematic theology, God's freedom precedes human freedom because our freedom is a divine gift. Paul Jewett, *Election and Predestination* (Grand Rapids: William B. Eerdmans, 1985) discusses the relation of divine and human freedom as seen in various doctrines of predestination.

5. The "will of God" is debated in Reformed theology as the paradox of his will for the salvation of all (1 Tim. 2:4) and his will to harden some (Rom. 9:18). See Jewett, *Election and Predestination*, pp. 97ff.

6. The teaching of the church fathers concerning faith and fate are reviewed by Albert Outler in chap. 4 of *Who Trusts in God: Musings on the Meaning of Providence* (New York: Oxford University Press, 1968). An exhaustive analysis of the themes of evil and good in Ireneaus and Augustine are provided in John Hick's *Evil and the God of Love* (New York: Harper and Row, 1978).

7. Paul Tillich, *The Courage to Be* (New Haven: Yale University Press, 1952). For a theocentric working out of these themes, see Albert C. Outler, *Who Trusts in God*.

8. See the discussion of the new life of believers and the divine will *(thelema)* in Schrenk.

9. In the New Testament, the "will of God" *(thelema)* is almost always used for his saving and protecting activity (especially in the Gospel of Matthew, where it is consistently linked with the title "Father": 6:10; 7:21; 12:50; 18:14; 21:28–31). Schrenk. In relation to believers, the will of God is a readiness for the renewal of the mind and the making of choices according to this insight (Rom. 12:2; Col. 1:9).

10. This example of Jesus is given by Jürgen Moltmann as the great commission of any church that seeks to provide unmistakable witness to their belief in Jesus as the Christ. Jürgen Moltmann, *Hope for the Church* (Nashville: Abingdon, 1979), pp. 24–25.

11. The assurance of God's will must bridge the gulf between our limited will and God's infinite power. In covenant theology, God voluntarily limited himself to interact with his creation through a covenant (Deut. 6:20–25). Those who faithfully live within the restrictions of his promises will receive his constant love (Deut. 7:12ff). Without these assurances from God, the Israelites feared death if God came near to them (Deut. 5:23–33). This awareness of God's tremendous power is a theme of Rudolph Otto's *The Idea of the Holy* (London: Oxford University Press, 1950).

    Covenant theology was an important part of the Reformed theology of John Calvin (*Institutes of the Christian Religion*, 2.6.2; 2.10.2–3). In the seventeenth century, Johannes Wollebius emphasized the covenant in *Compendium of Christian Theology* (1626), as did William Ames, *The Marrow of True Divinity* (1623). Ames, an English puritan, was influential for the New England understanding of the relationship between the awesome power of God and the mercy of God in fellowship with those whom he had created. For a summary of covenant theology, see Geoffrey W. Bromiley, *Historical Theology: An Introduction* (Grand Rapids: William B. Eerdmans, 1978, pp. 310–16).

12. Robert Hazelton in *God's Way With Man: Variations on the Theme of Providence* (New York: Abbeydon Press, 1956) develops the theme that the fateful boundaries of human life become the frontiers where God provides ultimate succor.

13. Jonathan Edwards, *Religious Affections* (New Haven: Yale University Press, 1959), p. 34.

14. Now what is the place of accidents in our understanding of providence? See the discussions in William Pollard, *Chance and Providence* (New York: Scribner, 1958) and in Harold Kushner, *When Bad Things Happen to Good People* (New York: Schocken Books, 1981).

15. Living with circumstances that threaten the meaning of our existence is described from the viewpoint of Ecclesiastes by Harold Kushner, *When All You've Ever Wanted Isn't Enough* (New York: Simon and Shuster, 1986).

16. Outler, *Who Trusts in God*, pp. 79–80.

17. H. H. Farmer, *The World and God* (London: Nisbet and Company, 1935), pp. 43–49.

18. The more general discussion of God's purpose for the universe and the system of causes for his decisions is called *teleology*. It is a term coined by Christian Wolff in 1728 as part of his argument for his belief in God. A more restrictive term is *theodicy*, an explanation for the presence of evil in a world created and under the providential care of God. G. W. Leibnitz developed the term in 1710 from a combination of *theos* (God) and *dike* (justice). For some discussions of these theological terms, see Leo Scheffczyk, *Creation and Providence*, tr. Richard Strichan (New York: Herder and Herder, 1970); H. H. Farmer, *The World and God*; and G.C. Berkouwer, *The Providence of God*, tr. Lewis Smedes (Grand Rapids: William B. Eerdmans, 1952).

19. See Colin Brown, *That You May Believe: Miracles and Faith: Then and Now* (Grand Rapids: William B. Eerdmans, 1985), pp. 62–77.

20. Our impulsive call for instantaneous healing can be tempered by a belief in God's prevenient grace, his activity in running before us or reaching out to us with guidance and strength. In this sense the free will of the believer is conditioned by the freedom of God, as Albert C. Outler wrote in *Who Trusts in God*, "freedom is less the power to intervene in the causal process than it is the power to act in the presence of that Provident Mystery that encompasses our lives," p. 51.

The confidence of the Christian is in his election by God to salvation in spite of the sin that brings God's judgment. See Jewett, *Election and Predestination*, pp. 115ff.

21. Perhaps, as in Paul's statement to the Philippians (1:21–26), death is related to our mission in life as God understands it. From a godly perspective, we already have eternal life. This is God's will, that we never be separated from him (Rom. 8:28). From a human perspective, we wonder about relationship and mission. But what will the *timing* of our death have to do with these?

See James Barr, *Biblical Words for Time* (London: SCM Press, 1962).

22. If we are going to understand the place and occasion for miracles in Christian counsel, there must be more faithful interdisciplinary reporting of what has actually occurred. Then we would know how to relate faith, death, and miracles. A model for this kind of reporting may be found in an example of miraculous healing, see David H. Barlow, Ph.D.; Gene G. Abel, M.D.; and Edward B. Blanchard, "Gender, Identity Change in a Transsexual: An Exorcism," in Matthew and Dennis Linn, *Deliverance Prayer* (New York: Paulist Press, 1981).

23. For further study on miracles and healing, see Colin Brown, *That You May Believe: Miracles and the Critical Mind* (Grand Rapids: William B. Eerdmans, 1984); Morton Kelsey, *Healing and Christianity in Ancient Thought and Modern Times* (New York: Harper and Row, 1973); Francis McNutt, *Healing* (Notre Dame: Ave Maria Press, 1974); Louis Monden, *Signs and Wonders: A Study of the Miraculous Element in Religion* (New York: Desclee, 1966); Klaus Seybold and Ulrich B. Muller, *Sickness and Healing* (Nashville: Abingdon, 1981); Martin E. Marty and Kenneth L. Vaux, eds., *Health/Medicine and the Faith Traditions: An Inquiry into Religion and Medicine* (Philadelphia: Fortress Press, 1982); John Wilkinson, *Health and Healing: Studies in New Testament Principles and Practice* (Edinburgh: The Handsels Press, 1980); W. J. Sheils, *The Church and Healing* (Oxford: Basil Blackwell, 1982).

9

The Power of the Spirit

Fellowship in the Spirit provides a balanced perspective on God's will in relation to our will. In fellowship there is a sharing of power that compensates for the preoccupation of deprived people with their peculiar needs. In Christian counsel, the needs are met through honest and open sharing. The power of the Spirit is manifest in the overcoming of separation and deceit. In the power of the Spirit of Jesus those who were once strangers to each other, to God, and to themselves are now "brought near" through the sacrificial love of Jesus. It is a workable, demonstrable spirit of relationship. But we have this power only insofar as we repeat Jesus' relationship to God and his disciples with humility and insight.

In an age of personal control, the power of the Spirit is much sought after. This is most obvious in churches or counselees that have discarded the "New England self" in favor of the "California self." The New England self had integrity without intensity of feeling, duty with few desires, social conformity as the price of abiding community. It was a minimal self in which theology gave direction for the reduction of sin and incentives for community control.

143

The California self expanded awareness without many restrictions on choices, abandoned any sense of sin that diminished sensations, esteemed confidence in individual potential more than mutual service with esteemed friends. It was a maximum self in which theologies of power supported soaring expectations of success.[1]

The rise of the California self coincided with decreasing confidence in national leaders, fragmentation of the extended family, and skepticism concerning organized religion. In the midst of unparalleled opportunities for material acquisition and an exotic variety of experiences, personal choice was maximized, but so were the chances for failure—but with no support system to soften the fall.

I sat among several thousand worshipers in a California congregation which was enthralled by one pastor's answer to the threat of personal failure with no one to help: "More power, Lord, more power!" The pastor thrust forth his arm like the driving rod of a steam locomotive and people were empowered.

Empowered by what? By the Spirit, we trust. This is what they desired and this is the function of the Spirit—to empower humans.

For the Spirit that God has given us does not make us timid; instead, his Spirit fills us with power, love, and self control.

(2 Tim. 1:7)

The association of the Spirit with power is especially attractive in a time when personal control means ability to acquire and consume products and experience personal sensations with individual tenacity. We desire power to actualize our acquisitive instincts in a society where our personal significance is threatened. Those who are threatened may use verses about the Spirit to strengthen their self-confidence and diminish (or deny) their dependence upon the opinions of others:

Whoever has the Spirit . . . is able to judge the value of everything, but no one is able to judge him. (1 Cor. 2:15)

Power from Where?

Paul's words may sound like justification of an isolated and very human "cosmic consciousness," but the text does not support that interpretation of spiritual power.

144

The context of 1 Cor. 2:15 is "a message of wisdom to those who are spiritually mature" (2:6). The spiritually mature distinguish their own spirit, "that knows all about him," and God's Spirit, who "knows all about God" (vv. 2:11–12). It is the Spirit that gives us precision in "searching everything"—which we cannot accomplish without "God's secret wisdom." (1 Cor. 2:7–10).

The challenge of this message to the Corinthians was to discriminate between human assumptions about power and the spiritual power that is manifest despite our fear and weakness (1 Cor. 1:12–13; 2:6–16; 3:3–9).

The foundation of spiritual power is confession of weakness and desire to work humbly with others. These ingredients are major challenges to counselors or counselees who will only admit enough weakness to obtain someone else's power, and who expect to use self-actualization for their own advantage without too much thought for the community good.

So we must ask where the power comes from. Is it confirmation of our desire for dominance, absolute assurance that covers massive threats of failure, or acceptable language for social approval in a world of strangers?

These are the questions of spiritual discernment by which the work of our spirit may be distinguished from the power of God's Spirit.[2] The goal is to determine the range of the Spirit's work in enhancing our humanity and to detect the restrictive work of human deception, pride, and defeat. The criteria for "enhancement" is inner stability in the mind of Christ and communion with God and his people (Eph. 2–3).[3]

But these requirements of "full disclosure" and interdependence with others are often resisted by counselees who ardently desire "spiritual" power. They use spirituality to conceal rather than to reveal the kind of power they desire, as well as to hide the hidden sources of their own weaknesses. They often are so frightened and bewildered by unacceptable forces in the self that they seek a superficial covering of "spirituality" as an acceptable disguise for their true motivations ("angelic" seducers are the object of withering scorn in 2 Pet. 2:1–3, 9–22. See also Rom. 2).

In a defensive maneuver, which is as old as the Corinthian church, the transforming power of the Holy Spirit is reduced to a few "showy" gifts (1 Cor. 13:1–6). To expose these restrictions, Paul wrote some soul-searching questions to the church which was so "filled" with showy gifts that they did not examine immorality in their midst or selfishness at the Lord's table (1 Cor. 4:18-20; 5:1-2, 6-11; 11:17-22, 28-32).

The remedy for this deception is reflective and sacrificial love in the power of the Spirit. When the Spirit is allowed to operate completely within us, we will share our complete self with others in a humble and open way (1 Cor. 13:4ff.; cf. Rom. 2).

An open reception of the Spirit without the hindrance of hidden restrictions takes place when power comes from *charis* (grace) and precedes *charismata* (spiritual gifts) in our lives. Grace is primary because it is the decisive movement of God that establishes a positive interaction with those who have faith (Rom. 3:24; 5:15-21; 1 Cor. 1:4f.; 15:10; 2 Cor. 6:1; Gal. 1:6, 15; 2:21; Eph. 2:5, 8). Grace is power, the result and evidence of divine work in human life (Rom. 5:2; 6:14; Col. 3:16; 2 Cor. 1:12).

Grace is not only the power for spiritual gifting; it is also the explanation for the variety of gifts and for the harmonious relationship between gifts and human individuality. Paul speaks "of the grace given to me/you." (Rom. 12:3, 6; 15:15; Gal. 2:9; Eph. 3:2, 7f.). Each commission by the Spirit is particular. There will be differences in the "measure of faith" that comes to each of us and there should be some awareness of our individual gifting (Rom. 12:3-8).

When grace is seen as the precondition of gifts, we not only receive gifts in their proper spiritual setting, but we also recognize the futility of specializing in gifts and elevating the "showy" gifts above all the others.

Any attempt to categorize or arrange spiritual gifts according to our own needs for power or praise is preempted by Paul's words about grace in relation to gifts. First, Paul considers "grace" to be a summary word for the great gift of God, which is eternal life (Rom. 6:23). Any particular gift must be a part of this great gift. Second, grace may have a unique and personal meaning as a "gift," such as the ability to say no to sexual passions (1 Cor. 7:7). Third, any rampant individualism should be held in check by Paul's perspective of grace in the community of faith as the setting within which any spiritual gift is to be bestowed (1 Cor. 1:7; 12:7-10).

Spiritual gifts are ways in which grace may operate in particular circumstances for the building up of the body of Christ (Rom. 12:1-13).

146

How do we see this relation between the preeminence of grace and the actualization of gifts in a counselee? We may consider, for example, the gift of prophetic utterance, which may be spoken of as prophecy (1 Cor. 14:1–6), "word of knowledge" (1 Cor. 12:8), or "discernment between spirits" (1 Cor. 12:10). The relation between this gift and grace is evident in Paul's insistence that those who prophesy will build up the understanding of the entire congregation without puffing up the prophet at the same time (1 Cor. 14:1–6). It is the sacrificial love behind the prophetic utterance that humbles the prophet, making this person aware that we stand before God as his vulnerable, limited, honest servants (1 Thess. 2:4; 1 Cor. 14:23–24). This humble, undefensive honesty is the sign to others that there is grace in the gift, and it is this that brings the convicting power of God (1 Cor. 14:24f).

How is this conviction brought into Christian counsel? A pastor faced this question as he sat down with Helen Rahner for consultation about "an embarrassing problem." Mr. and Mrs. Rahner had been members of the congregation for two years and would attend the church several times each month for morning worship and occasionally be part of some social event. The pastor wrote up his conversation with Helen because he was not encouraged by it:

Helen Rahner came to see me on Monday afternoon. When we shook hands I noticed that there was cold sweat on them. She began talking even before we shook hands.

Helen: It is so terrible to have to admit this to a man of God. I am close to the Lord and I know that he tells me what to do. But ever since George (my second child) was born, I have blushed whenever a good-looking man came into the room. It's not because I'm not getting satisfaction with my husband. Some people might say that, but it's not true. Sex is a gift of God. God finally told me what it is: it's the result of my husband's punishment of me. He made me pregnant when I didn't want to be. How did I figure that out? I never had this problem before and now I have it all the time. So it's a sign of my resentment against my husband and of his cruelty to me.

Pastor: Cruelty?

Helen: Yes, he knew that my sister had an unwanted child. He knows the misery that it caused her. He wanted me to be miserable in the same way. Now he has done it and he will not take any responsibility for it. He denies that it was this way. He says that we talked about it, but we did not. I have had it up to *here*. I cannot take any more of this. But I have talked to the Lord about this and he has sent me an answer. My purpose in life is to bear the cross he has put upon me. It was his purpose that I should conceive. It's cruel. It's punishment for my sins. But I must accept it as God's will.

Pastor: Let's stop and look at that statement for a minute—

Helen: God's will always makes good sense—

Pastor: But people do not always make good sense out of God's will. That's why I stopped you, so that I can say that it makes no sense for you to say that God is punishing you through conception. The act of becoming a parent is a gift of God and is not, in his order of things, cruelty. I don't think you can blame conception and cruelty upon God.

Helen: Well, some people understand God's will in one way and some understand it in another way. I cannot stand any more of this cruelty from my husband. He thinks up ways to make me miserable. Sometimes he denies this, but I know it.

There are many things that I know because God shows them to me. I can read my husband like a book. He pretends to be something that he is not. He says that he likes his work, but he hates it. I question him and he has to admit that I am right. He denies that he thinks up ways to make my life miserable. I tell him what he has done. He has no answers. This is God's way of strengthening me. He has given me the gift of reading my husband's mind.

Pastor: I may look a little puzzled because I'm trying to think if this reading of the mind is ever mentioned as a gift in the New Testament. I don't think so—

Helen: It says in the Bible that God will give you wisdom. That is what this is.

Pastor: Is it? Now that I think about it, there is one mention of Jesus knowing what was in the mind of man—

Helen: That's it.

Pastor: But that is a statement in the Gospel of John, I believe, in which the apostle is showing that Jesus is really divine. He is different from us. He knows what is the mind of man, but the implication is that we do not. I don't think of any New Testament passages in which that divine attribute of the Saviour is passed on to his disciples. So, whatever ability you have to read your husband's mind must not be coming from God.

Helen: Well, it certainly isn't coming from the devil!

Pastor: Well, whoever it comes from, it seems to create a hellish situation. I don't think that anyone can completely read the mind of another person, except Jesus, so you probably create much resentment in your husband when you tell him that you can read his mind.

Helen: Yes, that's exactly it. He always has resentments. That's how I know this is a gift from God. He has to admit that I am right. I can see it in him and when I insist that I'm right, he begins to show how much anger there is down inside him. I can't take that from him much longer. I am to the breaking point.

Pastor: Are you concerned enough about this to have a series of conferences with me or with some other counselor?

The pastor handed this case to me because he thought it was a "failure." Some of the fellow pastors who looked at this verbatim were also convinced that he "went wrong" somewhere in the interview. One said, "You should have been more empathetic and established a friendship with Helen." Another said, "You argued with her. She felt rejected." A third said, "Pray! pray! Why do you seek a secular counselor when this woman's problem is a misunderstanding of prophecy?"

There is some wisdom in each of these comments; the last one has some possibilities for pre-counseling. As I see it, Helen thinks that she has "words of knowledge," but no one seems to agree with her. Why not? From what I can tell from this brief verbatim, Helen is an insecure person who tries to establish her position by dominating others. She is so insecure that she must use "God-talk" to get attention. It doesn't work, but the defense is so important to her that she cannot hear any rational arguments.[4] Something must be said to her about the value of prophecy and words of knowledge that will get her interest and perhaps her confidence. But it must be a correct teaching that shows her the difference between the way that she uses these "spiritual gifts" and the way in which true gifts were originally intended to be used (without ignoring the value of empathetic listening, once we get her attention). Could Helen be shown, by words or attitude, the setting of gifts within the context of grace? If so, Helen will have an appealing reason to continue the dialogue. Does she value spiritual gifting so much that she is willing to learn how to be gracious? Will she admit her defensiveness, fear, repression, domination—all the "unspiritual" parts of self—including sex and rage?

If Helen will accept correction, she is ready for counsel. The Spirit can now do a work of grace in her heart. Paul speaks of this as the work of the Spirit to build up the inner person (Rom. 2:28f.; 2 Cor. 3; Gal. 4:6; Phil. 3; Eph. 1:15–23; 3:14–19). When this occurs, prophecy or any other gift would no longer be superficial and showy. The gifts will then show the grace that comes from the work of God's power in our inner being.[5]

Power for What?

Grace will probably not be manifest in Helen if she continues to exercise power over her husband. She needs an opportunity to expand love toward some meeting of masculinity and femininity. Then spiritual power will have height and breadth in her life.

The expansion of love into all parts of the self is a continual challenge to theories or practices of male or female dominance. In theology, the dominance of male channels of power is just now being questioned.

The traditional purpose of power in systematic theology has been to restrain pride and maintain responsible action. But, as Valerie Goldstein noted in the 1950s, male theologians seemed to be preoccupied with their own major problem. They showed little awareness of the way in which women needed power as self-confidence. The problem for women was defeat and depression rather than pride.[6]

Research of the 1970s and 80s showed variations in the means and ends of power for men and women: men define themselves through power of separation from others, while women feel power through attachment to mother, sister, female friends. The threat to male power is intimacy, while for females it is separation.[7]

The relevance of these studies for modern theology is painful to admit. One of my favorite theologians was Paul Tillich, because he could correlate theology with psychology. But Tillich didn't correlate masculinity and femininity. He wrote *The Courage to Be*, a thoroughly masculine study of autonomy. Now I wish he had written on "The Courage to Embrace," so that intimacy and affiliation could be correlated with affirmation and autonomy.

There's something about the structure of traditional theological writing and lecturing that exalts male channels of adequacy: logical organization, clear definitions, lists of power figures who continually show how they are different from each other. There's no room in the tour de force of a propositional theologian for intimate sharing, no direct relevance of the writing for personal relationships, no continual desire to embrace other opinions without loss of personal integrity.[8]

The "Jesus movement" of the sixties, which continued into the post-Vietnam War period has offered more opportunity for feminine expressions of spiritual power by both men and women. Casual dress and relaxation of ritual have encouraged familiarity. Group prayer during a worship service and "kinship" or "house church" gatherings during the week were a step toward sharing and affiliation.[9]

Most of all, mood music filled the worshipers with subliminal rhythm, heart-felt affirmations, hypnotic repetitions, and continuous lyrics about filling, embracing, comforting, and caring. The worship service blended into after-care, where nurturing and healing were encouraged in intimate testimonies, prolonged embraces, and supportive prayer. Grown men were encouraged to weep and women were exhorted to discover and actualize their "gifts of the Spirit."

These churches made exclusive claims to being "Spirit-filled." My translation of their spiritualized language is: We have a place for feminine channels of power that male-dominated churches have forgotten. But, as a veteran English charismatic leader warned, charismatic churches have "forgotten the Father." Thomas Smail sought in the 1980s to bring back the fatherly elements of theology: creative power, the balance of mind with spirit, order and stability for the realistic continuation of emotional disclosure.[10]

Wisdom could broaden an understanding of spiritual power by a correlation of masculine and feminine approaches to adequacy.[11] Each person should be enriched by both. The opportunity for mutual enrichment would come through a Christian fellowship in which the power of the Spirit is known in masculine emphases upon externality and transcendence, combined with feminine mysteries of internality and immanence.[12] Can counselors find this kind of church for counselees, and themselves?

NOTES

1. I first read about the New England self and the Californian self in an article by Martin E. T. Seligman, "Boomer Blues," *Psychology Today*, October 1988, p. 52.

2. For a listing and discussion of New Testament passages on the Spirit of God, see Geoffrey Wainwright, *Doxology: The Praise of God in Worship, Doctrine, and Life* (New York: Oxford University Press, 1980), pp. 88–93. Discernment is defined in Jacques Guillet, et. al., *Discernment of Spirits* (Collegeville, Minnesota: Liturgical Press, 1970), pp. 51–52.

3. This is the theme of H. H. Farmer's *The World and God* (London: Nisbet and Company, 1935).

4. I have just described a self-defensive maneuver through the use of distortion and deceit. These deadly processes were exposed in Freudian interpretations of religion and were incorporated into ego psychology, which added an adaptive formulation to explain some movements of the self in response to anxiety and threat.

   James Fowler seems to have ignored the tendencies toward distortion and deceit in his exclusive orientation toward growth and adaptation through *Stages of Faith* (San Francisco: Harper and Row, 1981). Although his formulations assist counselors in the positive relation of life stages to Christian maturity, they do not alert counselors to the misuse of spirituality. See Carl D. Schneider, "Faith Development and Pastoral Diagnosis," in Craig Dykstra and Sharon Parks, ed., *Faith Development and Fowler* (Birmingham, Ala.: Religious Education Press, 1986).

5. I would suspect that Helen is probably suffering from a frustration or deprivation neurosis along with some repression of desires for intimacy. I would

suggest to the pastor a reading of Conrad Baars and Anna Terruwe, *Healing the Unaffirmed: Recognizing Deprivation Neurosis* (New York: Alba House, 1972). My reason for this recommendation comes from a review of literature on "showy gifts" which notes a contrast between the faithfulness of Pentecostal congregations and some persons who misuse spiritual gifts. See Samuel Southard, "Sectarianism and the Psychoses," *Religion and Life,* XXIII (Autumn 1954), pp. 580–90.

For a discussion of the defenses used by dominant people like Helen, see Karen Horney, *Our Inner Conflicts* (New York: W. W. Norton, 1945), chap. 12, "Sadistic Trends."

6. Valerie Goldstein, "The Human Situation: A Feminine Viewpoint," Simon Doniger, ed. *The Nature of Man* (New York: Harper and Brothers, 1962), pp. 167–68.

7. A summary of research that leads to these definitions is contained in Carol Gilligan, *In a Different Voice* (Cambridge: Harvard University Press, 1982), pp. 7ff.

8. Or perhaps we have to wait for propositional theologians to become older and less strident before they will accept aspects of nurturing in themselves that will embrace intimacy and relationships. At least this seemed to happen in the writings of Karl Barth, who concluded his monumental tomes of logic and erudition with a very human discussion of relationships between people. *The Christian Life* (Grand Rapids: William B. Eerdmans, 1981), pp. 92f.

9. The possibility of masculine and feminine aspects of power in theology is most possible through theologies of mediation, such as Wolfhart Pannenberg's *Anthropology in a Theological Perspective,* tr. Matthew J. O'Connell (Philadelphia: Westminster, 1985).

10. Thomas Smail, *The Forgotten Father* (London: Hodder and Stoughton, 1980).

11. My New Testament colleague, Frank Shirbroun has helped me see that attention to both the Gospel of John and the Synoptics is necessary to recognize the spiritual adequacy of both men and women.

   In John, Martha is the first to proclaim that Jesus is "the Christ, the Son of God" (John 11:27). Mary Magdalene is not only first to see the risen Christ, but the only one to believe the resurrection until Jesus makes a second appearance to the closeted apostles (John 20:11–19).

   In the Synoptic tradition, the spiritual insight of women is not so significant. Simon Peter is the first to proclaim: "You are the Christ" (Mark 8:29). The resurrection narratives do not include Jesus' appearance to Mary Magdalene; her report to the apostles is considered to be an "idle tale" (Luke 24:11) until two walk with Jesus to Emmaus and he later appears to the eleven apostles (Luke 24:13–43).

12. James B. Nelson, *The Intimate Connection: Masculine Spirituality* (Philadelphia: Westminster Press, 1988), p. 36. For other studies of spirituality see Irvin T. Hulmes, *Spirituality for Ministry* (San Francisco: Harper and Row, 1982); William M. Moreman, *Developing Spiritually and Professionally* (Philadelphia: Westminster, 1984); E. Glen Hinson, *A Serious Call to a Contemplative Lifestyle* (Philadelphia: Westminster, 1974); Morton Kelsey, *Discernment: A Study in*

Ecstasy and Evil (New York: Paulist Press, 1978); Myron Augsburger, *Practicing the Presence of the Spirit* (Scottsdale, Penn.: Herald Press, 1982); Roger Hazelton, *Grateful Courage: Adventure in Christian Humanism* (Philadelphia: Fortress, 1985); Thomas Merton, *Contemplative Prayer* (Garden City: Doubleday, 1971); Henri Nouwen, *Reaching Out: The Three Movements of the Spiritual Life* (Garden City: Doubleday, 1966); Gerald May, *Care of Mind: Care of Spirit* (San Francisco: Harper and Row, 1982); Tilden Edwards, *Spiritual Friend* (New York: Paulist Press, 1980); E. E. Thornton, *Being Transformed: An Inner Way of Spiritual Growth* (Philadelphia: Westminster, 1984).

10

The Community of Faith

Our conscious awareness of the power of the Spirit is greatly enhanced in a fellowship of faith where there is mutual expectation that God will work freely through our freedom to be who we are and to change into what we can become. The church is to provide the accepting climate for personal change.

But where do we find this kind of a church in which the mind of Christ meets the secrets of the heart? We are looking for a worshiping community, which is a church in which there is freedom to receive the power of God among people who honestly experience his grace.

Our humanity is enlivened by the wisdom that comes through a Christian community.

In modern American life this means encouragement by others to express the highs and lows of our experience. When a significant group evaluation and enduring relations are added to the initial encouragement, individual members report a new sense of power. It seems that inner and outer reality have been connected in a way that is different from the usual associations of work, parties, ballgames, trips to see relatives, or talk with a spouse in front of the TV. The group has not only accepted the story of a person, it has added norms that help order the rest of a person's life into meaningful narratives.[1]

This sounds like group therapy, especially the self-help groups who posit dependence upon a higher power (as in AA) or who teach psychological findings about the dynamics of addiction. Is this the wisdom of the Christian community?

In some churches this has been an integral part of ministry. At least it used to be. The "pre-scientific" predecessors of self-help groups were the weekly class meetings of Methodists and the discipleship groups of Presbyterians and Baptists on the American frontier.[2] Early in the twentieth century, the Reverend Elwood Worcester began support and evaluation groups in his Boston church. This "Emmanuel movement" (named for the church) provided the strategy for the group therapy that developed before World War II.[3]

This historical connection between a very human therapy group and a theologically orthodox church may sound strange. Where are the churches today that encourage the acceptance of highs and lows in humanity through open discussion of personal frailty?

The question was put this way in the initial ferment of freedom and change after World War II: What would be the source of power for self-actualization in the face of authoritarian social structures? In the 1950s the answer was to be found in the human power for acceptance of self and others. When a leader of clinical pastoral education, Anton Boisen, grappled with the development of new religious communities through the inspiration of charismatic leaders, the analysis was always in terms of interpersonal dynamics. Boisen, under the influence of Henry Nelson Weiman and other teachers at the University of Chicago, saw God as a "social process." Without minimizing the importance of a cohesive group structure as a power for instigating and maintaining personal freedom, Boisen could not think of the church as anything more than a social institution which used religious mythology to explain the power of human acceptance.

As theologians of the 1950s looked for a community of acceptance, they saw instead that the "mainline" churches of their day served as monuments to institutionalized oppression of women, the mentally ill, homosexuals, and anyone else who did not meet the success standards of a white, male-dominated society. When theologians considered the churches that ministered among the poor, as Boisen did, they found fanaticism and the repression of normal instincts.

Were these practical theologians rekindling interest in the church which Paul described as "the body of Christ" (Eph. 1:23)?

In some ways the modern adaptations are clearly in the spirit of Jesus' life and words. Consider this challenge in the Sermon on the Mount:

> So if you are offering your gift at the altar, and there remember that your brother has something against you, leave your gift there before the altar and go; first be reconciled to your brother, and then, offer your gift. (Matt. 5:23–24 RSV)

The experience of human love is so intimately connected with the revelation of God's steadfast love that his worship can be interrupted by the need for reconciliation with a brother.

The saying has powerful implications for those who sincerely seek the will of God through worship in the church.[4] Whether they look for answers through counsel with a member of the congregation, meet in a group for discussion, or pray for guidance during a service of worship, they are opening themselves to the possibility of insight and action that may break through their natural defenses of security, pride, resentment, self-pity, or procrastination. For, to worship is to be in the Spirit of Christ which is love, compassion, forgiveness, and reconciliation. Revelation is so intimately associated with experience that the inspiration of God's love cannot be inwardly contained during faithful worship. Some commitment must be made through attitude and action to share love, effect reconciliation, ask for forgiveness—now!

What's the power to overcome human deceit and the secrecy that defies sharing? The answer of Christian faith goes beyond group therapy in the assertion that the worship of God is the power for full fellowship and healing through the body of Christ.

The Wisdom of Worship

This is the way of wisdom. Statements of belief must be authenticated in action. The inevitable deceits of the human heart must be identified and redeemed through loving relationships that encourage repentance and reconciliation.

But there will be objections! Propositional theologians will insist that the purity of the church be maintained by concentration on assent to doctrinal statements. Sensational religionists will recoil from insight into the self ("That's psychology"; "It's of the devil," etc.).

I partially agree. Some propositions or statements of belief must guide the church in the fulfillment of a godly mission. My problem with the dogmatists is (1) their selective inattention to central statements in Scripture, such as "If someone says he loves God, but hates his brother, he is a liar" (1 John 4:20); (2) their inability to connect the revelation of God through his Son with the way we respond to him, to ourselves, and to each other (why, for example, in writings and preachings about the Last Judgment do we find so few references to social action as required by Matt. 25:31–46?).

How about the sensationalists? They're right in looking for something beyond group therapy in the church, but they are in denial about the way that God works through human emotions. Frightened by their own feelings, they deny humanity both to themselves and to Jesus. If they could have a clear head about the meaning of the Incarnation, they could receive a more humane way toward purity of heart. The answer to wayward emotions is not repression, but transformation of the way we think about ourselves and God (Rom. 12:1–21).

But how do we learn to think about ourselves and God with wisdom, that is, with a realistic assessment of our own condition in the light of God's intentions for us? We find the answer in a body unified through "true worship" (or "spiritual service") as described in Romans 12 and 1 Cor. 12–14.

Worship is divine-human communion in which the revelation of God and the experience of the worshiper are attuned by the Spirit. When this occurs in a fellowship, intimacy can be combined with realism in mutual confessions of faithful experience.[5] The power of a worshiping community is manifest in a new quality of relationships (Eph. 2:11–22). To be transformed by the "mercies of God" is to become a person of spiritual *leitorgia*, which means both worship and service.[6] Paul presents the interpersonal requirements of this worship in Romans 12.

In the New Testament, worship unites spiritual strength with human need through fellowship in the Holy Spirit. L. S. Thornton comments on 2 Corinthians 13:14 on the church as a new fellowship, defined by participation in the Holy Spirit (see also 1 Corinthians 12:13). The Spirit is the focus of our common interest, that in which we all share.[7] This is similar to the translation of 2 Cor. by Alfred Plummer in the International Critical Commentary: "The sense of membership which the Holy Spirit imparts to those who are united in one body."[8] In this paraphrase, Plummer supports Thornton in a new definition of fellowship. Christian fellowship is not so much a participation of our lives in the lives of other believers as it is the participation of all believers in the Holy Spirit. The closest analogy would be the second chapter of Ephesians in which Christ is spoken of as the chief cornerstone, by whom all of the members are held together. The arch is not an arch without the cornerstone and a fellowship is not a fellowship without the presence of the Holy Spirit.[9]

The indispensable nature of the Spirit of Christ in a fellowship can be seen in Paul's "deposition" ("for I receive from the Lord what I also delivered to you," 1 Cor. 11:23). The assembling of Christians for an observance of the Lord's Supper is an unworthy (1 Cor. 11:27) and dangerous (1 Cor. 11:30) fellowship without the presence of the Lord's Spirit. But if we are judged by the Lord, then there will be a "discernment of the body," an awareness of the factions and selfishness that can fill any human gathering. These must be confessed and forgiven so that we may continue to be directed by the Spirit in the solemn act of repeating the Lord's fellowship meal with his disciples.

"Assembling" to hear the "deposition" provides an internalization of power from beyond ourselves. We become new knowers of old things. Writings from the first century become letters written in our hearts today—personal testimony from the apostles. Historical teachings of theology become our history. The group process is complete when the mystical sense of communion with God becomes the prophetic reality of action in our world, including the transformation of our view of the world and ourselves.

When the mystical becomes prophetic, inner experience is connected with history. To be connected with history in Christian consciousness is to be a part of the church, for the church is the historical continuation of the apostolic witness to the resurrection. Our new knowledge must be conformed to the old way, by "testing the spirits." Does our testimony ring true with that of other believers? Do others see the mind of Christ in our attitudes, or only a projection of our own desires?

These are the questions of wisdom, the quality control of experience by the submission of our unique and fallible experience to the common confession that Jesus alone knows the will of the Father.

Wisdom through the Church

What qualifies a church for this kind of spiritual monitoring? The common assumption of all must be the coming of the Spirit as a sign of the reign of God upon earth—a reign that has begun but is not yet complete.

This tension between "already" and "not yet" is the spiritual climate within which the will of God can be appropriately sought. In such a fellowship, church organization and status are temporary aids to the primary goal of life as a pilgrim—always looking for God as he comes toward us.

This is an eschatological gathering, a group of believers in the future through God's faithful acts in the past; inspiration by the Spirit in the present and future consummation of his kingdom in the age to come.

The understanding of spiritual power in such a fellowship would be very compatible with the need of counselors to find a caring congregation for conspicuous failures. For such a congregation, open to God's future, has enough flexibility to receive "different" people— and enough rejection of security to disregard a loss of status when unsuccessful individuals appear in their midst.

Should we define a congregation in this way—as people who enter the kingdom of God through admission of failure in personal experience, and who gather to consider God's future for their broken lives? The answer begins in the reading of the Gospels, when Jesus announces that the kingdom of God is at hand and those who repent will be gathered into the kingdom (Mark 1:15). Those who receive the kingdom into their hearts are also those who are receptive to something more. In his resurrection appearance, Christ sets the consummation of the kingdom in the future and commands his disciples to wait for the time when they will receive the Holy Spirit (Acts 1:6–11).

When the Spirit is poured out upon diverse people at Pentecost, there is both fulfillment and expectation. The very image of "pouring out" (Acts 2:17, 33) defies any static definition of the Spirit's work.

160

The continuation of the book of Acts is a chronicle of surprises, seen especially in the outpouring of the Spirit upon Gentiles (Acts 10:34–48; 15:19). It is this sense of continually becoming more than we ever expected that leads Paul to describe the revelation of God's will as a mystery kept until the "fullness of time" (Eph. 1:7–10).

The relation of the kingdom to the organized gathering, the church, is through this mystery. A church is both the institution in society (an organization) and a fellowship of believers (an organism) through which individuals and society can be lead toward fulfillment in the kingdom of God. Paul locates this leading in the awareness of Jewish Christians that the Spirit would break all the boundaries of human security: Jewish-Gentile, male-female, slave-free, or any other "elemental spirit" (Gal. 3:23–4:7).

The plan of God to unfold the mysteries of the kingdom through the church led Hans Küng to describe the disciples as "the eschatological community of salvation."[10] They have come together because of a single decisive event, the resurrection of Christ, and they expect more power to be fulfilled through them in the very process of congregating. Küng defined "congregation" both as the actual process of congregating and as the congregated community.

> An *ekklesia* is not something that is formed and founded once and for all and remains unchanged; it becomes an *ekklesia* by the fact of a repeated concrete event, people coming together and congregating, in particular congregating for the purpose of worshiping God.[11]

It is this tension between the decisiveness of the resurrection event and the promise of future events that maintains the spiritual perspective of revelation and experience. That which has been revealed is the guarantee of salvation as well as the boundary for experiences that authenticate God's work of grace in our hearts.[12] No validated experience can go beyond the revelation. But at the same time, the continuation of revelation in our hearts and minds is a source of surprising change in ourselves and in our congregation, as the Spirit breaks the boundaries of human habit and hope with a power beyond ourselves.

It is within this range of fulfillment and expectation that a congregation interprets the will of God. For all persons there is a reliable witness to the "mystery of his will" in the life of Jesus and in the interpretation of his life and teaching by those who were directly inspired by his Spirit. The inspiration that came to his disciples was a "pouring out," a breaking of boundaries between Jew and Gentile, male and female, bound and free. As a result, the church was composed of many who came from backgrounds and experiences that were not directly referred to in the Gospel account of Jesus' walks through Galilee and Palestine. It would not be possible for Gentile converts to literally "walk in his steps."

This is the function of the church, to apply the mind of Christ to the daily habits of persons whose personality and circumstances have not placed them in the right place with the right thoughts at the right time, according to the established criteria of holy habits, social success, or self-actualization.

The church is defined by its purpose rather than by its place. The purpose is to plant and nourish the seeds of faith that are scattered among us by the wind of the Spirit. The seed is the gospel, or as Augustine wrote, the "kernel" of the kingdom.[13] This seed of the Spirit is the arena within which the new freedom of Christ is tested for each believer.

At the same time, the church itself is tested by the Spirit concerning the authenticity of the faith that is proclaimed. To what extent is each assembly free from sin, pride, contentiousness, prejudice, social conformity, and cultural stereotype (Rom. 14, 1 Cor. 10)?

The Spirit as judge of the church is an ever-present protection of individual believers against legalistic leaders. It is clear from the New Testament record that the Spirit may depart from a particular congregation (Rev. 2–3), but the preponderance of New Testament evidence is against any departure of the Spirit from those who have placed their trust in God through Christ (John 10:7–30; Rom. 8:31–39; contra, Heb. 10:19–39). Those who threaten others with a loss of salvation through disobedience to legalistic demands may one day be judged unfaithful themselves.[14]

Characteristics of a Worshiping Community

What are signs of the Spirit's power in a church? The early church characterized congregations as faithful to the purposes of God when they possessed unity, holiness, catholicity, and apostolicity. This

162

meaning in the making of Christian community was formulated in the Nicene Creed as an indication of the transformed character of a community that is graced by the Spirit of God.[15] We know the effectiveness of worship through these four criteria.

Unity

Unity is the first sign of a worshiping community. This is evidence that we know the will of the Father (John 17:6–26, especially 20–21).

Unity within a congregation and between congregations is not the same as conformity. This distinction is quite important in the socialization of a counselee into a community of faith. If the church has truly understood the biblical marks of unity, then persons with a diversity of backgrounds are accepted. There is a freedom from conformity in these congregations that builds up the integrity of an individual at the same time that fellowship is enhanced.

In contrast, a conforming congregation may speak many words about the "Spirit" as a means of coercion. Those who question or ignore codes of dress, prescribed rituals, and ways of speaking, find themselves to be "objects of prayer." (Paul was probably considered such an object after the Colossian church read the second chapter of his letter to them!)

The dynamic for unity is the power of the Spirit at Pentecost. Here, amid diverse nationalities, the apostolic message was understood by each person in the native tongue of that person. This is a model for wisdom as unity. It is a common message to people who appropriate the gospel from individual, exclusive, competing, or tribal backgrounds. Those who are "wise" train themselves in acceptance, congruence, and positive self-regard as human resources for the divine dynamic.

But when we recognize the importance of the content that was in the apostolic message, we find a problem in the modern approach to facilitating communication through "acceptance." This may be little more than tolerance of attitudes and behaviors different from our own. Acceptance will not facilitate the understanding of the Christian message unless it is influenced by the Christian doctrine of repentance and justification. When this happens, acceptance is much deeper than tolerance. Tolerance may be no more than a superficial indifference to another person who is "accepted" so long as one person does not get in the way of another.[16]

Acceptance is a measure of the depth of our judgment of another person and our sacrificial service to the person in spite of that judgment.[17]

Holiness

The criterion for repentance and justification is holiness. This is an acceptance of God's standards as our measure of life in community. We identify holiness by the ethical content of new life in Christ in a congregation of his disciples (Rom. 6, Col. 3). But the besetting problem is, Does a congregation define holiness in terms of revelation or primarily in terms of experience? We often find extreme answers to this question.

One extreme is the congregation that considers holiness in terms of identifiable agreement with propositions of the faith, without reference to individual experience and interpretation. Proper language and conceptual structure is valued so far above experience that the new life in Christ is little more than "Lord, Lord" with no attention to loving obedience in heart as well as head. (Consider the question of Jesus: "Why do you call me Lord, Lord, but do not do the things that I tell you?" Luke 6:46).

The other extreme of holiness is an exaltation of experience with little reference to revelation through scripture or the guidance of a Christian group. On one hand, persons may be subjected to merciless introspection and warned that only those who "feel right" are "within the will of God." Spirituality is equated with successful denial of fatigue, anger, despair, impatience, hunger, and thirst—which were part of Jesus' witness to his humanity upon earth. On the other hand, sensationalists concentrate on specified emotional states as guarantees of spirituality. At times the certainty of "godly leading" through these sensations may be seen by others as pride and error, but the enthusiast claims to be above human judgment in the church (cf. Col. 2:18-19).

The biblical doctrine of holiness is a balance between revelation and experience under the power and guidance of the Spirit. It was this balance that led the church in the Jerusalem conference to declare by inspiration of the Spirit that certain experiences or customs would not be required of Gentiles, and at the same time required certain ethical standards for both Jew and Gentile. This was also the balance provided by the apostle Paul in his struggle between the Law of his former life and the faith that gave him new life (Gal. 3:28).

This freedom for diverse circumstances under the unity of Christ's Spirit is of special value in dealing with persons who feel oppressed in tradition-oriented churches or exploited in sensational assemblies. The task of the Christian counselor is to help these people find some group in the church where they will be accepted in the spirit of Paul's statement in Galatians 3.

> For you were baptized into union with Christ, and so have taken upon yourselves the qualities of Christ himself. So there is no difference between Jews and Gentiles, between slaves and freemen, between men and women: you are all one in union with Christ Jesus. (vv. 27–28)

If we should read this Scripture to a counselee, there should be some discussion about the difference between holiness and wholeness. Those who have been conspicuous failures or who have some minority status in a church will often feel on the outside or like second-class citizens, no matter what Paul may have written in the first century. They are not made to feel "whole," or "self-actualized," as it is defined in modern society. Will they find people in the church who encourage their struggle toward wholeness by defining holiness as a quality of life that identifies the grace of the Lord Jesus within us and in our relationship with others? The question alerts people to find prophets and fend off Pharisees in a congregation. Prophets proclaim a broken heart as most acceptable to God. They have a message for the "poor in heart": the very weakness of the broken-hearted enables them to see the pretensions of those who think they are "whole" in society. The broken-hearted become the purifiers of the church, for they show how God's wisdom and strength come to us in the midst of our admitted weakness.[18]

Catholicity

A congregation that accepts human diversity without anxiety is catholic. To be catholic, or universal, in the faith is to rejoice in the differences that relate to experience under one revelation. The unity of the faith and the diversity of gifts are one.

This sign of a church that knows the will of God will be especially attractive to Christian counselors who are talking with people who need to combine autonomy with homonomy. That is, these counselees struggle with their need for personal identification and for some respect from people who are the same and/or different—but one in faith. How is this major task of maturity to be performed?

One counselor defined the task as comparison and contrast of Jesus' relationships with others and that of a troubled friend with her husband. This was wisdom, an attempt to bring the outline of an individual (the image of God) into conformity with the true substance of God in the humanity of Jesus.

But there were difficulties. Quin, the wife-in-trouble did not want any examination of human diversity. She wanted complete conformity to her ideas of a godly marriage. She insisted that she wanted guidance from the Scripture, not from "godless psychotherapy." Her friend, a "lay counselor" in the same church, agreed to start with Scripture. She advised Quin to remember the central issues in their conversation and to compare these with specific Scriptures that would be agreed on by both of them. So, at the end of the first hour the counselor said: "You say that Josh (Quin's husband) never has any time for you. He disregards your desire for companionship. This gives you the feeling that you are without value in his eyes—and in your own. Now, if we are going to start with Scripture, why not begin in the third chapter of John, where Jesus talks to Nicodemus. Think about yourself as Nicodemus and see how Jesus talked to you. Then compare the way that Jesus makes you feel with the way that Josh makes you feel. Can we talk about that next time?"

Quin agreed to this procedure. After all, she was committed to communion with God, and here was an opportunity for the revelation of God in Scripture to inform her feelings about self and family. So, she proceeded with the biblical meditation and analysis, and, with some prompting, was willing to describe in the next session her contrasting feelings.

Well, it seems like Jesus really treated Nicodemus as someone who had some important ideas, even though they needed to be corrected. Now, Josh corrects me, but somehow it is different from

Jesus. He explains a lot, just like Jesus does, but then he always says that I do not understand, so he gets tired of talking to me. Also, I notice that Jesus gave Nicodemus a choice. Josh never does that with me. He just explains why he is right, and he thinks that I am wrong if I don't mirror his opinion.

The second session was devoted to the difference that Jesus made in the way that a person would value self. Quin became enamored of and agitated by this idea. On the one hand she thought that this was the way that she should feel about herself, but she was very apprehensive of any change in herself that would appear to be defiant to Josh. As she said, "If I begin to argue with him, he will leave. Maybe he won't come back."

The counselor-friend agreed that this was a very serious issue and that they should again seek some biblical message upon which Quin could meditate and receive guidance. She suggested the fourth chapter of John, in which a woman was actually argumentative with Jesus. Again, she requested that Quin compare conversation that she would have with Jesus, in keeping with the fourth chapter of John, and the expression of her own ideas to Josh. With some reluctance, Quin agreed to this devotional task.

In the third interview, Quin spoke with joy about the change in her relationship to Josh. She had just finished a day's seminar on "The Complete Woman in Christ." From this seminar she had learned "to take all my disagreements and troubles to the Lord and to leave them with him." Consequently, whenever Josh made a demand of her she would nod and begin to pray that God would give Josh a new heart. Or, if he made some statement about the children or her work that was not in keeping with her own ideas, she would tell him that they should pray about this and seek an answer from the Lord. Since Josh was an active church member, he was pleased with this reference to prayer and would join her in a brief time of devotion.

"Did this change either one of you?" asked the counselor. Quin replied, "Well, at least a higher power is over Josh. I don't say that he has changed his mind. No, he would not do that. But now we don't argue, we just pray." "And does he still have his way?" asked the counselor. After a moment of hesitation, Quin answered, "I guess so. But I also guess that it must be God's way, since we have prayed about it. I shall always give in my way to God's way, isn't that the Scripture?"

The counselor seized this opportunity to ask about the Scripture meditation that had been assigned for this session. What had Quin learned from the study of the fourth chapter of John? Quin had some doubts about the reading. She felt that there was too great a contrast between the way that Jesus treated the woman at the well and the way that Josh had been treating her. So she thought that no comparison would be realistic. When asked for specifics, she said: "Well, my husband uses much bad language all the time and it annoys me very much. He is even more garbage-mouthed when I don't agree with him or if I contradict him. If I ever present my point of view on something, he's provoked to an even stronger attack than before. I don't think he would ever treat me with respect like Jesus treated that woman. He doesn't give me any choices. I think Jesus may have been provoked by the stupidity of that woman, but he didn't attack her. I couldn't imagine Josh having that kind of restraint."

"Well," said the counselor, "I guess that you will just abandon the idea of Scripture as a model for your relationship to your husband and . . ." With this, Quin broke in, "Oh no! I'm going to pray. That's what I learned in the seminar. It's the only way. That's the way that God provides me with guidance. The Scriptures are too confusing."

Counselor: Are you sure that the Scriptures are confusing? Maybe they create too many problems because you might be led to choices that make you uncomfortable.

Quin: Uncomfortable! Do you want me to ruin my marriage? If I were to act like you—or like Jesus acted toward that woman, I would have a divorce.

Counselor: So you see that as the worst consequence of acting as a person who is respected by God? I can see that a real dilemma is developing.

Quin: We are not using the right Scripture! Let's turn to the demands of Jesus that I can understand. He says that God created men and women to live together in marriage forever. Jesus hates divorce. Do you think I should do something that would lead to divorce? That couldn't be the will of God!

168

Counselor: I'm not quite sure where we are going, but I do know that we will find more about ourselves at the same time that we're finding out more of God's will for us. I mean, He will give us self-understanding at the same time that we gain understanding of Him. Am I talking about anything that makes sense?

Quin: Well, I'm not sure that I follow you. I hear you talking sometimes like one of those psychiatrists. You say things about "knowing yourself." Well, I think that too much knowledge is dangerous. We should just seek God's will and let it go at that.

Counselor: Maybe I have gone too far. I guess I've been pushing you too much to talk about your own feelings. But here is my dilemma. How can I help you find the will of God unless you are willing to know yourself as one of God's children?

Quin: Oh, so that is why you've been so anxious for me to talk about the way I would react if I were that man Nicodemus or that woman at the well! (Pause) I guess you mean well. Yes, you do. I do want to feel better about myself. I know that Jesus can give me strength to be the kind of person that he wants me to be. But I can't be that way with Josh!

Counselor: So, as you see things right now, it is more important to keep the marriage intact than it is to do all of this psychological exploration about yourself.

Quin: Well, I just think that you're asking for too much. I don't think God asks anything of us that would lead to sin. It's like I said, if I keep thinking about myself after reading those Scriptures, I'm going to get all stirred up and some of it will come out when I'm talking to Josh. Then what do I do? He leaves and I have no marriage. *That* is not God's will.

Counselor: Well, maybe we could talk some about ways in which you could feel stronger in yourself, whether you confronted Josh or not. Or, maybe we could get to the place that you could confront Josh in a way that would let him know that you were still anxious to agree with him, but that there was some power beyond yourself that led you to say what you thought. (Quin nods) So maybe we could talk about some of that next week.

There was only one more conference. In that session, Quin became more and more uncomfortable about insight, especially when it was linked with the will of God. She said at the conclusion of the interview that prayer was helping her to reduce conflict with Josh and that this would be her continuing spiritual resource. She did not need to talk to anybody but Jesus about her conflicts now.

Quin has refused wisdom through the church. One reason for this is her denial of human feelings, which she justifies through conformity to propositions about male dominance. She is unwilling to be catholic, to compare her differences honestly with another in a spirit of respect. She breaks the counselor's attempt to do this in a commonly-shared faith. Faith for Quin is obedience without insight.

Apostolicity

Quin also rejects the apostolic function of the church. Her friend performs this function by connecting the experience of Quin to the continuity of experience with the living Christ as recorded by those who were witness to his resurrection. The revelation of God in the Incarnation of his Son became the transformed experience of the apostles. Their written witness to the life and teachings of the Lord is the rule by which the revelation is transmitted to the church of any era. By the inspiration of the Spirit, our experiences of the living Word (the Spirit of Christ) are brought into conformity with a true understanding of the written word.

This understanding of apostolicity may confront a Christian counselor in several ways. One is a concern for the integrity with which experiences are interpreted to a counselee in a church. Is there a balance between revelation and experience? Is the counselee subjected to demands for submission to institutional authority without regard for diversity of feelings? Or does the counselee return to the counselor with interpretations of experience that encourage projection, denial, and displacement—with no attention to discipline, insight, and the historical record of Jesus' life as a model for our own?[19]

Another concern is more personal for the counselor. What is the apostolicity of the Christian counselor as a representative of the church, which is the corporate work of the Holy Spirit which is the wisdom of God?[20] When a counselor assists a person to find the will of God through the church, what is the authority of the counselor in this process? The issue is inevitable when the counselor is also in the church where a counselee is seeking fellowship.

In part, the answer is found in the wise counsel that a friend offered to Quin. Human feelings are discussed as a block or a channel of the will of God.

In part, the answer is worship, confession of both counselor and counselee that we are humans seeking communion with God. When his spirit instructs and intensifies our relationships, worship unites all our human strivings through honest sharing and sacrificial service.

Worship is the power and wisdom through which our humanity is confessed and celebrated in the church.

NOTES

1. John Biersdorf, *Hunger for Experience* (New York: Seabury Press, 1975), pp. 34–38.

2. Samuel Southard, *Pastoral Evangelism* (Atlanta: John Knox, 1981), pp. 25–31.

3. Charles F. Kemp, *Physicians of the Soul: A History of Pastoral Counseling* (New York: Macmillan, 1947), pp. 114ff; Elwood Worcester, *Religion and Medicine* (Moffatt Yard and Company, 1908).

4. Jürgen Moltmann, *Hope for the Church* (Nashville: Abingdon, 1979), pp. 21–33, 42–46.

5. For definitions of Christian worship, see Gerhard Delling, *Worship in the New Testament* (Philadelphia: Westminster Press, 1962), p. 24; for the decisiveness of the Holy Spirit in worship, see Karl Barth's *Church Dogmatics*, vol. 2, p. 524. This is a discussion of Rom. 8:15 and Gal. 4:6 as the work of the Spirit in the community. Also see William Nicholl's, *Jacob's Ladder* (Atlanta: John Knox Press, 1958), pp. 65ff. for discussions of worship as living devotion to the Son of God. For a theological and ecclesiological study of worship, see Geoffrey Wainwright, *Doxology: The Praise of God in Worship, Doctrine, and Life* (New York: Oxford, 1980).

6. William Barclay, *New Testament Words* (Philadelphia: Westminster Press, 1974), pp. 176–78.

7. L. S. Thornton, *The Common Life in the Body of Christ* (London: Dacre Press, 1950), pp. 69–72ff.

8. p. 84.

9. For the total application, see P. T. R. Kirk, *Worship: Its Social Significance* (London: The Centenary Press, 1939); Willard L. Sperry, *Reality and Worship* (New York: The Macmillan Company, 1925); see also Paul Hoon, *The Integrity of Worship* (Nashville: Abingdon, 1971), to whom I am indebted for many of these references and who has many others for the discerning reader.

10. Hans Küng, *The Church* (Garden City: Doubleday, 1976), p. 116.

11. Ibid., p. 120.

12. The church has a reliable memory of the events of the life of our Lord—with nothing being more important than the record of resurrection. Here is the crowning event by which all action and attitudes are to be judged. The person who proclaims that through this action there has come salvation and sanctification will be confirmed in the church. The person who denies the resurrection and its significance as the ultimate testimony of Jesus as the Christ will be condemned. At the same time, the assembly-in-expectation will offer no condemnation according to the mores of the community or the peculiarities of preferences for leadership and recognition in a particular congregation (1 Cor. 4).

13. Küng, *The Church*, p. 128.

14. The continual temptations of the church to legalism, rigorism, and asceticism have been documented by K. E. Kirk, *The Vision of God*.

15. For a discussion of these marks of the Church, see Wainwright, *Doxology*, pp. 118–48.

16. Joseph Sittler warned of this tendency in a chapel address at the divinity school of the University of Chicago in 1958: Joseph Sittler, "Acceptance, Human and Divine," *The Divinity School News*, May 1, 1958.

17. A psychiatrist, Hanna H. Colm, noted this astute theological observation in the writings of Paul Tillich (Colm, "Healing as Participation," *Psychiatry* 16 [1950]: 99–111]).

18. Reinhold Niebuhr in *The Nature and Destiny of Man*, vol. 1, has proposed the realistic thesis that it is no sin to be human. Sin comes when we yield to anxiety and pride. The result is a descent into sensuality, which is less than human, or ascent into pride, which is to have more than human expectations as a creature in the image of God.

    For reverent and perceptive interpretation of Jesus' humanity from the Gospels, read Otto Borchert, *The Original Jesus* (London: Lutterworth Press, 1933); and Harry Emerson Fosdick, *The Man from Nazareth* (New York: Harper and Brothers, 1949).

19. The problem is an ancient one in the church. Saint Augustine sought to reduce excessive "spirituality" by insistence upon honest self-knowledge, which is still the cure for pharisaical spirituality. See Rowan Williams, *Christian Spirituality*, chap. on Augustine, "The Clamour of the Heart."

20. Apostolicity might also be thought of as the test of effectiveness. The test of effectiveness as a church responds to the Spirit is given in 1 John as love, the sign of Spirit's guidance in human affairs (1 John 2:1, 10–11; 4:7f.). This love becomes the basis of fellowship (1 John 1:3), holiness (1 John 5–10), and service (1 John 3:18). All the marks of the church, which we have just considered, move toward the manifestation of love in relation to one another, to self, and to God.

11

The Christian Hope

Worship opens our awareness of another world in which we will find the fulfillment that is frustrated in this life by anxieties, fears, twisted relationships, and ambiguous rewards. The openness is a hopeful answer to a preoccupation of wisdom literature: How do I keep myself from misfortune, especially from premature death?[1] Wisdom is a realistic basis for worship and worship is a window to brighter worlds for wisdom.

Both worship and wisdom contribute answers to a continual question in counsel: Will we ever find certainty and clarity in a world of compromise? The Christian hope is for an unambiguous future in God, guaranteed in this life by the testimony of the Spirit within us and in the Christian community.

But our conceptualization and realization of that hope is wisely ambiguous, time-bound, limited, even when we are trying to process our apprehension of that which is final, complete, or unambiguous.

How can we think and talk with hope and wisdom of a coming reality beyond our understanding? This is the central question for an affirmation of Christian hope through counsel.

Christian counsel has a beginning and an ending. The beginning is an expectation that the Spirit will flow through our interpersonal

174

relationships with the power and clarity of communication that fell upon the apostles at Pentecost.[2] The ending is courage to affirm life despite ambiguity and approaching death, because the kingdom of God, already in our hearts, will have final victory over sin and death in the return of Christ at the end of the age.[3]

These are the existential bounds of Christian counsel: Pentecost and *parousia*. They are spiritual delineations of life that infuse the meaning of earthly existence with an eternal significance. The *chronos* of earthbound time is swallowed up in *kairos*, the decisive fulfillment of time through acts of God in history.[4] The measure of our days is now the eternal rule of God.

How do we communicate the content of this hope as finite human beings who are "between the times"? The question arises in Christian counsel as it did with John the seer, when facing the restrictions of personal freedom and the destructiveness of society (Rev. 1–3). Under such conditions, John first provided a realistic analysis of the human problems of the churches in Asia Minor and the specific sources of divine strength with which they might overcome evil from within and without. Then, in the fourth chapter of Revelation there is an "open door" to heaven and a flow of spiritual strength from a throne that is above any power of the Roman world.

It is this combination of spiritual revelation and realistic human analysis that produces the types of thinking which characterize the Christian hope as well as the topics for the fulfillment of that hope.

Human Thought and Other-Worldly Topics

The opening up (apocalyptic) of a world beyond our experience will be a challenge to our way of thinking and our discussion of mystery in counsel. Here, more than in any other area of theology, our human attitudes are decisive in accepting, rejecting, and altering our system of doctrine. Why? Because our resistance is high whenever we sense the direction of a discussion toward death. Death is the original question of all religious thought and the most hidden question of modern technological society.[5]

Attitudes and thoughts are also prominent because of the topics themselves: the Last Judgment, heaven and hell, the return of Christ, resurrection of the body, new heaven and new earth. These are the topics of two worlds in conflict. There are inevitable paradoxes in the interfacing: the tension between "now" and "not yet," flesh and spirit, Christ and Satan, heaven and hell. To think of these things is to be bifocal in vision, correlational in decisions.[6] This way of thought characterizes "eschatological" imagination, an attempt to understand how God is moving toward us in present events as preparation for a future hope of glory.

An example of eschatological thinking is found in Reinhold Niebuhr's classic, *The Nature and Destiny of Man*. Niebuhr saw the paradoxes of "last things" as a threat to the meaning of human life, for they introduce the peril of meaninglessness. How are we to face the seemingly abrupt and capricious termination of the development of life before it has reached its true end? The paradox is between (1) the end of a task or of life without meaning (*finis*, the finality of chronological time) and (2) the "end" of meaning (*telos*) which is fulfillment, the consummation of life and work.[7] The Christian faith asserts that it is not within our power to solve these tensions, for our freedom is always partial, always bounded by the fluctuation of time and events. The Christian hope is an affirmation that fulfillment of life has already begun in the kingdom of God that has been revealed in Jesus Christ. As citizens of this kingdom, we participate in the power of God to provide direction and courage in an evil age, while we wait for the consummation of God's kingdom in an age to come.

The topics of the Christian hope participate in this tension: the return of Christ, the Last Judgment, the Resurrection.[8]

These have always been the topics for Christian hope in the midst of life's dilemmas. But before they can be related to the Christian counsel of people in these dilemmas, we must consider the capacity of individuals to use the particular type of thinking that is paradoxical, bifocal, correlational.

I first faced this question as a chaplain to mental hospital patients who, because of their illness, were impaired in eschatological thinking. The majority of my conversations were with schizophrenics, persons who had lost the power to correlate symbol with reality. Consequently, their thinking about last things was literal. All symbols became concrete. In their impaired thought there could be no tension between now and not yet, and no realistic acceptance of wheat and tares in the same field. They could only accept absolute distinctions. Battles raged in their minds between heaven and hell, God and the devil, good and evil.

The patients thought of themselves as pawns. Some spoke nothing of their own feelings except in response to this cosmic drama. My challenge as a chaplain was to encourage the development of a self that could stand the tension of this battle, and in this way contribute to reduction of the extremes of conflict that characterize schizophrenic thinking.[9]

The same problem appears in work with more or less normal people. In a previous chapter, a pastor discussed his confrontation with Helen, who had reduced the dilemmas of life to extremes. She was always right and her husband was always wrong. She received direct messages from God that made her correct and invulnerable.

We often refer to this type of thinking as "apocalyptic" (an unveiling) because it is so final, so extreme and impulsive. It is not characterized by realism in thought or discernment of God that we find in the revelation of John. Instead of the centrality of God seen in John's visions, a human system of thought becomes central. Or, a mysterious prophecy in Scripture may receive more attention than the great event of Christ's death and resurrection.[10]

How may we avoid a human distortion of divine prophecy concerning the end of the age? The answer is in faith, hope, and love—the spiritual resources for anxiety and ambiguity in life.[11] When we are nourished by these theological virtues, we can tolerate the paradoxes of last things.

What is toleration of paradox? It is faith for solutions to the ambiguities of life, hope in the actualization of power and meaning of the kingdom of God, which unifies our life around symbols that transcend us.

Do we claim too much in such attempts to meet human ambiguity with unambiguous spiritual resources? Wouldn't we be more realistic to refer to the promises as symbols?

Is the kingdom only a symbol? In biblical theology, kingdom is more than symbol; it is a mystery hidden in events, a combination of event and explanation which is unknown to the world, but known to those who receive Christ as the supernatural evidence of God's message (Matt. 13:10ff.). To know the meaning of the kingdom is to acknowledge the King, the revelation of ultimate reality made known upon earth. He is the unity of earthly and heavenly worlds (Col. 1). All that was revealed before him was a shadow of reality. He alone is the substance of God (Heb. 1). There is always a mystery in God's answer to our ambiguity, but his answer is a clue to ultimate reality, a world more powerful than any symbol.

When we accept a reality beyond ourselves as the unambiguous answer to life's ambiguities, we have grounded faith and hope in our love for the manifestation of the mystery of the kingdom in the content of God's revelation in his Son.

What is the impact of this primacy of revelation for Christian counsel? It is a corrective to our incomplete answers to "last things," whether they be the sophisticated rejection of ultimate reality in the mystery of the kingdom (Tillich) or our complete answers to questions that Jesus would not answer: "Lord, will you at this time give the kingdom back to Israel?" (Acts 1:6).

In Christian counsel, the doctrine of last things places revelation from God above experience in human life, but includes sensitivity to human perceptions. The revelation of God is an historical account through human experience. All of our particular and finite experience is given the realistic analysis and hopeful courage that John provided the churches of Asia Minor in the first three chapters of Revelation, but all this is caught up in a vision of the reality of God that will fill our human experience with guidance and courage in areas of ultimate significance. This is the purpose of the visions that flow from the throne of God in chapter 4 and following.

The mission of Christian counsel goes beyond an open sharing of hope and faith in attitudes and actions for the present "now." There must also be a shaping of our attitudes and thoughts by the content of God's revelation of "not yet" that will help a client to close upon that which is final and fulfilling in the midst of suffering and uncertainty.

When we consider the dichotomies of a bounded existence, there is both fulfillment and frustration in Christian counsel. There is fulfillment as the content of the events of the future become realized in the attitudes and actions of our life today. But there is frustration in the thought forms that bring these supernatural realities into our time-bounded existence, for they participate in the very ambiguities that cry out for an unambiguous solution. If we are willing to live with this tension between the unambiguous event and the ambiguous thoughts with which we comprehend the event, then we have been faithful to the correlation of supernatural revelation with human experience in Christian counsel.

Case studies of previous chapters illustrate this tension between the promised event which is not yet and the realism which is "now." From them we can draw out four proclamations of the Christian hope. Each of these is placed *in situ* in the living situation of ambiguous thought about an event that will be unambiguous and complete in God's fulfillment of our future. That which was revealed as a shadowy outline in the past has become the full revelation of God in the age of the kingdom (Heb. Chaps. 1, 11, 12). How can we think and talk of these things?

Incisiveness Despite Defensiveness

The very dimness of the outline provokes extremes of thought in relation to that which is most definite in the biblical doctrine of last things: the Last Judgment, heaven and hell.

One extreme may be seen in Mac, the nonchalant husband (chaps. 3 and 4) who refused to judge himself in any way—although the pastor, using a combination of judgment and acceptance, seemed ready to go as deep as Mac was willing to go. Mac seemed interested in no more than gaining his wife's accommodation to his own schedule for financial success and security. The pastor rightly sensed (and said) that some supernatural power would have to move into Mac's life before he could be realistic about himself in the present and plan for a responsible future. Theologically, the pastor was calling for a recognition of the Last Judgment, the time when God's criteria for relationships will be decisive (Matt. 25:31–46).

The other extreme reaction to God's final judgment is represented by Helen, the strident wife who was reported in chapter 9. Far from ignoring God's judgment, as Mac did, Helen incorporated both God and judgment in herself. She was the final arbiter of all decisions about the life of her husband. She continually declared God's guidance for herself in judgments upon an erring mate.

For Helen, the psychologically attractive aspect of this usurping of God's final responsibility is the chance to escape any responsibility for what she does here on earth. She receives some impressions about her husband and her own needs, and with these she controls anxiety about the devastating effects of disappointments in her life. For, in her opinion, these feelings are the final and true judgments of God upon everyone that she meets. Her only responsibility is to declare that which has been communicated to her by a divine Spirit.

The pastor in that case responded rightly to Helen Rahner with an apostolic mode of counsel. He challenged her validity. Who was she to preempt the final judgment of God, who alone can say that some will have eternal fellowship with him and some would be cast into everlasting darkness?

As we can tell from the cases of both Mac and Helen, our response to any doctrine of the Last Judgment is conditioned by our experience with the "brutal facts of life." This was the phrase with which Reinhold Niebuhr described the development of his own thought concerning the judgment of God upon modern industrial civilization,[12] which he first experienced as a pastor in industrial Detroit. Out of the crushing impact of collective evil came Niebuhr's theological statement concerning the Last Judgment. It is a proclamation that there can be no fulfillment of meaning or achievement of virtue by which people in this world can escape a final judgment.[13] Niebuhr dedicated his mind and ministry to an insightful analysis of human evil. He contrasted immoral society with the only "good," the fulfillment of the will of God "with all our might and our full possibility."[14]

The use of judgment in this pastoral approach is both incisive and humble. The ambiguities of life are cut through with clear statements of the goodwill of God that can give us both freedom of action and clarity of judgment in an unfulfilling world. Clarity is manifest in an attitude of humility. The "cutting" is humble in two ways. First, it is an awareness that humans are always striving in their anxiety to be more than human (Helen) or less than human (Mac), and thereby miss the vision of God as Father. The other kind of humility is found in the personal and social prophet who participates in the judgment. Those who warn of judgment for others must first repent of God's judgment upon themselves and continue to identify with others in that repentance (Matt. 7:1-5; Rom. 2). Jesus ends his descriptions of the Last Judgment with the shattering conclusion that those who judged themselves to be in his kingdom were separated from him, and those who had no hope of his acceptance were actually received by the Father (Matt. 25:31-46).

The incisiveness of the Last Judgment cuts away the hostility or fanaticism of those who condemn all differences of thought as a way to magnify their own certainty. It lays bare the ambiguities of human judgment, our inability to know the precise application of God's decrees in any moment of time. It is an admission that God's judgments are righteous and unerring, in contrast to our confusion concerning the application of his judgment (Rom. 2).

What do these sharp, unambiguous statements of Christian hope mean for Christian counsel in the midst of ambiguity of understanding and application?

The Christian doctrine of Last Judgment and of heaven and hell is a challenge to accept people in the extremity of human ambiguity. Hanna Colm understood this in one of the first psychiatric evaluations of the writings of Paul Tillich (*Psychiatry*, 1950). From Tillich she had learned that we are to participate in the depths of human experience as well as the heights of ecstasy. She concluded that, from a psychiatric point of view, the depths of our acceptance of persons in trouble can be measured by the depths of our judgment of them. If we know how far they have gone into sin and yet accept them "in spite of" their condition, then they are prepared to receive the deepest acceptance of God.[15]

The counselor for Robert and Linda (chap. 7) was faced with this challenge of acceptance. On the one hand there was the problem of his own judgment of these quarreling people and on the other hand there was the dilemma of their inability to accept each other or themselves. In that particular case, mutual condemnation or manipulation was a block to the couple's acceptance of each other and of their own individual failings. The barriers erected by their inadequate and misguided judgments were seen in their extreme reactions: blaming, beating, submission, and seduction. The quarreling couple could always see the sin in the spouse but were very incomplete in the confession of their own unrighteousness. From reading the case, it appears that both husband and wife were in terror of their own private self-judgments, and also they were defending themselves against the judgments of others. They steadfastly resisted the incisiveness of the pastor's statements that the particular misconduct of one was no worse in God's sight than the misconduct of the other. Both must be open in confession before God, themselves, and each other.

In that case study, the content of judgment and our thoughts about judgment were intertwined. Robert kept telling the pastor that one topic of judgment (adultery) was all important and the pastor continued to say that our thoughts, our unforgiving attitudes, are also primary.

The comments of the pastor to the quarreling couple would also illustrate *a second implication of judgment for counsel, which is the quality of experience.* It is the issue with which Jesus confronted the "righteous" people of his day. Did their experience in life have the saving quality in it that would bring them eternal fellowship with God? If they had the quality of love that Jesus had in relation to those to whom he ministered, then they would enter the kingdom of God forever (Matt. 25:34-40). Jesus lived with this same judgment upon himself. The evidence of his Messiahship was his care of those who needed a physician (Luke 7:22-23; John 9:39).

This emphasis upon quality of life as an expression of the Last Judgment is especially hard upon people like Helen, who justify themselves on the basis of pious projections of their impulses. It is equally devastating for any counselor who is so fascinated by experiences, relationships, and attitudes that no questions are raised about the qualitative distinctions between these feelings and faithful commitment to God. The shocker for all who place their entire faith in experience, without qualifying experience by the Spirit of Christ, may be found in Paul's abrupt statement to the Corinthian church that they are "ignorant" (KJV; "unaware," NASB, 1 Cor. 12:1). This is followed by a listing of the gifts of the Spirit that would demonstrate the quality of life that builds up a congregation and witnesses for Christ and the world. Chapter 13 of First Corinthians warns that the experience of inspiration, or the filling of a person with power, is not in itself evidence of a living relationship with Christ. James D. G. Dunn summarizes the thought of Paul.

> Only when charisma is expressive more of Christ's love than of inspiration, only when charismatic experience bears the mark of the paradox of death and life, of power in weakness, only when it is stamped with the hallmark of the Crucified and Risen One is it a positive and constructive experience [cf. 2 Cor. 5:13f.]. Only when charisma *expresses the distinctive* charis *of Christ is it a gift which builds.*[16]

The third impact of the doctrine of the Last Judgment upon Christian counsel is a question: What type of polarities will lead us toward eternal life despite the ambiguities of our present existence? It is a question that follows inevitably from statements about the quality of life and experience. How did these qualities shape the concerns of our everyday existence? Or, what does the knowledge of God's incisive judgment for the future mean in terms of the present ways in which we think about that which is important and unimportant?

The very choice of polarities in biblical language will preserve the qualities of life that are of eternal significance in the Christian hope. Essentially, these are statements of the contrast between this world and the world to come, between the gods of this world and the God revealed in Jesus Christ.[17] For example, the doctrine of the Last Judgment provokes a variety of clarifications and choices at the present time.

(1) How much do we help people adjust to a materialistic culture and how much do we center on reaching out to others without regard to status and security? (Matt. 25)

(2) Do we see in ourselves, and assist others to recognize the fulminating effects of evil which will culminate in spiritual death? Or do we leave people with a contented acceptance of ambiguity and no urgency to choose spiritual life over death?

(3) What power is proclaimed as victorious over evil and death? Do we acknowledge the supernatural concentration of evil in some persons and admit to our clients that the power of the risen Christ is our only sure defense? Or does the divine-human drama deteriorate into a sideshow of the unconscious, where we show and tell the limited effects of misshapen impulses for evil and instinctive desires for the good?

(4) All our efforts for analysis of the unconscious are valuable as proximate expressions of an eternal struggle, but do we go on to see the supernatural forces that are dimly known in the depths of our existence? One day—the "Last Day"—will show the results of our perception, choice, and attitude.

The penetrating quality of the doctrine of last things will continually prompt an incisive question for our counsel: How are we led by the categories of thought concerning the Last Judgment and the finality of the events that they proclaim?

The Last Judgment and the separation of the righteous from the wicked, in God's sight, is a final act so far as human existence is concerned. The finality, the quality, and the depth of this action is dramatized in the triumph of Christ over Satan. This eschatological emphasis is portrayed in the exaltation of Jesus: "I saw Satan fall from heaven" (Luke 10:17–18). But the assurance of the disciples in this life was not to rest upon the beginning of that triumph over the Evil One, but rather upon the assurance that their relationship with God was secure: "But rejoice that your names are written in heaven" (Luke 10:20).

The battle of Christ with Satan participates in the ambiguities of "now" and "not yet." Satan is the summation of the super-fleshly powers that rule the world in connection with human sin (1 John 5:19; 2 Cor. 4:4; John 12:31). His potential presence in any ambiguity of life is seen in Paul's references to "principalities and powers" (Col. 2:15), the extension of wickedness into the world through "spiritual hosts" (Eph. 6:12).

The human opening for satanic influence is in the way we respond to death as a threat to our significance as creatures of God (Gen. 3:4). Only when this manipulator of human ambiguity is cast out does the judgment of the dead proceed with the unchallenged power of God (Rev. 20:14–15; 1 Cor. 15:25–26).

Deception about death is often accomplished through the association of a traumatic event with human failure, divine displeasure, thoughts of abandonment, and overwhelming depression. At least this was the constellation of emotional and spiritual problems that emerged in therapy and exorcism for "Naomi," a young woman who was first confronted at age six by "Friend" who appeared as her dead grandfather (this case will be presented in chap. 15). The family secret—unknown to Naomi until therapy as an adult—was the suicide of the grandfather.

Is there an overarching perspective by which we, as Christian counselors, can look upon human reactions to the doctrine of Last Judgment, heaven and hell? Our objective, both for the counselor and the counselee, is to accept the incisiveness of this Judgment in the midst of ambiguities in this life. The incisiveness is a valid sign of the finality of God's judgment. It must cut through the anxious defenses that we develop either by pretending that there is no godly criteria for control of our lives or that there is no mystery in our understanding of his ways. These anxieties in both counselor and counselee must be ultimately faced and submitted to the only true Judge.

Inclusiveness without Insecurity

The challenge of paradox is to live in, but not be of the world.

The threat to this paradox is a reduction of our capacity to recognize the distinctions between the kingdom of God and the kingdoms of this world, and to live by faith and hope in the midst of this tension (John 17:3–19; 1 Cor. 5:9–11).

One threat to this capacity to live with paradox is from within ourselves. It is a blurring of good and evil, divine mission and human need. The resulting devastation of perception may require both therapy and exorcism, as it did for Naomi (chap. 15, on evil). Her blurring began at age six when the "friendly" image of a deceased grandfather appeared as an answer to her loneliness. For years afterward this fantasy reduced her life to a constant struggle between a desire for acceptance by others and a desire to make a contribution by herself. It was not until she was in the midst of a divorce and confronted with some of her needs during psychotherapy that she admitted these paradoxes. Soon after this admission, she "remembered" the manifestations of the grandfather that had continued with her through adolescence and now were returning with increasing force as her capacity for paradox was developed through therapy. She realized that the fantasies were more powerful than would be possible through the human mind. Some force from beyond herself was responsible for her distortions of life in this world. When the psychiatrist was also convinced that transpersonal evil was present in her life, then he agreed with her to an exorcism.

Our capacity to live with spiritual ambiguity is threatened not only by the collapse of the paradox of good and evil in ourselves but also by the blurring of these distinctions in the world about us. The lure of the "world" is to substitute security and sensual delight for submission to God and a life of sacrifice for the sake of God's kingdom.

The insecurity that comes with these threats is met by the power of the kingdom of God as a present and a future source of strength for all those who live in, but not of the world. The Christian answer to insecurity is realistic hope. It is realistic in that it includes our responsibility to live as a part of two worlds. It is hopeful in our affirmation that we have permanent citizenship only in the world to come. Our Christian eschatology maintains this inclusiveness by a proclamation that the kingdom is already in our midst (Luke 11:20, 17:21), but is also in the future (Matt. 16:28, 24:7–14, 26:29; Acts 1:6ff.).

How does Christian counsel face the human insecurities that arise before this inclusive type of life in the kingdom? The first requirement is a capacity for ambiguity. Just as the doctrine of the Last Judgment determines the polarities of life that are of eternal significance, so the doctrine of a coming kingdom of God provides hope and faith to live with the tension of these dichotomies.[18]

The paradox of the kingdom—as among us and yet to come—is a continual stimulus to Christian growth. Like the principle of homeostasis in physiology and in family relations, a balance of forces must be maintained within any living being, whether the force be spiritual, social, personal, or physical. The Christian hope is that conversation will not only provide the believer with incisive judgment concerning the warfare between Spirit and "the law of sin" (Rom. 7), but that it will also provide guidance and power for moral development despite the ravages of the flesh, the world, and the devil (Rom. 8). Despite anxiety, inclusiveness can be maintained by the power of the Spirit.[19]

What resources of the Christian hope overcome anxiety as we face these divine-human paradoxes? Hope and faith are our principal resources.

Strength against any reduction of our tension between-the-times will come from continual personal hope in the dawning of God's kingdom.

The risen Christ accepted this tension for himself in the statement "It is not for you to know times or seasons which the Father has fixed by his own authority" (Acts 1:7 and Mark 13:32 RSV). His answer to the anxiously expectant disciples was one of power by the Holy Spirit to live in the ambiguities of this present life (Acts 1:8).

It is by this powerful hope that we are rescued out of darkness into the fulfillment of a new life (Col. 1:13f.). But how much hope can people maintain as they become more spiritually sensitive to good and evil in themselves and in the world? This is a key question in Christian counsel concerning last things. What is the capacity of an individual to maintain faith in God's order despite the disorder of our own lives? If we think back to the case of Helen (chap. 9) we can recognize that she had no capacity for ambiguity. She could not tolerate the thought that she was wrong and she would not suspend judgment when she overheard conversations about herself that might be interpreted in more than one way. Always she plunged—without hope or faith—toward a final decision.

How much of the world-to-come can we include in our present hope for this world? Jesus answered these questions with compassion for our human limitations. In the eighth chapter of Luke, the varieties in reception of the Word are presented by Christ as a mystery of the kingdom. Some persons are so hardened that they have no human capacity to receive the Word of God. Some are so shallow that they can only maintain a fruitful Christian experience under ideal conditions. Some are so preoccupied with a variety of responsibilities that their capacity to hear and do the Word is severely restricted. Some have a capacity to bear fruit consistently, but even then it may vary among them from thirtyfold to a hundredfold.

The application of this parable in our own ministry is illuminated by the work of developmental psychologists such as Erik Erickson, John Piaget, Lawrence Kohlberg, James Fowler, and Daniel Levinson. Their research has demonstrated the capacity of individuals to tolerate some type of ambiguity, such as trust versus distrust, if there has been a prudent mixture of acceptance and frustration in their own human development. The value of these research reports and theories for Christian counsel is diagnostic as well as prescriptive. Diagnostically, the concepts of developmental psychologists provide definitions of and explanations for strengths or weaknesses of a person's character at particular times in life.

Prescriptively, developmental psychology is a part of judgment and comfort in Christian counsel. That is, we can comfort a person with the knowledge that their capacity for trust or distrust is strongly conditioned by events that raise the same problems for many other persons. But at the same time there is a prescription of faith and hope that challenges them to confess those areas of life in which they have been hardened, made shallow, or unable to choose the best in the midst of many good and bad things.

When we have gained access to our human capacity to tolerate the ambiguities of life, we are ready for realistic strengthening of our thought and character. Perhaps this is why Mac (chap. 3) was so unwilling to look very deeply into his lack of capacity for faithfulness, intimacy, and sacrifice. To openly admit his weakness would have presented an opportunity for the pastor to discuss God's power to meet that weakness with a change in Mac's character.

How do we develop a capacity for inclusiveness, a sense of patience and courage and expectation in the midst of ambiguity? Paul presents an answer to the tension-filled Thessalonian church. As he exhorts the church to continue an expectant spirit concerning prophecy, he also requires that they "test" everything: "hold fast what is good, abstain from every form of evil" (1 Thess. 5:21-22 RSV). In this admonition, Paul presents the necessity of having categories of thought by which we can know what is good and what is evil in the present age, according to the light that shines into our darkness from the age that is coming (vv. 5f.).

What are the forms of thought that maintain realistic tension with godly hope? To speak of the kingdom of God and the kingdoms of this world, of heaven and hell, of Christ and Antichrist is both a recognition of the separations in our existence and the way of reconciliation. A poetic presentation of these dangers and possibilities is found in John Bunyan's *Pilgrim's Progress.* In this Puritan classic, the journey from the City of Destruction to the City of Light is filled with paradoxes, each of which are described in earthly detail and surmounted with heavenly grace. The biblical statements of consolation and condemnation, earthly destruction and heavenly bliss are focal points for power to move through the ambiguities of this life with assurance of the life to come.

The challenge of Christian counsel is to correlate the language of another world with the thought forms of this world. This will always be an incomplete undertaking, for prophetic language participates in the mystery of the kingdom and earthly language participates in all the ambiguities of our human vision. On the one hand we must speak with finality about the reality of events that are to come, but never with certainty about our ability to describe these events in human language or to correlate them exactly with the human condition.

Our calling is to greet the feelings and events of human life as parables of the larger drama of a life to come. We need training in bifocal vision, by which we may evaluate our feelings and actions today by a second sight that comes from a world beyond our vision.

Some of this other-worldly conception was present in the conversations with Michael (chap. 2). When Michael analyzes his feelings of self-indulgence and raises a question about the reason for his restlessness, this is an opportunity to talk about a perspective that goes beyond human insight. His restlessness may be a sign that he is made in the image of God and that he has a purpose in life beyond himself. Also, when Michael talks about his desire to help others, there is an opening to speak of the life of discipleship that was demonstrated by Christ.

In these and other examples, there is a deliberate focus upon insights in this life as they symbolize a reality that is beyond this life. In the process, there is no absolute equation between the two worlds. They are still separate. In fact, one of the breakthroughs in Michael's thought was a confession that he was not God. There was a definite separation between his desire to be like Christ and the thought that he *was* Christ.

Intimacy without Indecisiveness

How do we make choices that are realistic in terms of our human condition yet faithful to our vision of a heavenly kingdom? The answer comes in the development of a new concept of the self, by which the feelings and events of our life are viewed in light of our identity as citizens of the kingdom of God.

In one of his teachings concerning last things, Paul presents death as the last ambiguity to be overcome in this life (1 Cor. 15:54–57). This is followed by an exhortation for "beloved brethren" to be "steadfast, immovable, always abounding in the work of the Lord, knowing that in the Lord your labor is not in vain" (1 Cor. 15:58). This is the eschatological hope, that we remain decisive in our discipleship despite the fear of death.

Intimate involvement in life is the Christian answer to indecisiveness. In biblical language, this is the longing of the Bridegroom for the bride (Matt. 9:15), the desire of Christ to return (Matt. 25:6), the assurance from Christ that he will prepare a place to receive his disciples (John 14:3), the prayer that Christ will return quickly for his own (1 Cor. 16:22).

These longings are expressed in the biblical context of crucifixion and separation. They are poignant requests that are only partially fulfilled in the present time. They must also be a part of separation-anxiety and trust in the return of the beloved (John 16). As his disciples, the constant threat to our intimacy with Jesus is a "drawing back" from self-disclosure, especially if our character is called into question during "testing" (Luke 22:31-34). Indecisiveness pushes against godly assurance through our involvement in the bruising dichotomy of spiritual reward versus earthly reward, confidence in Christ versus confidence in the flesh, fellowship with God and his saints versus safety and security in the power structures of this world.

An awareness of and participation in these tensions is the basic meaning of Christian suffering. During imprisonment, Paul exhorts the Philippian church to a manner of life that is worthy of the gospel of Christ, one that is bold in the presence of frightening opponents. It is inevitable in such a life that those who believe in Christ would suffer for him in the sense that they are engaged in the same conflicts as any other follower of Christ (Phil. 1:27-30).[20]

The confirmation of godly affection in the midst of these tensions is made possible by "participation in the Spirit," an acceptance of the mind of Christ Jesus, who was obedient to all the limitations of life, including death (Phil. 2:1-11; 1 Pet. 2:21f; John 15:18-21). The life of Jesus is our example of a completely unambiguous relationship with the Father in the midst of all the ambiguities of earthly existence. Our encouragement is to seek a similar life of obedience to God through an increasingly intimate fellowship with his Son. In this way we "work out our salvation" in the midst of fear and trembling, for our fellowship with God through his Son is an opportunity for God to will and work his good pleasure (Phil. 2:12-13).

But the closer we draw to Christ, the more we are drawn into the service of a "crooked and perverse generation" (Phil. 2:15). To be a disciple in the midst of life's dichotomies is to run the continual risk of drawing back from the intimate fellowship that is required with Christ and those who suffer with us for his sake. The indecisiveness that is always before us is the cause of Paul's warning: "Hold fast the word of life, so that in the day of Christ I may be proud that I did not run in vain or labor in vain" (Phil. 2:16 RSV).

The eschatological hope is that intimacy in the midst of suffering will purify us of ambiguity so that we may steadfastly see the Father who comes toward us. Intimacy demands fulfillment, especially in the midst of tension. God's fulfillment of our obedience will be "the day of Christ," the time when the ambiguities of earthly suffering pass away and all things become new (Rev. 21:3-5). The eager longing of disciples for that day will be consummated in the event of Christ's return for his own, the judgment of "the dead, great and small," the new city of God in the midst of a new creation (Rev. 20:11-21:5).

How do we bring this fulfillment to counselees in the midst of indecisiveness? The answer emerges in those very crises where intimacy is most threatened by the temptation to draw back into the self.

Indecisiveness draws us away from a clear focus upon such intimate and existential issues as death. We repress fear by denial; we never have to make a life or death decision. As Ernest Becker has shown in *The Denial of Death*, sophisticated Americans in an affluent society want all the joys of life with no recognition that they fear death.

The biblical solution to this repression is freedom. Those who have died to this life in the new life of Christ will rejoice in their sufferings as an expression of life (Rom. 5:3-5; 2 Cor. 12:9). The Christian life is so abundant that we live "through" death, we burst the bonds of the fears of human limitations. This is done not by repression, but by the recognition of death's hold upon us and divine strength in the midst of this weakness.

The power for this recognition of weakness is the earthly life of Jesus, the complete substance of God upon earth (Heb. 1), who suffered as a person in all the ways that any of us would suffer (Heb. 4:14-16). He is the new man, the Second Adam who recapitulates in himself the temptations of the first Adam without falling into disobedience (Rom. 8:3; 1 Cor. 15:27; Phil. 2:5-8). When we identify with his life and death, we have the courage to look at our own death in the light of the new life which comes from him.

Without this courage, a Christian counselor is instinctively drawn into the inhibitions of modern society against open declarations of death. The professional training of counselors in the post-World War II era has unwittingly provided a hiding place, where the counselor was safe against commitment to the challenges of eschatological categories. It was really a strange scene in the period between World War II and the Vietnam conflict to see counselors adroitly leading counselees to discuss all of the psychological topics that were considered to be sources of psychological health, while passively refraining from any reinforcement of spiritual categories such as physical death and eternal life. A blatant example of a professional person's repression of the fear of death was one psychiatrist's decision to lie to a very capable patient about her approaching death. His excuse for contradicting the private medical report on the patient's condition was his feeling that she would "go to pieces" if she had to face death. Yet the lady intuitively recognized the deception by an internist and the psychiatrist, and prepared openly for her death in a realistic way that defied the anxieties of the therapist.[21]

Indecisiveness also appears in the chronic anxieties of "other-directed" people. Popular religion seeks to cover their free-floating anxiety with the cult of reassurance. Joshua Liebman's *Peace of Mind* was a best seller in the 1940s and has been followed by a series of popular writing and teaching on "positive thinking," possibility thinking, and "name it and claim it" thinking. In all of these soporific success-oriented reassurances, the dichotomies of life and death shift to the tension between success and failure in this life, health and illness, psychological serenity and insecurity. The spoken or unspoken message is that life is abundant when the self is centered upon itself. Life, in the cult of reassurance, is to be saved by claiming everything. We do not make the choices that would lead us to sacrifice some pleasure and reassurance.[22]

The challenge of Christian counsel is to move beyond those categories of security/insecurity, health/illness that promote "boasting" and "foolishness," into the life-productive dichotomy of affirmation in Christ versus secular success (cf. 2 Cor. 11:21). To place this in the intimate language of the book of Hebrews, we are to have "confidence to enter the sanctuary by the blood of Jesus" (Heb. 10:19–22 RSV) rather than to shrink back from the public exposure of our purpose in life and participation with those who affirm life in the same way (Heb. 10:32–39).

The entire book of Hebrews is summarized as "a word of exhortation" (Heb. 13:22). There is a continual alternation between the risks that come in identification with others and the rewards that we receive through fellowship with others. The direction of the Christian life for these people was to be a continual involvement in the horrendous ambiguities of a persecuted minority (Heb. 13:1–6, 12–16).

The Christian hope for any who are reaching out toward God and toward others is the vision of a heavenly fellowship (Heb. 12:22–24).

The Christian Hope

In the midst of anxiety and turmoil in this city there is the assurance of a heavenly city to come (Heb. 13:14).

In the interim, we see ourselves as we are seen by a "cloud of witnesses" (Heb. 12). We do not draw back into a self-concept of isolation and of communion only with God. Instead, the eschatological hope changes the very way in which we see ourselves, for we are seen by others who identify with our sufferings and we are to identify with them. Isolation and self-sufficiency have no part in the self-concept of an active Christian-as-participant. Instead, the Christian hope is full of action words in the exhortation to fellowship: "Go forth" (Heb. 13:13), "run" (Heb. 12:1), "do" (Heb. 10:36), "seek" (Heb. 13:14), "continually offer up" (Heb. 13:15).

Intensity without Rigidity

Do we push people too far when we bring these expectations, these exhortations into our ministry? The answer depends upon the reality of the Resurrection appearances of Christ and our expectation of a resurrection body.

The question and the answer are joined in Rom. 8:18–25, in which the uncertainties and futilities of this life are contrasted with the hope of "the redemption of our bodies." This is the guarantee of our salvation. Christ who is risen from the dead as the first fruits of the Spirit maintains this hope in us that our adoption as sons of God will bring us into the presence of God as the first fruits of Christ (Rom. 8:28–30; 1 Cor. 15:20–23).

This is an intense belief, not only because of the existential contrast between death and resurrection, but also because of the concentration of contact between our existence in this life and fulfillment in the life to come. Intensity is increased by the sacrifice of Christ which brought him into direct confrontation with sin, hell, and the grave. His victory over these evil forces is the Resurrection power that proclaims a decisive victory. Our reconciliation with God and with one another is made possible through his public, decisive, personal confrontation of the "principalities and powers" of this world through the Cross and the Resurrection (Col. 1:15–23).

But the decisiveness of the resurrection of Christ and the intensity of our belief in the resurrection of the body does not produce rigidity.

Paul proclaims that the redemption of our bodies is the hope in which we are saved, but hope that is seen is not hope: "But if we hope for what we do not see, we wait for it with patience" (Rom. 8:25).

The destruction of any rigid human formula for resurrection is proclaimed in Paul's preamble to the doctrine of the resurrection of the body: "Lo! I tell you a mystery" (1 Cor. 15:51). That which is to come through Christ's return is known neither through a precise timetable nor through complete explanations of the way in which the body as we know it today is related to the glorified body with which we will meet the Lord at the end time.

The corollary of intensity is faith, not rigidity. The doctrine of the Resurrection is most significant when human power is least certain and the consequent expectation of God's power is greatest. Times of sudden tragedy, grinding despair, chronic deprivation become the natural opportunities for God's impelling power to be received most eagerly.

Yet it is the "eager longing," as Paul describes it, which creates difficulties in Christian counsel. There is such a grasp for certainty, so many questions about the details of the life to come, so many complaints that life is ending before a person is ready. At such times, Christian counselors may long for some specific answers, some sensible and factual solution. But the resurrection of Christ and of our bodies is a mystery to mortals. It is to be embraced in a leap of faith which internalizes the Spirit as a guide to all things.

If *the hope of the resurrection of the body is a leap of faith,* then what is the basis of our assurance concerning this event? Our faith without sight is based upon the faithful testimony of those who saw the resurrection of Christ. These include the appearances of the risen Christ to his disciples in the time between Easter and the Ascension, along with the appearance, after the Ascension, to Saul on the road to Damascus.[23] The essential distinction between our belief and the belief of the apostles is their witnessing to an event in which they participated and our belief in their testimony to that event, guaranteed by the inner counsel of the Spirit.

Unless these distinctions are clear, our Christian counsel can participate neither in the faith that is founded upon a historical event nor in a hope that is an eager longing for a future event in history.

If we assume that the apostles "saw" the resurrected Christ only in their "eyes of faith"—as we do—then the spiritual power of the event has been lost and our present and future hopes are bounded by human concepts and power alone. This is the besetting problem of counseling that has been correlated with process theology. Process theology is by its very name an emphasis upon process rather than upon historical, definable events that begin and end in history.[24]

In this philosophical religion, there could be no definite, historical Resurrection; the apostles could believe only as we believe in the "myth" of Christ's rising from the dead. So, the emphasis of process theology would be on *how* we have faith rather than in faith-events, the *what* and *who* of our belief.

Since process theology has no beginning and no ending, so far as human events are concerned, there is a vague, "floating" sense to all conversations about the future hope of those who die in the Lord.

At the other end of the faith-fact spectrum, we find people who speak of the resurrection of the dead as an event which should be described as a present, observable experience. Their exact chronologies, elaborate explanations, and contentiousness with other theories is a lamentable sign of rigidity. They have forgotten the plain words of Paul that the future resurrection is a matter of faith because it is not something that we can "see" in the present time (2 Cor. 5:7).[25]

The concept of faith, in contrast to sight, will always contain both the idea of knowing and the idea of not knowing fully.[26] On the one hand, a Christian does not say: "I know nothing about the Resurrection," for there is both the record of the Resurrection in the Bible, in the growth of the Church, in the lives of people around us, and there is confirmation through the internal work of the Spirit. But, at the same time, the Christian must say, "Now I know in part" (1 Cor. 13), because our present knowledge of future events is incomplete. We live with eager longing, anticipation, humble admission that our knowledge of prophecy is imperfect (1 Cor. 13:9).

The hope of a Christian for a glorified body is not an abandonment of the earthly body. The argument of the apostle Paul in 1 Corinthians is that, because the body is to be glorified in the future life, we are to glorify God in our body now (1 Cor. 6; Rom 14:6–8). Our physical existence is glorified and given a new perspective because of its participation in the life to come.

This intimate connection between a physical and spiritual body is necessary for hope to be maintained in the present life of physical decay. In 2 Cor. 4 and 5, Paul describes the gradual changes from a predominance of physical strength in the body to a predominance of spiritual strength in the same body. This is the earthly approximation of the mystery of the resurrection of the body in the Last Day. We cannot understand the process that will take place then, but we can benefit from the preview of that event in the surge of God's strength through our physical weakness at the present time.

At a time when many dying or disfigured persons have a tendency to hate their own bodies, the doctrine of the resurrection of the body is a guarantee of our unity of body and soul in the present life. There can be no absolute rejection of the body in the present life or in the life to come. The movement from one to the other is theologically described as transformation of the body rather than as abandonment.

This was the theme of my last prayer with our administrator at Church of the Savior, West Hollywood. He was dying of AIDS.

One Pebble's Prayer

Dear Jesus:
    I feel like a pebble on the beach, washed in and out by waves of
        pain and relief
            fatigue and rest
                fitful sleep and alertness.

What am I supposed to do about this? I want to maintain some control of my life. I need some anchor, some mooring. So much is breaking loose!

Let's plan together. I'll live with this sloshing back and forth if you'll keep some deep ballast in me so I don't tip over. You be the anchor within that holds me fast to you. Then I'll be upright even when I must flow in and out of consciousness, rock to-and-fro with pain. You're the solid foundation that keeps me from panic when I lose a grip on myself.

So this is where I am right now. My outer security is washing away, but my eternal security is more reliable as I fix my heart and mind upon you.   Amen.

This is the work of wisdom, to give coherence and courage to life in the face of approaching death.

NOTES

1. Walther Zimmerli, "Concerning the Structure of Old Testament Wisdom," in James L. Crenshaw, *Studies in Ancient Israelite Wisdom* (New York: KTAV Publishing House, 1976), p. 193.

2. For discussion of the historical beginning of the Christian community at Pentecost, see James Dunn, *Jesus and the Spirit*, pp. 136–46.

3. The definitions of the end time were subject to debate by the "dialectal" theologians of the post-World War I period. Barth, Thurneysen, and Gogarten thought that it was impossible to speak of God and his kingdom in terms that would be understood in this world. Their theologies were concerned about the discerning of that which is truly the Word of God. They did not think of the time between Pentecost and Parousia as a present that awaits fulfillment. Rather, they emphasized the continual paradox of living in the present moment with an awareness of God's eternal moment. The paradox was heightened by their insistence upon God as "Wholly Other" and absolute. His kingdom was not to be contaminated by human time and the human spirit. Their concept of counsel would be limited to proclamation of faith and guidance from the Word of God. They did not regard this as any restriction, for they considered the Word of God to be a force for freedom, radical newness, and otherness in this world. This did not take Christians out of this world, but actually made the Word of God more concrete because it came with a freshness from outside of time into a present time that was cluttered with cultural and philosophical assumptions. For a discussion of the beginning of this movement, see the biography of Karl Barth by Eberhard Busch, *Karl Barth: His Life From Letters and Autobiographical Texts* (Philadelphia: Fortress, 1976). For the opinions of other theologians on issues in eschatology, see Donald G. Bloesch, *Essentials of Evangelical Theology*, Vol. II, "Life, Ministry and Hope" (San Francisco: Harper and Row, 1979), pp. 174f.

4. G. Ernest Wright, *The God Who Acts* (Chicago: Henry Regnery, 1952); Oscar Cullman, *Christ and Time* (Philadelphia: Westminster, 1950). The question of *kairos* in relation to *kronos* has varied from the compartmentalizing of time in the Scofield Bible to the condensation of all *kairos* within *kronos* in the "realized eschatology" of C. H. Dodd, *The Parables of the Kingdom* (London: Nisbet, 1935).

5. A noted anthropologist, Malinowski, claimed "death, which of all human events is the most upsetting and disorganizing to man's calculations, is perhaps the main source of religious belief" ("The Role of Magic and Religion," in W. A. Lessa and E. Z. Vogt, editors, *A Reader in Comparative Religion*, New York: Harper and Row, 1965, p. 71). A sociologist, Milton Yinger, proposed that "the most significant of the tendencies with which religion everywhere grapples is fear of death" (*The Scientific Study of Religion*, [New York: Macmillan, 1970], p. 123). For a discussion of these and related studies, see Bernard Spilka, Ralph W. Hood, Jr., and Richard L. Gorsuch, *The Psychology of Religion: An Empirical Approach* (Englewood Cliffs: Prentice-Hall, 1985), pp. 126f.

6. The techniques and theory of correlation are discussed by Paul Tillich in vol. 1 of *Systematic Theology* (Chicago: University of Chicago Press, 1951, pp. 59–65) but without the reverence for God as "Wholly Other" (Karl Barth) or adoration of Christ as the only mediator in the gulf between God and humanity (Emil Brunner).

7. Reinhold Niebuhr, *The Nature and Destiny of Man* (New York: Charles Scribner's Sons, 1953), p. 287.

8. These are the categories as discussed by Reinhold Niebuhr. However, Niebuhr does not discuss these as events, but as symbols. For, in his thinking, "if the symbol is taken literally, the dialectical conception of time in eternity is falsified and the ultimate vindication of God over history is reduced to a point in history" (Ibid., p. 289).

9. The theme is presented by a mental hospital chaplain who became a professor of pastoral care, Carroll Wise, *Religion in Illness and Health* (New York: Harper and Brothers, 1942).

10. For example, Southern Presbyterians accused dispensationalism of an exaggeration that ". . . attacks the very heart of the theology of the Church, which is unquestionably a theology of one Covenant of Grace." Quoted in Oswald Allis, *Prophecy and the Church* (Philadelphia: Presbyterian and Reformed Publishing Company, 1945), p. 296. His main argument is that the Cross rather than the return of Jews to Palestine is the central event in God's plan of salvation.

11. These are the classic theological virtues. They are weakened when the *Theos* of the virtue is reduced to human experience without supernatural power, as in the "empirical" theology of Paul Tillich. Tillich abandons "supernaturalistic" interpretations of the symbolic language of hope. *Systematic Theology*, vol. 3 (Chicago: University of Chicago Press, 1963), p. 114. For Tillich, all of our hope is to be confined to the existential categories of human dilemma. Any Christian doctrine that promises completely unambiguous existence in an age to come would be a contradiction of the tensions between ambiguity and the hope for unambiguous life in our present existence. Heaven and hell are unacceptable as final solutions to ambiguity. They are all relative terms and cannot be absolute (pp. 400–08). All Christian symbols for the end time are provisional answers to the meaning of contradictions in our political, social, and personal life, but they are considered by Tillich to be ineffective as final solutions to ambiguity. The answer of Tillich is a "merging of individual destiny into the destiny of the universe" (pp. 356–59, 418). For Tillich and pastoral psychologists who were influenced by him, the symbols of the Christian hope are useful in the service of an ego that seeks courage in the face of some ending in life.

12. Hans Hoffman, *The Theology of Reinhold Niebuhr* (New York: Charles Scribner's Sons, 1956), pp. 13–15.

13. Niebuhr, *Nature and Destiny of Man*, vol. 2, p. 293.

14. Hoffman, *The Theology of Niebuhr*, p. 229.

15. Hanna Colm, "Healing as Participation," *Psychiatry* 16:99–111.

16. Dunn, *Jesus and the Spirit*, pp. 341–42.

17. The contrasts are made in a variety of New Testament proclamations. The proclamation may be of the various contact points of this world with the world to come. For example, Hans Conzelmann's *The Theology of Saint Luke* (New York: Harper, 1960) separates the theology of Luke-Acts into three periods of events in the kingdom of God. The first period of proclamation, which concluded with John the Baptist, was to Israel (Luke 16:16). The second period, the earthly ministry of Jesus, was a proclamation of the future kingdom through the miraculous signs of the Messiah (Luke 11:20; 17:21). The third period is the filling of the church with the Spirit, by which power and patience may come to the faithful as they look for the appearance of the kingdom in glory (Luke 19:12; 23:42; 24:26).

18. See the discussion of warfare between Spirit and flesh as discussed in Dunn, *Jesus and the Spirit*, pp. 312-18.

19. A tendency to reduce anxiety about the end time may be found in various attempts to divide all of revelational history into compartments and provide absolute certainty from this compartmentalization concerning the time of the Parousia. Dale Moody carries on a running battle with dispensationalists in footnote and text of *The Word of Truth* (Grand Rapids: William B. Eerdmans, 1981). The extremes of organization of Revelation 20 for the Christian hope are demolished by George Ladd in *The Blessed Hope* (Grand Rapids: William B. Eerdmans, 1956).

20. A resolute Christian life may or may not involve physical suffering. Paul considers it foolish to speak of the physical hazards of his apostolic ministry (2 Cor. 11:21-12:11). His teaching is in direct opposition to the popular religious explanation of disease as a sign of God's cursing and of health as a sign of blessing. The Gospels record Jesus' specific repudiation of these inferences (Luke 13, John 9).

21. K. R. Eissler, *The Psychiatrist and the Dying Patient* (New York: International Universities Press, 1955), pp. 144ff.

22. The beginnings of the reassuring literature after the Civil War and until World War II has been traced by Louis Schneider and Sanford Dornbusch, *Popular Religion* (Chicago: University of Chicago Press, 1958).

23. For a discussion of all these testimonies, see the chapter on "Resurrection Appearances" in Dunn, *Jesus and the Spirit*.

24. Alongside this central deficiency we should place some values of process theology for psychologically-oriented counselors, such as those given by Gordon Jackson, *Pastoral Care and Process Theology* (University Press, 1981).

25. A warning against this presumptiveness is issued by Wolfhart Pannenberg in "Analogy and Doxology," chap. 7 of vol. 1, *Basic Questions in Theology* (Philadelphia: Westminster Press, 1970).

26. The difference between knowledge and certitude has been explored by John Baillie, *The Sense of the Presence of God* (New York: Charles Scribner's Sons, 1962) especially pp. 4f.

PART II
FRIENDSHIP

Friendship is the context for communication of the wisdom of God under special circumstances. These circumstances are:

(1) An exercise in choice, an acknowledged association that is special. At times the friendship may take precedence over inherited obligations such as kinship (Prov. 18:24; John 15:16).

(2) A restrictive covenant between two persons that deepens intimacy and privileged communication. Sacrifice of time, energy, and even life itself may be a part of this exclusive investment (John 15:13).

(3) An acknowledged set of values that commands mutual respect (John 15:14). Friends see in each other the highest values of self and society, to which they are mutually pledged and for which they will take risks (Luke 22:28).

(4) An equalitarian relationship that is strengthened and identified by spontaneous sharing of the highs and lows of life (John 15:15). There is honesty and authenticity in communication that is sustained by trust. The threat to this relationship is betrayal and holding back (Matt. 26:49-50; 22:11-12).[1]

A recognition of and commitment to these circumstances is essential for the communication of wisdom.

Without choice, there can be no call for commitment.
Without restrictive investment, intimacy is threatened.
Without values, there is no common ground for sharing
     and growth.
Without equality, there will be holding back.

Defining the Relationship

There is both freedom and restriction in these circumstances. This is a characteristic of any therapeutic relationship. It is a marking off of psychological space within which two or more people can pursue the good with minimum anxiety and resistance.

What is a "good" interaction for purposes of helping another? In traditional analysis, individuation is the good; in wisdom it is righteousness which carries individuation into relations with others and with God.

The good of each therapeutic interaction defines its freedom and limitation. In psychoanalysis, interaction of ego, id, superego is stressed and references to the ego of the analyst are minimized. In wisdom, interaction with others is an integral part of internal growth, so dialogue and mutual sharing are expected.

There are many similarities and some striking differences between the definitions of freedom and restriction in wisdom and in professional therapy.[2]

The freedom of expression desired in friendship is close to that of many modern therapies, especially those which stress congruence, empathy, positive regard for another.

The restrictions of friendship as the context for wisdom will be less than the conventional boundaries of a "professional relationship" in traditional office practice of therapy. Professional restrictions are usually of three types: (1) ethical neutrality and an aura of personal reservation and noncommitment in the presence of clients; (2) a reliance upon academic degrees, professional accreditation, and approved supervision for recognition of competence; (3) the use of a support structure which includes fees, appointments, offices, diplomas on the wall, meetings of professional societies, and identification of the counselor with a professional group rather than with the church or a parachurch organization.

In contrast, a therapeutic relationship based on friendship would be recognized by other assumptions.

First, there would be an *open dedication to a godly mission*, known by a sense of worship in the conversation between Christian counselor and counselee. Paul Pruyser has explicated the "holy" concerns of such counsel in a series of questions in chapter 5 of *The Minister As Diagnostician*.[3] These questions or others create an open expectation of spiritual power that will deepen wisdom and guide the healing process.

Because the true source of good is beyond either counselor or counselee, there is an *essential equality and mutuality* in the search of wisdom for emotional and/or physical healing. Both parties are called to seek God's power as a source of wisdom in the solution of personal difficulties. There is openness and vulnerability in the counselor so that the counselee may see how God has worked in the life of the wounded healer who is helping.[4] This expression of gratitude and adoration of God is implicit in all of the counsel and there will be opportunities for it to be explicitly stated from time to time. There is an open expectation of spiritual power that will bring salvation and healing.

Equality extends beyond the counseling session to the organization of care-giving services, so that the church utilizes counselors according to their calling and talents rather than according to their academic degrees or membership in a professional organization.[5]

Reliance upon the Body of Christ, the Church, characterizes Christian counsel above any identification with a professional organization that provides training for counselors or any society that maintains fellowship and continuing education for counselors. The reliance of the counselor upon the Body of Christ is shown both in identification with a specific Christian fellowship and in concern that counselees should also be identified with a church that embodies the Spirit of Christ.

These elements of demand and release, freedom and responsibility are included in the biblical term "wisdom."[6] Wisdom balances the free, mysterious work of the Spirit with the responsibility of the counselor to share the wisdom known in the Christian tradition, contemporary community of faith and the inner life of the counselor.

Loving within Limits

Wisdom proclaims the necessity of both freedom and restrictions, for wisdom is loving within limits. The most common limitation to be used in counsel is our human way of learning. We do not possess ultimate knowledge of good and evil. What we do attain in discernment comes through confession that we are creatures, not Creator.

Wisdom works among us as created beings by a move from specific friendship toward the universal love of God. We begin with our strengths and weaknesses, and hope that others will accept us—even as we accept them—as continually incomplete and occasionally wayward incarnations of God's love.

God moves toward us within these limits. That which is eternal became temporal in the Incarnation. We learn about love beyond normal limits through the earthly example of Jesus with his disciples. The divine Word became human flesh to perfect in us the unseen universal love which comes only from God (1 John 4:7–21).

Friendship is an appropriate context for the progression of wisdom because it begins the work of love in a way that humans can appreciate without much deception. If friendship is satisfied in the accurate appreciation of truth and beauty in one intimate association, then love can nurture the next step in wisdom, which is the discernment of truth and beauty, good and evil among strangers as well as friends. The wisdom of love among limited humans is a movement from concentration upon one embodiment of ideals toward self-giving to many despite inevitable compromises and disappointments. The vertical walls within which we initially nurture friendship can become horizontal stepping stones across shaky ground to embrace strangers.

How do we communicate this wisdom through friendship in counsel? Here are some implications from each circumstance of friendship.

Restrictive and Redemptive Choices

Friendship is a relationship of choice. So is counsel or therapy. Early in a therapeutic relationship there is a growing awareness of special choices, as more and more time and energy is invested in one person. There is privileged communication, a sharing of family secrets—or an unearthing of them—in a context that reduces family condemnation for such "indecency" and for the breaking of family mores.

But alongside this search for insight there may appear the distortions of over-dependence, transference, and counter-transference. What is to be done?

In part the answer is a traditional analysis of the way in which a hurting person has invested a therapist with deep emotional ties to parents or to significant others. In part the answer is a challenge of love: can restrictive, possessive choices give way to redemptive choices? This was described by Augustine in On Christian Doctrine as the acceptance of particular friendship in anticipation of our finite pilgrimage toward universal love.[7]

The close bonding of a therapeutic friendship becomes the occasion to teach universal principles that penetrate heart as well as head. A part of this penetration is painful. The counselee cannot possess the counselor as a friend, for the friendship of Christian counsel moves toward a sharing of nonpossessive love.

Wisdom in the context of friendship begins with restrictive choices and, through love, changes them into covenants of grace toward others. This is the movement we will describe in chapter 12.

The Exclusive Invitations

The movement of friendship begins in exclusive invitations. The invitation may be rooted in a perceived need, such as companionship, insight, healing, redemption. It is exclusive because one person admits something that should claim the intimate attention of another. Sometimes the call is an open cry for help; sometimes it is a gently growing admission that one person is drawn toward the qualities of life in another.

The invitation invites obligation. The invitation may take the form of a person's confession of need in one area of life; an acceptance by the other of that need and a desire to meet it for their mutual benefit is a response of willing obligation. Each is expected in some way to measure up to acknowledged benefits of the growing relationship. If expectations are not met, the friendship may cease.

Therapy as a form of friendship may be undermined by hidden expectations, either in counselor or counselee. How can there be some clear statements of expectations as conversations begin? How can these be brought into the continuing dialogue in ways that will enhance understanding and acceptance of responsibility for the way we present ourselves to others?

The questions are especially pertinent for the relation of wisdom to friendship. People may seek a Christian counselor in order to gain exclusive attention—which soon is revealed as a neurotic, extractive misdirection of friendship. The needy persons may become increasingly resistant to wisdom, the movement of friendship toward vulnerable and self-giving love.

There is some clarification of expectations in New Testament words and phrases that proclaim Jesus' invitations to the helpless as well as descriptions of the ways in which Christians are to respond to cries for help or searches for companionship. Chapter 13 will study several of the key biblical words for both invitation and obligation toward an exclusive helping relationship. The purpose is clarification of counsel expressed as wisdom in the context of friendship.

The Communication of Virtue

A cry for help implies dependence, and an answer may mean that one person is more adequate than another. This may be the first move toward friendship, but the relationship must soon "right itself" as equalitarian, or it should be redefined as something else.

Equilibrium is obtained through mutual openness in increasingly intimate conversation. In the Last Supper discourse, the disciples become friends rather than servants of Christ because he has told them all that he has heard from the Father (John 15:15).

But we are not equally communicative at all stages or circumstances of life. Self-awareness will vary. At times, threatening circumstances may lead to defensiveness between friends. Friends either help each other to mutual maturity or they eventually separate.

What holds friends together, moving toward maturation? Depth of character is a key element in this bonding. It is known in the way that friends communicate that which is mutually valuable. In Christian counsel the values are expressed as character. The elements of character are usually known in each other as virtues. These remain constant, while circumstances and patterns from the past stimulate or deflect growth in one or another area of character.

How do we develop consistent respect for self and the other in counsel through awareness of and allegiance to these virtues? This is the question of chapter 14.

The Power of a Higher Loyalty

There are threats to friendship in the passage of time, the movement from one place to another, the development of new and engaging relationships (such as marriage). All of these are limiting factors which alter and often diminish the intensity and fulfillment of friendship.

Is there an ultimate loyalty that will sustain friendship? The question often occurs in counsel when a person must decide between two questions: What does life owe to me, and What do I owe to life? The answers to these questions will vary with personal history and circumstances. They also will vary between male and female. But in one way or another, these values call us beyond ourselves and beyond friendship.

The call beyond ourselves is to spiritual maturity that is directed and strengthened by God's grace in our hearts and by the graciousness of those who participate with us in faith, hope, and love.

The call is also to commitment beyond friendship. The fulfillment of the self in relationships is a proximate value, and in counsel it often appears as co-dependence rather than interdependence. Equalitarian friendship is constantly threatened by anxiety to maintain human bonds for their own sake.

In counsel, there are two major threats to the balance between responsibility for individual maturity and gratitude for a faithful companion in this growth. The first threat is secrecy, which undermines sharing and stimulates opportunities for evil. The second is dependence upon some power less than God for the ultimate strength to be a person-in-relationship. These are the issues to be considered in chapter 15.

NOTES

1. Inspiration for these characteristics comes from Gilbert Meilaender, *Friendship: A Study in Theological Ethics* (Notre Dame: University of Notre Dame Press, 1981), pp. 1–3.

2. Roy Fairchild ("Is Psychology Dangerous to the Health of Ministry?" *Pacific Theological Review*, XVIII [Winter, 1985] 56–61.) suggests the possibility of fruitful dialogue between psychology and theology when a school of psychology is concerned with the following issues:

    a. Basic existential questions of life such as freedom, death, trust, isolation, meaninglessness, purpose in life.
    b. The symbolic world of images, expectations, motivations.
    c. Capacity for empathy, compassion, love in balance with autonomy and self-realization.
    d. Freedom for an individual despite external circumstances.
    e. The capacity of the ego to comprehend power from beyond the self, to participate in mystery and mysticism.

3. Paul Pruyser, *The Minister As Diagnostician* (Philadelphia: Westminster Press, 1976).

4. For an explanation of "wounded healer," see the writings of Henri Nouwen, such as *Creative Ministry* (Garden City: Doubleday, 1971).

5. Therapeutic support for this assertion comes from the studies of the 1960s and 1970s on effectiveness of lay counselors (Ernest Poser, "The Effect of Therapists' Training on Group Therapeutic Outcome," *Journal of Consulting Psychology*, 1966, vol. 30, no. 4, 283–89; Allen Bergin, "Some Implications of Psychotherapy Research for Therapeutic Practice," *Journal of Abnormal Psychology*, 1966, vol. 71, no. 4, 235–46; Robert R. Carkhuff and Charles B. Truax, "The Effects of Lay Group Counseling," *Journal of Consulting Psychology* 29, 5 (1965) 426–31. Later studies raise cautions, as in the evaluation of delinquents who were counseled and tutored by volunteers ("Volunteer Program Proves Ineffective, Researchers Find," *IRS Newsletter*, Winter, 1976, p. 2).

6. Ps. 16:1; Isa. 16:3; Jer. 49:7; Acts 20:27; Eph. 1:11.

7. Meilaender, *Friendship*, p. 21.

12

Restrictive and Redemptive Choices

Friendship is the embodiment of wisdom in decisions that endure. The wisdom of friendship is demonstrated under trying circumstances:

A friend loves at all times. (Prov. 17:17)

There is a realism in friendship that expresses the ability of wisdom to encompass both that which is good and evil, pleasurable and painful:

A friend means well even when he hurts you. But when an enemy puts his arm around your shoulder—watch out!   (Prov. 27:6)

Friendship has the intimacy that is associated with kinship, but it is an intimacy based upon wise choices rather than inheritance. The relation of choice to these relationships is shown in the wisdom literature of the Old Testament:

Some friendships do not last, but some friends are more loyal than brothers. (Prov. 18:24)

Most of all, chosen friendship shows the character of an individual. The values of life emerge in the associations that are made, especially those which may involve a sacrifice of status and security:

> When the Son of Man came, he ate and drank, and everyone said, "Look at this man! He is a glutton and wine drinker, a friend of tax collectors and other outcasts!" God's wisdom, however is shown to be true by its results.   (Matt. 11:18)

Ancient and Modern Associations

The results of friendship in Jesus' time were monumental. The choice of a friend might set a person apart from the most enduring identification of human values in society—the family. The consequence might be the loss of physical life (cf. Saul's conflict with David and Jonathan; Jesus' juxtaposition of family and discipleship, Matt. 10:34-39).

In a settled and stratified society, friendship was significant and much sought after. But most of the readers of this book are living in a changing kaleidoscope of cultures in which an individual may go up or down the social ladder in one generation. Successful businessmen have many associates and few, if any, friends.[1]

The multiplication of choices has made the difference. The variety of personal preferences came out of seventeenth century philosophies of universal benevolence which were in marked contrast to the ancient and medieval mores of allegiance to family, clan, tribe, mother tongue, and nation. This more universal outlook was made possible, and extended by, the emerging capitalism and exploration that opened myriad opportunities for economic, social, and political advancement.

The ancient, enduring choice of a friend was an encumbrance to entrepreneurs. The greatest offense to modern capitalism was the time-honored custom of "surety," in which a friend would pledge economic resources to secure a loan for a person. This was a personal restriction, a preferential trust in money lending that must yield to a new concept of marketplace relationships among men. Martin Luther sensed this difficulty in a time when individualistic, self-protective business practices were just emerging in the development of western capitalism.

There is a common error, which has become a widespread custom, not only among merchants but throughout the world, by
which one man becomes the surety for another.[2]

What is "surety"? It is the central motif of Shakespeare's *The
Merchant of Venice*. The hero, Antonio, is the true friend of a
carefree young lover, Bassanio. Antonio was willing to lay down his
life, his soul for his friend. The guarantee of this devotion is a
financial obligation assumed by Antonio on behalf of Bassanio.
When Antonio cannot cover the economic obligation to Shylock,
he is willing to sacrifice a "pound of flesh" to honorably fulfill the
terms of the loan that is in default. He has given himself as "surety"
for his friend.

The resolution of this difficulty reveals the social stratification
and racial prejudice that undergirded the ancient exclusiveness of
friendship. The moneylender, Shylock, is Jewish. He is not allowed
to shed any Christian blood. So how can he carve a "pound of flesh"
out of Antonio?

If the economic individualism of modern society has undermined
the social foundation of friendship, what is left? A century after
Luther, Jeremy Taylor wrote "A Discourse of the Nature, Offices
and Measures of Friendship." For the Reverend Taylor, ideal Christian character in a friend would justify the depth of friendship that
might include sacrifice of life. Moral elitism upheld friendship as
social and economic ties declined. But there still was a reluctance to
embrace the indiscriminate universal application of Jesus' command
to lay down one's life for friends. Taylor warned:

> It is not easily and lightly to be done; and a man must not die for
> humor [emotions], nor expend so great a jewel for a trifle . . . ;
> we will hardly die when it is for nothing, or no good, no worthy
> end, is served, and become a sacrifice to redeem a footboy.[3]

The elitist, restrictive elements of friendship have not survived in
an opportunistic society. How, then, can we recommend friendship
as the mode for discussion of wise choices today?

A more relaxed, less encompassing style of friendship can be developed out of the necessities of personal associations in an entrepreneu-
rial society. These associations may be called "peer networks," as in

Harvard demographer George Masnick's study of their emergence in importance as family networks recede. Whatever the new configuration or nomenclature, "You have to have something," said Yale University epidemiologist Lisa Berkman. "If the family disintegrates, substitute friends. If a marriage fails, affiliate in some other way with a church, neighborhood society, or club." The advice of Berkman was underlined by her finding that socially isolated people had a mortality rate 2.5 times higher than people with strong social bonds.[4]

With the decrease in traditional friendships and family ties, "networking" has become an urban necessity. It is a fashioning of relations around possible, personal preferences. Even relations among kin become a matter of choice as we reach adulthood.[5]

In an opportunistic blending of cultures, a more redemptive form of friendship may be built upon peer networks, church, school, and vocational associations. The theoretical basis has already been presented in the Christian belief that friendship is a schoolmaster for the creation of authentic intimacy that will be transformed into universal love. But there are some problems of application before us, such as the substitution of codependence for redemptive friendship.

The Problem of Codependence

In the light of our brief historical survey, codependence might be seen as a longing for the all-encompassing, absolutely dependable aspects of ancient and medieval friendship. The element of mutual responsibility and personal integrity is missing, but a codependent person is oblivious to this fact. He or she has a system of thought which excludes these elements of maturity.[6] So, counselors in our insecure, choice-oriented society often observe a distorted view of "friends" as a pattern of behavior in which security is maintained through clinging to other people. This often becomes a relationship addiction in which the counselee is not sure about differentiation between self and others. Meaning in life comes increasingly from external referents, and the counselee thinks: I am nothing without a relationship. Impressions upon others become increasingly important. But along with anxiety about dependable relationships there is also a desire to control everything. Codependent people feel a need to be involved in every aspect of the lives of those who are significant to them. Otherwise they feel abandoned.[7] There is no personal integrity to provide friendship between equals and the valuing of ultimate ideals above proximate relationships. A depleted self is not yet free to really choose responsible friendship.

The Decisions of the Sexes

The route to redemptive friendship in a multichoice-oriented society will probably be more internal than external. Changes in self-concept will produce a more flexible and inclusive definition of "friend" among associates and kin. The most strategic of these changes will be a broadening of the way in which men and women make decisions. Instead of a sex-specific solution to issues, men will become more aware of nurturing and bonding as factors in any important choice. These are traditionally "feminine" aspects of the self that men have neglected. Women will begin to include assertiveness along with affiliation as factors in their style of relationships. Precision and definition will have a place in their lives along with intuition and mutual support. Some traditional "male" characteristics in relationships will then be part of a broadened concept of femininity.[8]

Men and women will become more friendly with neglected parts of their inner selves. This will be the basis of redemptive friendship. A neglected part of the self will be restored, and our ability to combine precision of identity with capacity for intimate associations will be increased.

How will this change in our perception and range of decision-making begin? I would suggest a start with Jesus' statement that the disciples had become his friends because he was sharing with them all that the Father had told him. The intimacy of communication would nourish and condition their ability to fulfill his command to "love one another" (John 15:17).

A sex-specific society has made it easier for women than men to fulfill the intimacy requirement of friendship. Men are conditioned to an inhibition of emotional expression that Jack Balswick has described as a syndrome of the "inexpressive male."[9] In contrast, the studies of Lillian Rubin show that women share intimacies, self-revelation, nurturance, and mutual support. These seem to be workable dimensions of friendship in modern society, since three-fourths of the single women in a study by Rubin could identify a best friend, and almost always that person was a woman. Those who did not have a best friend were quick to say that this was a source of regret to them. But among single men, there were few who could name a best friend and most of them indicated that they did not worry about this lack. Besides, the men—married or single—didn't feel that they could share any pain with someone who was a friend.[10]

Rubin found that the feminine aspects of friendship could be cultivated in men who turned to women as friends. Here they found the nurturance and intimacy that was missing from their associations with males, who based their bonding solely upon shared activities. This may mean that friendless males will profit greatly from the counsel of women and that male and female counselors can work with an inarticulate male to find women who will be his friends. It might even be possible for these men to try friendship with their wives![11]

The object of this consciousness-raising is not to blur the distinctions between male and female or to "womanize" the male consciousness. Instead, as James Nelson has advised in *Intimate Associations,* the need is for men to become aware of the feminine component within themselves. There are elements of nurturing, vulnerability, and openness that will strengthen rather than blur male identity. Men do not need something added to them from women. They need to be aware of God-given resources already within themselves that have been inhibited by the tough orientation of a male-dominant culture.[12]

Self-Disclosure through Spiritual Discipline

The development of inner capacity for the full range of redemptive friendship will strengthen the content and the communication aspects of wisdom. The choices of life can combine intimate sharing with steadfast allegiance to virtues that transcend relationships. This joint venture is prominent in wisdom literature, especially the Psalms. Walter Brueggemann followed this twofold strategy in his study of the lament psalms and has continued to bring divine revelation and personal sharing together in such works as *Hopeful Imagination* and *Prophetic Imagination.*[13]

Biblical studies validate the combination of vulnerable communication that we associate with femininity and the task-oriented identity that we associate with masculinity. Can counsel follow this broadening direction for friendship through choices that demonstrate personal preferences along with intuitive awareness of our impact upon others?

One answer is to seek the broadest possible categories for our discussion of self-identity, disclosure, and decision-making with counselees. Are there categories which transcend the sex-specific styles of relationships that we find in our acquisitive, individualistic society?

In a mediated theology there is a vocabulary for divine demand and human response that moves us beyond our tight categories of choice. Consider these biblical challenges to decision-making: an awareness of the holy, the differentiation between chance and providence, the source of faith, the meaning of grace, the experience of repentance, the closeness of communion, the sense of calling. These are the topics through which persons may express the deepest longings of the heart in a way that brings self-identification, as well as community with those who share the same wisdom of God. When personal choices combine authoritative guidance with personal motivation in decision-making, a person is expressing "spiritual discernment."

The modern procedure of discernment is a mixture of theological belief with psychological assessment, especially prevalent in the writing of Paul Pruyser, *The Minister As Diagnostician*.[14] As director of graduate education at the Menninger Foundation, Pruyser had many opportunities to interact with pastors, chaplains, and psychiatric residents who were concerned about the religious dimension of life-changing decisions. Out of this interest came a series of diagnostic variables for assessment of the religious life of an individual.

First, *what is the person's awareness of the holy?* This may be known without direct questioning, for people often speak about feelings of awe or bliss. Here is a clue to that which is considered holy. Direct questions may yield answers to that which is most highly prized by an individual or that which would be willingly sacrificed in case of difficult circumstances. However the information were obtained, we would then have some idea of the "treasure of the heart," which might be an idol or might be God. This is a depth of being beyond role-models of "male" or "female."

How does a person think about providence? That is, what is God's purpose in relation to the life of this individual? Sometimes the counselee will reveal this by referring to some misfortune and asking, Why me? This may be followed by such questions as, What must I do? or, What should I try to change in myself? This is an opportunity to find out if the person believes in a God of forgiveness or just sees him as a God of condemnation. Does the individual wallow in depravity, or look up with hope for forgiveness? Is there an indifferent air, as though God did not care? Or is there a sense of God's outraged love that one of his creatures has departed from his will? Is the world an evil place in which God punishes those who are unwary, or is it a good place in which God strives with cosmic evil to bring us back to his original creation?

What is the source of faith in the life of this person? This would certainly follow from the person's doctrine of providence. Does the individual embrace life and its experiences, or shy away from anything that would involve a choice or a commitment? Is faith a source of courage to new activities, a stimulus to curiosity? Or is it a cautious belief in a power that will offer protection in an evil world, a way of testing those who can be trusted and those who must be rejected?

What about grace and gracefulness? Does the counselee report kindness, generosity, and forgiveness in stories of childhood? Does the person know about the beauty of giving and receiving? Or is the background of this person filled with thorny issues upon which the memory is continually impaled? Do viciousness, intolerance, and a lack of forgiveness appear continually in the conversations? Are they stuck at the adolescent level of "If I were a man I would—" or "Women have it easy—"?

A lack of grace will appear as self-rejection or as excessive narcissism. It may be seen in the "marketplace" personality, of one who is always getting and never giving. We also may listen in vain for some specific way in which a troubled person decides to help, bless, or forgive someone else, and then realize with sadness that they have never known these graces in anyone.

Does the person know the meaning of repentance? When a person begins to speak about trouble, is this done with anxiety about punishment or with a sense of sadness for having hurt other people and outraged the love of God? Does the person excuse self from any role in personal tragedy and project all blame upon others? Or, conversely, is there an upsurge of scrupulosity, a feeling that the individual can never be forgiven for all the sins that have been committed? Hopefully, the individual will show a more healthy form of contrition, in which personal responsibility is accepted with an awareness that circumstances and other persons are also partially responsible.

The individual will not be so concerned about repentance to avoid punishment as about the restoration of relationships.

With whom is the person in communion? Is this individual in some continuous and committed relationship with a group of persons— both men and women? If not, why not? If there is some sense of communion, what are the values of the group that is esteemed by this individual? Is this an active communion, which includes give and take, acceptance and rejection, fulfillment and disappointment? Or is there present sadness for past estrangement from the church or some other community of moral inquiry? How does the community of commitment explain the alienation and isolation of this individual or give hope for a reconciliation and forgiveness?

To what is this person called in life? What is the sense of vocation, the purpose for individual existence? How do work and love interact with each other as an expression of a person's sense of calling? Is there a high sense of involvement in work and love: zest, vigor, liveliness, dedication? Or has the individual suffered a loss of involvement because of ceaseless disappointment, interpersonal tragedy, attack from vicious or demonic elements in life?

These are the categories for redemptive choices. The questions are invitations to a self-concept and sharing that challenge our individualistic, marketplace power-plays, defenses, and self-imposed defeats. They unite sharing of our sense of inner discipline and our ways of communicating with others. Most of all, they establish open dialogue with the Father through the forms of thought revealed in his Son. Spiritual discipline is a habitual awareness of the kinds of questions that Jesus asked of the Father as his earthly decisions were made—ways of deciding that demonstrate our friendship with God and all those whom he would be friend through us.

NOTES

1. Daniel Levinson, *Seasons of a Man's Life* (New York: Alfred A. Knopf, 1978), p. 335.
2. Benjamin Nelson, *The Idea of Usury: From Tribal Brotherhood to Universal Otherhood* (Chicago: University of Chicago Press, 1969), p. 151.
3. Ibid. pp. 162–63.
4. Judy Foreman (Boston Globe) reprinted in *Star-Bulletin and Advertiser* (Honolulu) March 21, 1982.

5. Claude S. Fischer, *To Dwell among Friends* (Chicago: University of Chicago Press, 1982), p. 4.
6. The self-deceptions of co-dependency are discussed in Anne Wilson Schaef's *When Society Becomes an Addict* (San Francisco: Harper and Row, 1987), pp. 52ff.
7. Anne Wilson Schaef, *Co-dependents: Misunderstood —Mistreated* (San Francisco: Harper and Row, 1986), pp. 44–52, 57–60.
8. For summaries of research studies in the 1970s and 80s on masculine and feminine components of decision-making, see Carol Gilligan, *In a Different Voice* (Cambridge: Harvard University Press, 1982).
9. Jack Balswick, *The Inexpressive Male* (Lexington, MA: Lexington Books, 1988). See also the chapter on "Men, Women and Friends," in Lillian B. Rubin, *Just Friends* (New York: Harper and Row, 1985).
10. Rubin, *Just Friends*, pp. 62–68.
11. Literature on the difficulties of male intimacy includes: M. McGill, *The McGill Report on Male Intimacy* (San Francisco: Harper and Row, 1985); Leanne Payne, *Crisis in Masculinity* (Westchester, Ill.: Crossway Books, 1986); S. Osherson, *Finding Our Fathers* (New York: Free Press, 1986). See also the many references to research studies in Balswick, *The Inexpressive Male*.
12. James Nelson, *The Intimate Connection* (Philadelphia: Westminster Press, 1988), especially pp. 85–111.
13. Walter Brueggemann, "The Formfulness of Grief," *Interpretation* 31, no. 3 (July, 1977) pp. 263–75; *Hopeful Imagination* (Philadelphia: Fortress Press, 1986); *Prophetic Imagination* (Philadelphia: Fortress Press, 1972); *Hope within History* (Atlanta: John Knox Press, 1987).
14. Paul Pruyser, *The Minister As Diagnostician* (Philadelphia: Westminster Press, 1976), pp. 60–79.

13

Invitations to Sharing

The movement toward friendship begins in exclusive invitations, especially when a felt need is expressed. The exclusiveness is in the expectation of obligation: who will help in time of trouble? Specific concentration upon the need of one person is required. To whom are we obligated? Jesus' answer was, the stranger (Luke 10:25–37; Matt. 25:35, 42). This turned the ancient ideal of friendship in a completely new direction. The old wisdom gave no help to Samaritans or other strangers.

If you promise to pay a stranger's debt, you will regret it. You are better off if you don't get involved.   (Prov. 11:15; 20:16; 27:13)

Consider that exclusiveness beside the great surprise of the final judgment.

Come, you that are blessed by my Father. . . . I was a stranger and you received me in your homes, naked and you clothed me.
(Matt. 25:34–36)

The Christian invitation to help is only exclusive in the sense of focus upon the needs of individuals (or groups). They know our love

219

through a specific investment of time, energy, money, and affection. This makes the care personal. At the same time, our motivation is inclusive. We are inviting all people to share their burdens with us, so that strangers may become friends (Matt. 11:29–30; Gal. 6:1–10; Matt. 5:42).

How do we show counselees (and ourselves) that they can expect the close, preferential bonding that characterizes traditional friend-ship along with a movement toward sharing with self and others that is redemptive friendship? And how can they be inspired to make this combination in their associations outside the hour of counsel?

This bifocal approach is imbedded in many New Testament pas-sages. Sometimes an action of Jesus is described in words that combine diagnostic interest with disregard for social or moral barriers. Or the same words may appear in descriptions of the way that disciples are to befriend the needy or establish companionship among themselves.

A study of these words may explain the context for our helping relationship and dramatize the way that a counselee may make a friendly journey into the self and also journey out toward love for those who seem to be strangers. We will begin with the word that is most closely associated with counsel in the New Testament, *parakaleo*.

Parakaleo

Parakaleo as the Need for Help

The primary use of *parakaleo* is as a precondition for care and counsel. It is a cry for help, an awareness of distress and willingness to receive help. The first chapter of Mark contains the cry of a leper who "begged" Jesus to heal him (Mark 1:40, KJV). This is followed by calls for help from people in many conditions of life. A ruler of the syna-gogue, Jairus, "besought" Jesus to heal his daughter (Mark 5:22–23, KJV). The guides of a deaf mute make the same plea (Mark 7:32, KJV), as does a blind man (Mark 8:22, KJV). And, a demoniac "begs" to go with Jesus after he is restored to health (Mark 5:18).

Not only is the word used for the cry of troubled people to Jesus and Peter and other disciples, but it is also the Greek verb used for Jesus' statement that he could "appeal to" his Father for twelve legions of angels to save him in his time of trouble (Matt. 26:53, KJV).

There are at least three contextual guidelines for redemptive friendship in the New Testament uses of *parakaleo*.

The attention of Jesus is immediately directed toward those who will admit that they need help. He stops a triumphal journey toward his final days in Jerusalem to hear the cry of a blind man (Luke 18:13–43).

The willingness and power of Jesus to aid the afflicted is the primary evidence of his messiahship before the resurrection. It is so characteristic of his ministry that Jürgen Moltmann concludes that the Christian church and society must be judged primarily by the obedience to the commands of Jesus to care for the sick, the poor, and the disenfranchised.[1]

The cry for help usually, but not always, met the primary complaint of a person. Paul issued this cry to the Lord three times (*tris ton kurion parakalesa*), but he received no relief from his "thorn in the flesh." Instead, the answer of the Lord was, "My grace is sufficient for you, for my power is made perfect in weakness" (2 Cor. 12:9).

The cry of Paul was concentrated and insistent. He wanted help for an acknowledged need, but the answer was more inclusive than he had anticipated. God's answer was grace, the power to reach out to others in universal love.

In Paul's usage, *parakaleo* is continued awareness of God's affection despite the continuation of affliction (2 Cor. 1:3–7; 1 Thess. 3:7). The spirit of comfort despite suffering is similar to that of the Lord Jesus, who commanded his disciples to put up their swords and declared, "Do you think that I cannot appeal [*parakaleo*] to my Father, and he will at once send me more than twelve legions of angels?" (Matt. 26:53, KJV). Love of enemies takes precedence over exclusive protection as the Son of God.

Neither the cry for help nor the desire for help will automatically result in the relief of physical or emotional distress, although we are to ask for this healing and expect a manifestation of God's power. Something deeper and more pervasive will fill us. The comfort of God is his presence, his willingness to suffer with us in affliction (Heb. 2:10; 4:14–18). This is an affirmation that may be resisted among counselees who seek assurance through sensational theology. But neither God nor a counselor are obligated to meet the possessive, absolute demands of a person who plays helpless "victim."

Concern is for both the person in trouble and for those who care for the person. Our attention to one person's need does not exclude a network of influences, or the lack thereof. The same word is used for helping the leper (Mark 1:40), the mute man, and the blind man as is used for the centurion who pleads for his servant or by the elders of the synagogue who say the centurion is worthy of help. Biblical consolation is for all those who have interest in the problems that center in one individual. It is not isolated or secretive. Those who were sick unto death were to confess their sins to one another (presumably in the company of the church elders) so that they would be healed (James 5:16).

Parakaleo as Exhortation

Parakaleo is more than an articulate cry for aid from one person who suffers. It is also an awareness of diffuse and inarticulate needs. The obligation of redemptive friendship is to develop a fellowship of mutual encouragement, in which there is a winsome appeal to those who need help, whether they have expressed this cry or not.

Parakaleo is a *general exhortation* for all to come to Jesus, who knows they may be weary and heavy-laden. This proclamation may be explicit or implicit. The explicit appeal was made by John the Baptist ("many exhortations" Luke 3:18). The implicit call is through the personality of the disciple, who is an ambassador of God's appeal to a world in need (2 Cor. 5:14–21).

Exhortation is encouragement in a multitude of ways. The entire letter to the Hebrews is referred to as "a word of exhortation" (Heb. 13:22). Friendship becomes universal love when we realize the many ways in which people need help.

The message of Hebrews presents *the purpose of exhortation,* which is for disciples to provide a faithful witness to the suffering of Christ when there is testing in this world. It is the test of experience which duplicates the experience of Christ. He was tempted in every way as we are in our weakness, yet he was without sin (Heb. 4:14–16). He walks with us as a wounded friend, even as we do with each other. Sharing is the substance of redemptive faith.

The agent of exhortation is the Christian fellowship. Christians are to exhort one another every day lest they fall into self-deceit (Heb.

3:13). This is the guarantee of wisdom under trial. Friendship provides the courage to continue in honesty and faithfulness. The faithful are to "stir up" one another, lest any fall back into self-pity, isolation, and despair (Heb. 10:25).

A modern application would be a network of "life preservers" rather than one human "life saver" to those under trial. The support system of several friends is more essential than the care which can be offered by one designated leader.

Guidance and *exhortation is by the Holy Spirit*, which works through a clear mind. Exhortation in the church is primarily the work of a prophet, one who speaks for the good of all rather than for personal edification. This is a person of discernment, who can translate the incoherent sentences and buried feelings of others into statements that the entire community can understand and accept with edification (1 Cor. 14:1–5). Wisdom is made known in the way we explain needs to one another.

Parakaleo as a Sense of Urgency

Parakaleo is sometimes found in the context of urgent response to divine command: "And he testified with many other words and exhorted them saying, 'Save yourselves from this crooked generation'" (Acts 2:45). These words of Peter for all who heard him are also used by Paul for those who are to proclaim the word. His urging to Timothy is "preach the word, be urgent in season and out of season, convince, rebuke, and exhort, be unfailing in patience and in teaching" (2 Tim. 4:2, RSV).

The urgency of this appeal is both for personal relations and for action: "Finally, brethren, farewell. Mend your ways, heed my appeal, agree with one another, live in peace, and the God of love and peace will be with you" (2 Cor. 13:11, RSV).

Parakaleo expresses the integrity of wisdom, which is a gracious word embodied in loving associations.

The urging of *parakaleo* is serious but gentle. Paul uses the term with the Thessalonians as a father with children (1 Thess. 2:11). He writes as one who is gentle, a nurse who is "affectionately desirous" of their spiritual development (vv. 7, 8). His exhortation is not to put them down, but to build them up, that they may be steadfast in

223

the midst of afflictions (1 Thess. 3). They are to be comforted and established (2 Thess. 2:17), built up and encouraged by his words (1 Thess. 5:11).

These verses show the distinction between exhortation as a serious concern of those who are led by the compassion of Christ and "exhortation" as heavy condemnation by those who despise human weakness. The distinction should be kept in mind by every counselor who reads popular works by authors in the field of "biblical" counsel, some of whom condemn the mentally ill as sinners.[2] A more accurate biblical counsel would impart the spirit of gentleness and affection that characterized the ministry of Paul. He did not seize upon human weakness—the cry for help—as a chance to condemn anyone, but combined exhortation with encouragement, incentive, participation, affection, sympathy, common agreement, and love (Phil. 2:1).

Parakaleo is a correction to propositional theology in which human need is feared and repressed under the force of arguments that secure success for those who comply.

Parakaleo as the Supporting Spirit

In the writings of Paul, and in Hebrews, *parakaleo* often has the principal meaning of comfort. Paul writes in 2 Corinthians of the way that God comforts us and we comfort one another (2 Cor. 1:3ff.). There is also the comfort of the Scriptures that bring us hope (Rom. 15:4). The very words that we use with one another are a source of comfort (1 Thess. 4:8), for this includes a spirit of pardon and consolation (2 Cor. 2:7).

The letter of Hebrews seems to be a continual exhortation that builds up and comforts disciples in a time of difficulty (Heb. 10:23; 13). Comfort for one another is to be a daily habit (Heb. 3:13).

The supportive nature of *parakaleo* is summarized in the beautiful benediction of Paul to the Thessalonians.

Now may our Lord Jesus Christ himself, and God our Father, who loved us and gave us eternal comfort and good hope through Grace, comfort your hearts and establish them in every good work and word. (2 Thess. 2:16–17)

The support takes the form not of general sentimentality, but of specific fellowship that is guided by encouragement from the Scriptures (2 Cor. 7:5–7; Rom. 15:4). The full implication of comfort is to be found both in word and in deed (Col. 2:2). The embodiment of this friendship is Barnabas, who brings the "joy of encouragement" (Acts 4:36). As an intermediary between Saul and the church, he opened the doors for reconciling conversation (Acts 9:27; 11:22, 25, 30). This is redemptive friendship.

Oikodomeo

Edifying Conversations

The supporting nature of conversations as the "mind of Christ" is possible because the speaking occurs within "the sight of God" (2 Cor. 12:19). The presence of God builds up the believer even when he/she must contend with quarreling, jealousy, anger, selfishness, slander, gossip, conceit, and disorder (2 Cor. 12:20). The overcoming Spirit brings edifying conversation, which is one translation of *oikodomeo*, a companion word to *parakaleo*.

Oikodomeo is not only the strength of conversation because God is present. It is strong because of companionship. Those who exercise their gifts are "building up" (*oikodomen*) the body of Christ (Eph. 4:12). The purpose of the conversations is the unity of faith in submission to Christ. The goal of the conversation is maturity after the model of the son of God (Eph. 4:13–16). God in his wisdom knows our limitations and afflictions as humans, and has chosen to use human resources as channels of divine strength. This is the basis of mediated theology.

Hypotasso

The Attitude of Submission

When our conversations are conducted in the sight of God, there is no place for arrogance about our own ability or pride and our power over another. Counsel in the sight of God has a quality of submission both in the counselor and in the client. This is the meaning of *hypotasso*.

Hypotasso is the way God works to change us from lowliness to glory. Christ subjects all things to himself, including the remolding of our personality (Phil. 3:21). It is recognition of the creative power of God, who has made us with power over the rest of creation (Heb. 2:8).

The visible manifestation of *hypotasso* is humility toward one another (1 Cor. 16:16). There is to be humble constraint in the exercise of any leadership in the congregation (1 Pet. 5:1–11). This is wisdom expressed as mutual recognition of imperfection in all our attempts to draw near to God, to others, and to ourselves.

Noutheteo

Adequate Instruction

Counsel includes a sharing of wisdom that is embodied in the New Testament word *noutheteo*. The basic meaning is a competent teacher. This competence is demonstrated in several ways. One is an awareness of external danger. The counselor must acknowledge threats to an individual and assist him/her against them. Acts 20:31 uses *noutheteo* in the context of guarding a flock against wolves. The counselor is a shepherd.

But the word is not confined to any dependent relationship. The *International Critical Commentary* translates Col. 3:16 as "mutual instruction." Rom. 15:14 spells out the belief of Paul in the adequacy of those whom he would "admonish." They are good and knowledgeable servants of God, before whom Paul has a duty as an apostle to provide instruction. And, because of their adequacy, they are commanded to instruct one another.

In at least one of the seven uses of *noutheteo* in the New Testament, there is a touch of sternness or blame. This is in the writing of Paul in 1 Cor. 4:14 about the duty of parents.

These New Testament words for instruction, comfort, confrontation, and building up are aspects of redemptive relationships. Each demonstrates friendship in different circumstances of life or different phases of growth toward maturity. They are invitations to share a new kind of intimate association, in which we expend ourselves for an individual because Christ has given himself for us all. Since he has bridged the gulf of sin that made us strangers, we can extend his grace without the barriers of exclusive obligations. The only obligation left standing is inclusive, "to love one another" (Rom. 13:8).

In the freedom of this diversity of invitations, the church presents the "wisdom of God in all its different forms" (Eph. 3:10).

NOTES

1. Jürgen Moltmann, *Hope for the Church* (Nashville: Abingdon, 1979), pp. 21–36.
2. Adams, Jay, *Competent to Counsel*, pp. 31–35.

14

The Communication of Virtue

What do friends share in common as they seek wisdom and the solution of problems? The answer to this question is twofold. First, there must be some common definition of the values that bind us together in friendship. If these values contain eternal as well as temporal qualities, they would be considered a part of wisdom. The church has sought to communicate the meaning of these divine-human qualities in the "cardinal" and "theological" virtues. Cardinal virtues refer to the elements of character that would be esteemed by wise persons who follow Greek philosophers such as Plato and Aristotle. Theological virtues refer to the divine-human attributes of Jesus.

The second aspect of virtue in counsel will be longitudinal. When does a particular virtue become a central concern of our direction in life? In counsel this would be the question of a teachable moment. How do circumstances and personal maturation bring one to see the application of an ethical or spiritual aspect of character to self-actualization? In counsel this will mean attention to the multiplicity of selves within one personality. A person may be a servant in one setting and a friend in another, both at the same time. Some virtues

228

may seem more important to roles as husband or wife and others to leadership in the community or competence in work. A knowledge of these roles at any time in life will be affected by crises of illness and disaster, sudden success and economic freedom.

Whatever the circumstances, a common understanding of virtues will facilitate friendship. If we can come to some definition of these great words of grace, then intellect and intuition can work together. Also, the use of value-laden terms will increase the flow of spiritual power through understanding and commitment, for each designation of a virtue is a description of Christ. To concentrate upon these virtues is to place ourselves in a receptive frame of mind to receive him as he truly is.

The Christian community has presented the characteristics of Christ as the lines of spiritual force through which the character of individuals is conformed to the nature and will of God. Traditionally, these have been called the cardinal and theological virtues: prudence, justice, courage, temperance (or balance), faith, hope, love.[1]

But we must accept some limitations of our wisdom in communication and in the modeling of our character. The power-oriented words for the attributes of our Lord are not a series of equations with which we solve every puzzle in social interaction or assuage every uneasy thought. Dietrich Bonhoeffer called such obsessive searches for security "a pathological overburdening of life by the ethical."[2] The appropriate communication of virtue in counsel is by mutual negotiation. This is the function of friendship in relation to virtues, a mutual appraisal of our progress toward ideals, with joy in what we have accomplished with each other.

In the following discussion, each cardinal and theological virtue will be described in relation to one of the cases we have considered in this book. The purpose is not to provide an encyclopedia of all the meanings of virtue, or to list all that are significant in Christian counsel. Rather, we are establishing signposts by which friends may assess their character and agree on the goals toward which they move.[3]

Prudence

Is a person realistic in the perception of self, of associates, and of situations? This is the first question of prudence.

Prudence is founded upon foresight. This is realistic perception of goals. How do the intentions of this individual facilitate or inhibit the meanings that this person seeks in this world and in the world to come?

Both prudence and foresight are very appropriate attributes for counselees who complain about "not getting anywhere in life." This was a complaint of Mac (chaps. 3 and 4). Mac began his first counseling session with statements of what he wanted to get out of life: "I would like to be president of the company some day." The pastor replies with interest and Mac admits that another goal is not being met, the happiness of his wife. But, he doesn't "do anything about it." This provokes a brief speech from the pastor about the question of what Mac really lives for.

This exercise in prudence and foresight is a precondition of any passionate and caring friendship between Mac and his wife as well as the development of humane and reliable associations in his business. It is an attempt to define whether goals are realistic or unrealistic and to describe the ways in which Mac may move toward those goals. To do this, Mac must not only have foresight, but also be realistic about self and others. In one conversation, the pastor asks if Mac is indifferent to himself. Mac thinks that he is not, since he dresses well and tries to impress other people. But the pastor insists with a challenge: "But you don't act like someone who has been well cared for." This is explained in terms of Mac's anxieties about deeper relationships and leads Mac to admit that his father made a lot of money but "was not much of a man around the house." The pastor concludes from this that Mac did not have a model by which he could think out the way in which a power would mold him in the direction of lover and responsible husband. This is a move toward prudence. It is a discovery of the self. It is foresight. The self is defined in terms of goals that are sought in life.

Counselors can often facilitate a discussion about prudence and foresight through questions that are close to the following ones:

Am I honest with myself?
Am I frank with others?
Why do I take this action?
Should I act now?

Justice

Justice is action to make real that which is good. By "good" we mean the increase of love for self and neighbor. To make this good real, we must distribute the goods and services of this world in such a way that each person can perform the obligation that is owed to the Creator.

Certainly the question of justice blazed forth in the fights between Robert and Linda. In one way their desire for justice could be formulated as a question: What should I expect from life that anyone else would want to receive as a human being? Linda's answer is that a wife should not be beaten. Robert's answer is that a woman should obey her husband. Each of them is concerned with obligations of people in relationship and both of them are disappointed in what they have received from a partner. They do not know how to be "civil" with each other.

Fortunately, the pastor's replies do not lead toward a legalistic answer to these questions. He does not take sides or fix blame. Instead, he introduces the virtue of justice with the question of intentions in life. What is it that Robert and Linda want to get out of life? What does each of them expect of self and of spouse as a part of life's fulfillment?

Robert's answers lead to another dimension of justice: What demands must I meet in life? In answer to this question, Robert confesses that there has been great injustice in his life. As a child, he was an unwitting witness to adultery in his family and he had been determined that he would not let anything like that happen in his own marriage. In making this confession, he reveals the "ethical ledgers" that individuals keep in their memories of family relations.[4] Now, in adult life, Robert will do anything to prevent that particular kind of injustice, even if it means that he threatens his family and beats them. Dynamically, the question What demands must I meet? depends in Robert's case upon his previous experience with the question: What should I expect from life as a human being?

"What should I expect" is the "equalitarian" side of justice. This is the basic reason for rage in Robert, for he thinks that his fundamental rights as a human being have been violated. He is not yet clear about the impact of the other question (What demands must I meet?), or the relationship between these two questions of justice.

The question of demands is a question of "distributive" justice. It deals with the distinctions that are made between people on the basis of their talents and circumstances in life. Jesus explained justice in this way when he said: "To whom much is given, of him much is required." Robert, like many other people, will feel that he has not been given very much. Therefore, there is something "special" about the distribution of justice in relation to his problems. He needs more affection, more reassurance than persons who have grown up with a basic sense of trust in their family. Because he is so very needy in this area, he reacts to any injustice in a "dated" way, especially in the case of adultery, because of the horrible memory of what he experienced as a child. The unjust distribution of trust in childhood must be fully disclosed before Robert can define the kind of justice he is really calling for as an adult.

Of course Robert could reply that his basic need is for love, along with justice. He certainly is correct in this, but he may not realize that another term is of equal importance: power. Having been deprived of trustworthy love as a child, Robert is desperately seeking a reassurance from his family and others as an adult. But as an adult, he is using power in a way that is self-defeating. Could he learn through counsel to accept a deeper meaning of power as self-respect and utilize this power to increase the possibility of love and justice in his life? So far, Robert is stuck. He cannot forgive his wife or himself because of a fear that he will lose power. But he is enraged because power, as he knows it, has produced neither justice nor love.

What kind of questions can we ask of people that will disclose their intentions concerning justice, provide them with the realistic definitions they seek, and show how the "ethical ledger" can be balanced?

To whom am I responsible?
What demands must I meet?
How do I give and receive power?
Will I stand firm when it hurts?

Courage

The last question of justice is also the first question of courage: Will I stand firm when it hurts?

The issues of courage come after those of justice because courage is not a virtue in itself. Virtuous courage is always dependent upon some other value. We may lay down our lives for our friends (John 15:13). It is a marvel that Christ would die for us while we were unworthy (Rom. 5:6–11). He has made us his friends through this sacrifice (vs 10).

When we think of what we are willing to suffer for, justice and courage are combined. This was certainly in the mind of the pastor who talked with May (chap. 6). She wanted justice for herself in terms of respect and love from her husband. She also wanted respect from her children as a loving mother and faithful wife. But she was continually tempted to repeat the love fantasies of her adolescent years. This would have been an injustice to herself, to her children, to her husband, and to God.

May admitted that she needed courage to face this dilemma. The pastor's service to her was foresight. He looked ahead with her to what would happen if she fell into the arms of a high school lover. He kept asking questions that would build up her strength and self-respect. Together they considered ways by which she could maintain integrity and open communication with her husband. This requires courage, a willingness to deprive oneself of immediate pleasure on behalf of some value that can bring satisfaction in the future. Would May be willing to delay gratification for the sake of the values to which she was committed?

In asking about the future, the pastor did not neglect the present pain in May's life. He was very accepting of the sense of abandonment and frustration she experienced, even as he showed how she was handling these feelings inappropriately through a return to patterns of escape into fantasy. He seemed to know that the hurt was so deep that she needed these fantasies as a temporary way of relief. But the question was, would she make this her permanent response to blockage of affection with her husband? Was this to be her reward or could she look for the more adequate reward of a full giving and receiving of love with her husband?

The question of reward must always be a part of the lengthening and deepening of friendship. We cannot exhort anyone to stand fast with friends or lovers unless we can give them reasons for this that will provide satisfaction at some time in life. Is there any sense in which God can provide satisfaction for a person during a time when desires are delayed? The book of Hebrews is continually offering exhortations to cheerfulness as a present reward for those who seek values beyond themselves. Perhaps the pastor sought to lead May in this way as he injected some humor (which she refers to as sarcasm) into their conversation. Certainly she would be more attractive to her husband, Alfred, and the possibility of deeper reunion would be increased if she could be as joyous and free as she presumably was at age thirteen. If this should occur, then courage would be an important solution to her dilemma, for it would give her strength to live cheerfully with the burden of delayed gratification.

Four questions for fortitude in counsel are:

Will it last?
Did I count the cost?
Will I be rewarded?
Can I be cheerful?

Temperance

Friends are valued for their perspective on life even when we have lost our own perspective. They teach us how to preserve mature values under difficult conditions. This ability to be "even-tempered" is attained through inner discipline that is based on awareness of self, confident display of feelings, accurate assessments of who we are in the presence of others, and recognition of limitations as we move toward desired goals.

These qualities of character are necessary for mutual assessment of present problems and their impact on us. In such discussions, friends do not become hostile with each other, because they are trying to know themselves in relation to that which is valued in both. They are seeking some adjustment, balance, ability to even the load (the function of a yoke, Matt. 11:29; Gal. 6:1–4).

Michael and I shared this understanding in our investigation of the difficulties that he faced with consistent, responsible action. He asked for some assessment of himself and I assisted him—as a friend would. How much did he need to know about himself? With such a fragmented self, could he offer as much service to others as he would like? These are questions of temperance, a particularly apt

234

term for someone who had been diagnosed as a manic depressive. Psychologically, his condition was stabilized through medication and psychotherapy. Spiritually, the answer was being sought in "chastity."

When we speak of *chastity*, we introduce the positive benefits of temperance for Christian ethics. Chastity is accepting the joy of love without insisting on reward. It is a balance of self-respect and self-giving. This temperate love guided many of the questions that Michael and I debated. Would Michael respect the woman who was his therapist without seeking to exploit her sexually? Would he deny himself an attempt to seek a sexual reward for his emotional openness with her? What about his relationships with his parents? Would he care for them without requiring that they treat him as a very adequate person who did not suffer from the limitations of occasional manic flights into grandiose fantasy? And what about his love for himself? Could he recognize the loyalty, devotion, and sensitivity for others that was basic in himself without insisting that this lead immediately to the same psychological adequacy to be found in people who take no medication?

The steadfastness of chastity leads to *continence*. For Michael, this virtue was a sure sense of touch, the ability to be comfortable with what he knew about himself and others. It was his desired ability to identify what he felt without becoming overbalanced with grandiosity or depression. It was the ability to express his love for others in ways that would benefit them as well as him. In a sense, our conversation was a continual answer to the question: How do I see myself in relationships? In Michael's case my answer was: Seeking humility. I saw a continual desire to advance qualities in self that would portray something greater than self. The question was, could this be balanced with his urge toward grandiosity? To answer that question we first had to look with acceptance at his ideal self-image. Why did he think so highly of himself at certain times and so little at other times? What was beneficial about the urge toward grandiosity and how could it be reshaped in submission to God? Could he be temperate with self-image and his urge toward grandiosity?

Here we face one of the central issues in Christian counsel: Can we humble ourselves before God? Michael raised this issue several times as he told of his struggle to deal with the anger of being less than God. This is the great test of humility.

At the same time, submission to God is the sign of a move toward a stronger image of the self which is both realistic and goal-oriented. It is a feeling that we are adequate enough in God's sight to accept challenges by competitors or circumstances as well as to face some bold self-examination in our own private moments.

Friends who are dedicated to purposes beyond themselves are models for humility. Charles Darwin wrote in his autobiography that whenever a new observation or thought was published or spoken in opposition to his general results he immediately made a memorandum of it. He found by experience that he tended to forget that which was unfavorable to his own theories unless he immediately wrote down the observation. He asserted that owing to this habit, few objections to his views were raised that he had not already noticed and at least had attempted to answer.[5]

As we think about the way temperance operates in Christian counsel, we can easily see that it is associated with all of the other virtues. This will come out in the questions that we can ask about temperance:

What is in this situation for me?
Should my feelings show?
Can I see myself in action?
How do I use my strength, now and later?

Faith

Faith, hope, and love shape character in the image of Christ. These are the theological virtues, the preeminent characteristics of Christ that are channels of spiritual grace. When these virtues infuse prudence, justice, courage, temperance, then the human desire for that which is good is met with the incarnate power of God.

These are the qualities appreciated by the disciples as they saw the Lord lay down his life for his friends: "He had always loved them in the world who were his own, and he loved them to the end" (John 13:1). By his example, faith becomes the first of the theological virtues. It is a confident reliance upon God that fulfills our search

236

for self-identity and increases our openness to the type of relationships Jesus had with others.

Faith is the link between the revelation of God's love and our memory of loyal incidents in our own life (Heb. 10:32). The search for tested experiences is to be conducted within the fellowship of the church and in light of the history of those who have been saints. The Letter to the Hebrews urges courage today because of the history of those who have had courage before us and now are witnesses to our own faith (Heb. 11–12).

How do we see faith in our self-concept and relation with others? The counselor for Quin (chap. 10) was seeking faith in the testing of Quin's experiences with her husband. What could Quin reliably expect of her husband? What were her memories of the way in which she had acted in the past or during a trial and how would she act in the present?

To establish Quin's faith, the counselor opened the faithful record of biblical experience. She presented the conversation of Jesus with Nicodemus as a witness to faith and a tested experience from which we may learn. Quin was willing to make some comparisons between Nicodemus's experience with Jesus and her experience with her husband. But a week later, in the next exercise on a comparison with Jesus and the woman at the well, Quin rebelled. She was not looking for faith as the memory of tested experiences in which there was loyalty to that which is good, despite opposition. She retreated from godly reflection and took refuge in unreflective reassurance, apparently substituting submission to her husband for faith in God.

Quin probably made this compromise because she had no experience with faithful people. Faithful persons are the prototypes of faith, the guide to that by which we obtain assurance of God's support in our search for self-identity and commitment to godly purposes. The purpose of these witnesses is to show us how God works in human life. If we can understand the way in which his power is demonstrated in the problems and weaknesses, solutions and strengths of others, then we can have assurance of his work through the same channels of our own lives.

Christian counsel is this kind of faithful exercise. It is an examination of the trust and distrust we have developed in the past on the basis of relationships with others or circumstances of life.[6] It is a study of the questions: Why do I react to one person or experience in one way and not in another way? Do the choices that I make indicate that I have trusted in God or in myself or something else? What kind of evidence do I have from my relationship and circumstances that God is working in my decisions and in the integrity of my own existence?

We reflect upon our trust in God's involvement in our lives by asking several questions of faith:

What are my memories about conflicts from the past?
Who and what can I rely on from previous relationships?
How has God worked in my life up until now?

Hope

Hope is giving love time to take root, a confidence that the faithful lives of others might also be attained through our own lives. A hopeful person is passionately committed to that which is possible because of gratitude for what God has already done for us in Christ and those who are faithful to him.

Hope is built on faith. We begin by looking for the signs of hope in the past. What has happened in our lives that would give us a realistic confidence that God has always been coming toward us from the future? We then can ask realistically about our future. How have our intentions been met up until now and what hope is there of attaining them in the future?

Hope that is based upon tested possibilities from the past and the present will give us some clues as to the direction of our growth in the future. Will we continue to make the kinds of choices and respond in the same ways as we have until now, or will we seek some other direction, some different perspective and goal in life? Whether we seek to do the same or differently, what is the power that will sustain us?

Helen (chap. 10) is in need of this kind of hope. She needs to assess the direction of her thoughts and the possibility that relationships with her husband might be on a better basis than they have in the past.

But although Helen claims that she can always look into the future and discern the thoughts of her husband, she will not practice the virtue of hope as a faithful study of the past and a confident belief in a changing future. Instead, she adopts a hopeless attitude saying, "I cannot take any more of this." She has decided that her life is to be one of suffering. She must accept punishment for her sins. Nothing can change. This is "God's will," she says.

The pastor tries to confront this fatalism with a reinterpretation of those events in her life that Helen has decided are a punishment, such as her assertion that the conception of a child is a sign of God's cruelty. But she will not admit the possibility of any change in her opinions.

In defending herself against change, Helen adopts a curious but common interpretation of the "plan of God." She uses this phrase as divine sanction for being both passive and resentful. Nothing is going to happen in her life because God has already ordained the suffering that will be her lot in this life. If the pastor were to suggest any plan for change, Helen would immediately counter this with the assertion that God alone can direct her life. She already "knows" what his plan is and there can be no change.[7]

Such an attitude is the contraindication for faith and hope. A claim to know the "plan of God" is often used by insecure people to justify their caution and to maintain a closed future.

In contradiction to Helen's opinions, the biblical evidence for hope is active rather than passive. The first chapter of Ephesians, in which the plan of God is actually explained, refers to the faithful commitment of Father, Son, and Holy Spirit to bring unmistakable signs of God's salvation to earth through the Incarnation. This projection of divine plan into human life is to result in activity by human beings toward God and one another. Just as God through his action is breaking down barriers between himself and his creatures, so those who respond to his action are to break down barriers between themselves and other people (Eph. 2:11–22).

We can stimulate the movement of gratitude for God's actions toward the possibility of actions on our own through such hopeful questions as the following:

What can I realistically expect from my future?
What obstacles do I face in relationships?
Why do I persist in maintaining the relationships?
How can I work to make things better?
Do I see any plan of God for my life?

Love

Love is the power for change from restrictive to redemptive friendship. Love begins this work in the passionate, exclusive investment of ourselves in another. We live in and for the friend. It is love for our sake.

The possessive phase of friendship is a necessary risk, which we accept in counsel. There is a need for reaching out to another, talking with trust that hasn't been found in many others, guarding confessions from curiosity seekers. It is a time of schooling for change in a very small classroom.

Too intense a focus in counsel may encourage narcissism, dependency, elitism. That's the risk of an intimate relationship.

The prophylaxis for possessiveness is faith and hope. Faith is the link between our values (or idealizations) and the reality of individual differences and changing circumstances. It is reality-control over the continual projection of our sentiments into another. In what ways is the friend like us and how is he or she different? Faithful counsel might contain the sentiments of Bishop Ridding's prayer.

> Give us true knowledge of our [friends] in their differences from us and in their likenesses to us, that we may deal with their real selves, measuring their feelings by our own, but patiently considering their varied lives and thoughts and circumstances; and in all our relations to them, from false judgments of our own, from misplaced trust and distrust, from misplaced giving and refusing, from misplaced praise and rebuke, save us and help us, we humbly beseech thee, O Lord.[8]

We also need some prayers of hope, lest reality shatter a wounded soul and justify the "sickness unto death" which Søren Kierkegaard described as despair in our attempts to be a self.[9] Friendship that lives on faith alone is vulnerable to cynicism and the mood swings of sentimentality and recrimination. Hope is fervent belief that values are attainable in ourselves and in relationships despite a realistic testing of our strengths and limitations.

Hope turns the worst we can think of into the best that God can provide under the circumstances. The apostle Paul describes these circumstances as "the evil things we did and thought" (Col. 1:21).

240

The circumstances were overcome through the sacrificial death of God's Son. "By means of the physical death of his Son, God has made you his friends . . ." (Col. 1:22). Then Paul adds:

> You must, of course, continue faithful on a firm and sure foundation, and must not allow yourselves to be shaken from the hope you gained when you heard the gospel. (1:23)

Should we hope to love others at the same time that we love ourselves? The answer of friendship begins in the love of God. It is through God as Creator and Redeemer that we learn that we are made for each other and not just for ourselves. To live for others is to fulfill our original purpose and to find the satisfaction of a purpose in life that increases our communion with God.[10]

To find satisfaction and joy with ourselves in this harmony of relationships is to find such gratitude that we overcome the cost. We do not ignore the cost, for we must come to some acceptance of ourselves as having been created with limitations as human beings. Our idealized images of self and world must be reduced to a realistic acceptance of our limited capacities as creatures who will do the will of God on earth and as servants of God who will not be exceptions to the ravages of natural evil.[11]

Some of our questions to enhance realistic love of self and neighbor are:

Do I know my real needs and those of my neighbor?
What resources in myself are appropriate to meet the needs of my neighbor without reducing my own self-concept?
How may I help my neighbor without making my neighbor seem smaller than myself?
Does gratitude for God's love in others allow me to give without grudging, or inducing guilt?
What purposes of life are fulfilled despite frustration?

An Appropriate Word in Season

As we discuss examples of a specific virtue in any of the persons who were chosen for study, it might seem artificial to pick one virtue that was dominant in the life of an individual. Certainly we could find more than one aspect of Christian character in these people! And do we not need all of these virtues plus others to portray the full life of Christ in our own? The answer is yes, but with a knowledge of our own limits in communication as counselors. Our combining of a proclamation with healing is not meant to be a full course in Christian personal ethics. Our purpose is to discuss one or more of these signposts that point us toward a manifestation of the Incarnation in our own lives. If we treated these virtues as an end in themselves we would be reduced to legalism.

We can avoid legalism and rigorism by remaining faithful to the biblical spirit of growth in grace and the knowledge of our Lord Jesus Christ. The Christ toward whom we move is complete but we are incomplete. Step by step we seek to become more complete or perfect (Eph. 3; Phil. 3).

If we see the progress of faith as God has designed it for our lives, we will look for the most appropriate virtue that is called for at some crucial time in the life of an individual. In this way we will be saved from some mechanical recitation of all seven of the virtues in relation to every counseling emergency.

If we listen sensitively to the issues that people present to us, we will usually find that they need strengthening in some particular area of life that is closely related to an element of Christian character that we have just discussed. Or at least it seems this way from the cases that I have presented. When we examine each of these cases in turn, we find that there was some threat of failure in each one. This was the reason counsel was sought and this was the guideline that should be emphasized. Sometimes this is immediately known, as in the furious debates of Robert and Linda that pointed swiftly toward some need to understand justice. Or it might come more quietly in a series of interviews, as when Michael gradually understood that his greatest need was for temperance.

The threat of failure may come through a sudden crisis or it may come over a period of time as a person moves through this world from one crucial stage of development to another. All of the virtues would be important at any stage, but we usually find that there are questions at each stage that call for emphasis on the appropriate virtue necessary to continual growth and stability. I would like to use the descriptions of life-stages by Daniel Levinson as a way to illustrate the appropriateness of the different moral and spiritual questions at particular times in life.[12]

The Communication of Virtue

Moral Stages of Adult Life

Age	Psychological Stage	Cardinal and Theological Virtues
17–22	Early adult transition Task: exploration and initiation	Fortitude
23–28	Entering the adult world Task: first choices and commitments	Fidelity
28–33	Age thirty transition Questions: What have I done? What do I want to do?	Love
33–40	Settling down period Task: build on a few key choices, become one's own person	Prudence, faith, hope
40–45	Midlife transition Task: individuation and balance of priorities	Temperance, forgiveness, humility
45–50	Entering middle adulthood Task: building structure around forces that have meaning	Justice, charity
50–60	Later adulthood Task: maturity of judgment, self-awareness, magnanimity, integrated structure, breadth of perspective	Wisdom

1. Kirk, K. E., *Principles of Moral Theology*, pp. 41ff.; Carl Henry, *Christian Personal Ethics*, chap. 21, "The Distinctive New Testament Virtues." For a summary of cardinal virtues, see Joseph Peiper, *The Four Cardinal Virtues* (New York: Harcourt, Brace and World, 1965).

2. Dietrich Bonhoeffer, *Ethics* (New York: Macmillan, 1965), p. 264.

3. The general goal of all virtues would be "maturity in Christ." The criteria of maturity is a subject of much debate. In the early days of the pastoral psychology movement, self-actualization as defined by Abraham Maslow and others was considered to be maturity. Some wise distinctions concerning the matureness of religion were presented by Gordon Allport, *The Individual and His Religion* (New York: Macmillan Co., 1950), esp. p. 57. Unfortunately, these definitions tended to equate dependent behavior with immaturity. This has continued in articles such as those of Joseph Burke, "Mature Religious Behavior: A Psychological Perspective and Its Implications," *Journal of Religion and Health* 17:3 (1978) 181–82.

   The early movement in pastoral psychology also concentrated upon effectiveness rather than upon ethics as a measure of mature communication. Through the triad of unconditional regard, empathy, and congruence, the psychological researchers on effectiveness were quite explicit in their approach. Gerard Egan discussed genuineness "not as a moral or a metaphysical quality or property but as a set of counselor behaviors essential to a high-level helping process." (Gerard Egan, *The Skilled Helper* [Monterey, California: Brooks/Cole, 1975], p. 90).

   Alistair Campbell found this effectiveness orientation to be a characteristic of one of the leading theoreticians in pastoral counseling, Seward Hiltner. Above all else, Hiltner was concerned about competence. His dominant concern was the way in which a counselor communicated and the relationship between various roles that lent authority to the communication. In a search for "basic principles of shepherding," Hiltner lost sight of the Shepherd Himself. Alistair Campbell, *Rediscovering Pastoral Care* (London: Darton, Longmann and Todd, 1981), pp. 32–33.

   Is there a definition of maturity that can be made operational in Christian counsel? The material in this chapter on virtues is basic to such a definition, but incomplete. The necessity of such a definition arises out of the shift in Christian counsel toward theology, which implies some standard, some godly goals and expectations. It was faced in clinical practice by two psychiatrists who have developed "healing of the unaffirmed." Drs. Baars and Terruwe wrote: "As psychiatrists and as Christians . . . we want to go beyond solely utilitarian criteria of vocational performance or adjustment in business or profession, and assist our patients in attaining a level of happiness commensurate with their innate capacities and potentials."

   Then they offer a definition of maturing: "A greater sensitivity for a keener intellectual appreciation of what is true, good, and beautiful; a greater capacity to love and enjoy; a lesser emphasis on utilitarian pursuits with a decided tempering of the utilitarian emotions (fear, courage, hope, anger, despair); and a greater harmony of interaction between sensory and intellectual life." Conrad Baars and Anna Terruwe, *Healing the Unaffirmed: Recognizing Deprivation Neurosis* (New York: Alba House, 1976).

4. Ivan Boszormenyi-Nagy and Geraldine Spark, *Invisible Loyalties: Reciprocities in Intergenerational Family Therapy* (Hagerstown: Harper and Row, 1973). See also the favorable review in *Contemporary Psychology*, 20 (1975) 322. Ivan Boszormenyi-Nagy and Geraldine Spark consider these memories to be the burden of justice and injustice that are basic to the deepest interpersonal conflicts of individuals. For a theoretical presentation of this problem, see Paul Tillich, *Love, Power and Justice* (New York: Oxford University Press, 1954).

5. Charles Darwin, *Autobiography and Selected Letters* (New York: Dover, 1958).

6. Trust and distrust were the foundational issues of Erik Erikson's theory of integrity development: *Insight and Responsibility* (New York: W. W. Norton, 1964).

7. The tenacious defenses of people like Helen will make more sense if one reads David Shapiro's *Neurotic Styles* (New York: Basic Books).

8. The Southwell Litany for the Personal Life (Forward Movement Publications, 412 Sycamore St., Cincinnati, Ohio, n.d.).

9. Søren Kierkegaard, *The Sickness unto Death* tr. Walter Launie (Princeton: Princeton University Press, 1948).

10. Jonathan Edwards presented love for others and love for God as part of the original reality of human life. Therefore, to find ourselves in others is also to find ourselves as happy people under God's direction. Contrawise, those who dwell in selfishness are miserable because they do not love themselves enough. They do not realize that love is a way to personal welfare and happiness. Floyd Holbrook, *The Ethics of Jonathan Edwards* (Ann Arbor, MI: University of Michigan Press, 1973), p. 56.

11. Freud did not accept the possibility of any limitations in the Christian view of love. He therefore discounted the realistic basis of Christian teaching because he thought that it overlooked the hostility that the neighbor and the stranger have toward someone who is trying to love all persons with equal affection. The New Testament scholar Victor Furnish has argued that Freud did not see the realism and limitation of Christian neighbor-love. We are *not* to have the same deep affection for everyone. Rather we are to extend positive helpfulness to all people and to take our neighbor's needs and claims as seriously as our own. Victor Furnish, "Neighbor Love in the New Testament," *Journal of Religious Studies* 10 (1982): 327–29. Some of the same acceptance of limitations is seen in Emil Brunner's "Orders," in which there is an intimate expression of love within the family that would not be expected in the community of labor or in the state. Emil Brunner, *The Divine Imperative* (Philadelphia: Westminster Press, 1947).

12. *Seasons of a Man's Life* (New York: Alfred A. Knopf, 1978). See also James W.

Fowler, *Stages of Faith* (San Francisco: Harper and Row, 1981); George Vaillant, *Adaptation to Life* (Boston: Little, Brown and Co., 1977); Gail Sheehy, *Passages* (New York: E. P. Dutton and Co., 1974).

Donald Capps has correlated Erik Erikson's life-cycle stages with the deadly sins (p. 24) and the saving virtues (p. 78). Capps, *Deadly Sins and Saving Virtues* (Philadelphia: Fortress Press, 1987).

15

The Blessing of a Wise Balance

Wisdom is a balancing of the ethical ledgers of life. It is a satisfactory adjustment between two questions: What does life owe me? and What do I owe life?

Friendship makes the balancing worthwhile. Intimate, reliable companions are not only a reward for wise interpersonal decisions, they are also sources of incentives to keep trying, to mature in the face of defeat and deceits.

But no friend can completely balance the ledger for us. Always there is doubt, fear, injustice, and hypocrisy to unbalance either question:

What does life owe me?
What do I owe life?

The realism of wisdom always brings up a final question:

When is the account settled?

The final question can only be answered by a power beyond friendship. It is found in worship and prayer.

THEOLOGY AND THERAPY

What Does Life Owe Me?

But we may be deceived if the final question obliterates the first. Unless we can admit what we require—and have or have not received—we may settle for counterfeit worship.

Counterfeit worship is the substitution of a false answer to our real question: What does life owe me? But the substitution will not be satisfying unless we conceal our real needs. Why? Because the false answer does not show us how we hurt, or where we feel deprived, or challenge the validity of our perceived needs. It is false because it satisfies our fantasies and obscures our limitations. We are deceived with such thoughts as: I don't really need friends. I never need to share with anyone, anyway. I'm sufficient in myself.

Such were the thoughts that confronted "Naomi," a lonely grade-school girl who was comforted by "Friend." He (it?) appeared to her in the image of a long-dead grandfather that she had never known in the real world.

The Substitute "Friend"

The desperation of life without friends was dramatized for Donna and me in the video review of a thirty-six-hour exorcism of "Naomi" in 1985. Before the viewing, Naomi's psychiatrist provided this background. A year before the exorcism she had told her psychiatrist that life had been unbearably lonely as a child. At age six, she found a companion in the real/unreal appearance of an elderly gentleman who identified himself as her grandfather. She knew he was physically dead, but psychologically he was alive in her mind. It was a shadowy form who sometimes was only identified by his words, "I am your friend." This was her only intimate associate in childhood and adolescence.[1]

Naomi married in her twenties, had a good job, and then bore two children. Life seemed good for her family in a church where they were leaders. But for reasons that she could not explain, she and her husband drew apart and were divorced. She became depressed, vindictive, and lethargic. By age thirty she had been in and out of several psychiatric facilities. Finally she accepted the invitation of a psychiatrist to talk about her feelings. In counseling sessions before this, she would vent anger on him for several minutes and then

248

spend the rest of the session with her back to him, eyes and ears covered with her hands.

Naomi admitted that she felt compelled to kill herself. When pressed for reasons, she replied: "My grandfather appeared to me in the old family barn and told me the date when I must kill myself as he did."

"But you said no one ever told you how your grandfather died."

"No one ever did. He also told me the date he did it. I've never asked about the date and never been to his grave."

"Let's go to that barn and see what the old boy will tell me—if he appears."

Naomi, her psychiatrist, and a social worker drove out into the country to an abandoned barn. Nothing happened—until the psychiatrist, who didn't consider himself to be very religious, decided to "stir something up" by offering to pray for guidance, since he admitted that he was sensing something for which his professional training had not prepared him. Naomi's face underwent a change to sheer hatred, an alien presence seemed to stare from her eyes and she sought to kill both the psychiatrist and the social worker. After a lengthy struggle, the three agreed that they were experiencing something evil beyond themselves. An exorcism was agreed upon.

A psychiatric team, which included an Episcopal priest, began to meet with Naomi so that they would all be friends at the time of the exorcism. During these weeks of meeting, the grandfather appeared again to Naomi. But on this occasion he separated into two figures, one of which appeared as the grandfather and the other as Friend. Naomi explained later that Friend was her childhood playmate, the "person" who appeared to her as an answer to her ever-growing loneliness.

This was the background for the exorcism. We watched six hours of excerpts from the videotapes of the exorcism in the presence of Naomi, her psychiatrist, and other members of the team. The exorcism began with the Eucharist. Then Naomi tried to get away. After several hours of physical struggle, she agreed with the psychiatrist that this was a diversion that kept Friend from being manifest. When the tape was stopped at this point, Naomi said that this was the time when she first had doubts about Friend's power, for he had promised her that she would have superhuman strength.

When Naomi was willing to stop her physical struggling, members of the group began to confess that they had become fragmented. They needed to seek power from God to continue their attempts to dispel something evil that had supernatural strength.

Then the videotape came to a dramatic moment. A second psychiatrist on the team said: "Naomi, you must release Friend yourself. To dramatize it, I suggest the team should stand back from the bed [on which Naomi was sitting]." Each of the team members stepped back after telling Naomi that they wished to be her friend, but that she would have to renounce Friend and come to them. After an agonizing inner struggle, Naomi replied to the prayers offered by the group: "I denounce Satan." Then she went to each member of the group in turn and earnestly said, "I pray in the name of Jesus Christ that I renounce my demon Friend and send him away."

The tape stopped at this point, and the team and Naomi talked about the after-care. They said that psychotherapy continued for several months after the exorcism, but with two differences. First, Naomi said she felt that she had a purpose in life which was to tell others of the way in which she had been gripped by evil forces. Friend, masquerading as grandfather, was her answer to the loneliness in childhood. He (it) also strengthened her tendency to project self-rejection upon others. With this awareness of her opening to evil, Naomi felt that she could speak to others about the need for exorcism in similar cases.

Second, Naomi said she became active in a church several members of the therapeutic team attended: "This is one place where I can come back Sunday by Sunday and find some acceptance and understanding, no matter what I may have thought and done during the week."

Team members nodded, said the exorcism had been worth the effort, but they couldn't take another weekend like that! So what were the benefits to them, I asked. One replied: "This has been a window for me into a world of good and evil that I had not really understood in previous experiences as a therapist."

What Do We "Discern"?

Donna and I admired the courage of this team to enter an area of therapy for which few are prepared—the identification and expulsion of radical evil from a suffering person. It is a necessary work of wisdom, but it certainly complicates our definition of reality. Did the evil "Friend" come from Naomi's unconscious? Did he personify the deceptive substitutes for friendship that we find in our society? Or was this a part of some force beyond human control that could only be overcome with divine aid?

Theologically, good and/or evil could come from any or all of the three sources just mentioned.

Let's look at the biblical evidence and ask: Could any or all of these sources be identified in some way today in therapy and exorcism as in Naomi's case?

In both the Old and New Testaments, the "heart" is considered to be the source of "good treasure" or evil motivation (Matt. 5:26; 6:21; 9:4; 12:34–35; 13:15; 15:18–19; 22:37). Thus, to make a modern application, the psychiatrist would be correct in holding Naomi responsible for the presence of evil within her, for the evil may have begun in her own thoughts and later become reinforced by an external evil presence. The root of *personal evil* is a distortion of natural desire in which human emotions are no longer used for the primary purpose of fellowship with God and others, but rather for our own glorification and satisfaction. This is the "human desire" that is most often referred to as a source of temptation in Scripture (James 1:13–14; Matt. 5:28; 5:21–24; 15:15–20; 18:5–9; 19:16–30; 21:33–46; 23:25–26; 7:16–21; 12:33–35).

However, neither the psychiatrist nor the biblical writers considered temptations to sin to come from human desires because the desires were evil in themselves. The New Testament distinguishes between the natural longings of a human being and the anxious self-seeking that leads to sin.[2] The former "longings" are acknowledged by Jesus and by Paul (Luke 22:15; Phil. 1:23–24). They express our need for human affection, companionship, creativity, accomplishment. There are also very basic needs, as for food and shelter, which the heavenly Father knows that we need (Matt. 6:32). Another basic need is sex, which Paul expressly commands a husband and wife not to neglect in marriage (1 Cor. 7:5).

"*Natural evil*" is natural human needs gone astray, as in adulterous lust (Matt. 5:28) or desire for material possessions above all other things (Mark 4:19). Then a God-given need is subverted by self-seeking anxiety. Reinhold Niebuhr uses this inordinate anxiety as the perverse force that pushes us to be more than human or less than human. His principle argument is found in volume 1 of *Nature and*

Destiny of Man. It is a reassurance that humanity within our natural limitations is not sin, but fulfillment of our purpose as servants of God. The constant danger to our humanity is similar to the dread and fear of authentic selfhood as described by Søren Kierkegaard.

The decision to pursue authentic selfhood does not occur in a social vacuum (although Naomi seemed to be in one as a child). Individual anxiety, dread, and fear are reinforced by the "cares of the world" (Luke 8:14) or by "principalities and powers" (Rom. 8:38; 1 Cor. 15:24; Eph. 1:21; 3:10; 6:12; Col. 1:16; 2:10; 15).[3] In biblical metaphors, personal and *social* forces toward *evil* are often connected when "lusts of the heart" (Rom. 1:24) create an unbalanced condition in which the individual is susceptible to the "desires of the world" (1 John 2:15-17) which then rule unchecked in the personality. The result is referred to as a "reign of wickedness" (Rom. 6:12-13).

Who "reigns"? The answer may be an internal desire that rises up above others (greed, sensuality, pride) or a combination of social and personal twisting of our original purposes in life. Or, in a few biblical references, there is a *supernatural* force of *evil* that may distort the structures of society and/or gratify human desire through something less than the power of God (as in the temptation of Jesus by Satan as recorded in Matt. 4).

Satan "reigns" as the organizing center of demonic powers which promise a person dominion over others.[4] The dominion begins when one part of the self rises up and dominates the rest of the self (John 12:31; 1 John 5:19; Eph. 2:2; Rom. 1:24-32; 1 Cor. 7:5-7). Then there is an opportunity for superhuman evil to "enter" (Matt. 12:45).

From the few scriptural references to the demonic we cannot deduce very much about the way that superhuman evil enters the life of a person, but in the modern case of Naomi there was a discernible time when she began to feel that a power beyond herself was the only answer to her loneliness. As she looked back upon the situation, she felt that she would have died of loneliness without her mysterious comforter. He provided the power to go on living that she did not have in herself. Ironically, by age thirty she was willing to admit that this power had drained her of humanity.

What twists or drains our power for authentic humanity? Any one of the three identifications of evil may betray a friendless person. The challenge of the therapist as friend is to remain faithful despite the confusion of identifying evil and despite the deviousness and depth of this menacing mystery. The maintenance of open and realistic communication under these circumstances may be the ultimate test of friendship, for it will be sacrificial. Sometimes in this hazardous journey with another we must ask: Is it worth the risk? This is the time to ask if a Power beyond ourselves is going to uphold us when we are at the point of rejecting another. With our friend, we must join in worship of a God who knows our weakness and restores our relationships.

Our prayers are for authenticity in a time when we are tempted with deception, for openness when secrecy seems the answer to self-protection, for commitment when isolation would cover a hidden hurt, for reaching out when the spiral of introspection becomes a maelstrom. These were the kinds of prayers that were prayed by the mental health team that worked with Naomi. The prayers were answered: Friend was openly identified by Naomi as an alien force in her and she "renounced" him. Then one of the psychiatrists asked,

"Friend," why did you finally decide to let go of Naomi? You knew we were making mistakes, and you'd been with her for years.

Naomi's face looked like a death mask. (Watching the tape, Naomi gripped the psychiatrist's arm and whispered: "That's him! I see him in my eyes. God! How he drained life out of me.") A hoarse voice spoke from Naomi:

Why should I keep on? We've got plenty more. We get all we want from those that the church rejects.

What Do I Owe Life?

After the deliverance, Naomi joined the church of several team members. She gave us this explanation:

I wanted to be in a place where I was accepted and I wanted to help others who were all bound up as I was.

The friendship is redemptive when both acceptance and service are essential. On one hand, Naomi's need to be accepted did not effect change in her until the team backed off in the exorcism and challenged her to give up a demonic substitute for their affection. Sacrifice and movement toward others were essential.

On another hand, Naomi felt a rush of gratitude for new life after the exorcism. Her friends had helped her toward realistic ways of thinking about her needs in life, and she wanted to encourage others to find love through honest companionship instead of secrecy and self-hate. Now she would be valuable to others in trouble because she had learned how to value herself through friends.

Naomi wanted to be a redemptive friend, and in our last report from her psychiatrist, she had spent two years as a resource to people in several states who wanted to know if they could be delivered from a demonic presence. Usually the consultations were by phone, first with a person's therapist and then with the person who needed encouragement. One of the strong points of the conversations was Naomi's statement that she was continuing in therapy. She was not abandoned after exorcism. The friends made on a mental health team before deliverance were still being active in the long-term reparative work that followed the exorcism.

Without guidance and encouragement toward mature thought, Naomi could have slipped back into the sick ways that preceded the deliverance, in spite of her well-intentioned actions. Her psychiatrist remarked about this after we saw the exorcism video. Naomi had just said that the church was essential to her, but that she had to learn a hard lesson. Some of the members wanted nothing to do with her. Could she continue to be relaxed and outgoing in a fellowship where acceptance was not assured with everyone? "Good question!" said her psychiatrist. "That's a hazard for you. You can think of more reasons for rejecting people than anyone I ever met. So let's be sure you're reading the people right—which in some cases you are."

Friendship in counsel and in church offers both guidance and incentive to ways of thinking and acting that combine gratitude and grace—gratitude for the healthy and righteous way that deep personal needs are met, and grace to show others the way to health and righteousness.

Guidelines for Maturity

Friends provide the context for faith as well as hope to share the outpouring of God's love into our lives. Friends are faithful in asking about and accepting our dreams and disappointments, satisfactions and deprivations. This is the "reality testing" aspect of friendship that is an antidote to the self-deception and distortion of the past that could poison our spiritual growth.

Friends are hopeful in the presentation of ways by which we can serve with grace and prudence. Then we are capable of practicing the unassuming love that Paul describes in 1 Corinthians 13. Without this hope in relationship, we fall prey to secrecy and isolation, the deadly foes of Christian discipleship.

Faith and hope give direction and stability to the "higher gift," love (1 Cor. 12:31; 13:13). Now, we know that this gift is the sign of spiritual maturity within us, but how can we identify it in ourselves and others? This is a central function of faithful and hopeful friends.

Spiritually maturing persons are in love with other people, just as God is in love with them and they are in love with God (1 Cor. 12:31–13:13). This love gives power to discerning persons as they move through personal fantasies and cultural deception toward the truth of Christ.

By contrast, unloving "discernment" is characterized by fascination with and fear of evil. Much of this evil must be in the self, for whenever obsessed persons are challenged about their morbid thoughts and projection of hate upon others, they turn on the questioner with hate and denounce all those who disagree.

Persons of spiritual maturity expect the power to come from God rather than from themselves. Their discernment is a humble alertness to the way in which the power of God wars against the power of evil in themselves and in others. They seek no credit for their own methods of discernment, the quality of cures, or the recognition that they receive (1 Cor. 13:4).

By contrast, persons who feel powerless are intoxicated with the appearance of power through momentary "signs and wonders" (1 Cor. 13:1–3). This instant reassurance not only mitigates the terror of an unfulfilled self, it also gratifies desires to cast out all those who lack this special display of power (e.g., "You would be cured—or cure others—if only you had faith.").

Spiritually discerning persons are not only aware that power comes from beyond themselves, but also that they have no power to decide what God is going to do in the life of another person (John 3:8). They do not "lord it over" others with specific pronouncements about the path toward God that another person must take (1 Pet. 5:3). If they have a gift of prophecy, they share insight for mutual appraisal without domination.

By contrast, power-hungry persons inappropriately pass judgment on others and seek control. Like the leaders of the Corinthian church, these people assume that they have a superior, special gift of knowledge above others (1 Cor. 2). But in the opinion of the apostle Paul, they need a reminder about spiritual gifts (1 Cor. 12:1). Since they probably attempted to tell the apostle Paul how he was to direct his life, the apostle answers forthrightly, "It is a very small thing that I should be judged of you, or any man's judgment" (1 Cor. 4:3). He waits only for the judgment of God, who alone will make manifest the counsel of the heart (v. 5).

Spiritual persons know the relationship between our human capacity and the spiritual power that can work in us, either for good or evil. They identify with the strengths and weaknesses of other persons, without praise or rebuke (Gal. 6:1–3). They recognize that all persons are tempted and that each of us is to identify with the temptations of others, just as Jesus did (Heb. 4:15). They do not think it is a sin to be human.

In contrast, persons who do not know or admit their natural longings reject in their bodies the desires that God has placed in all of us. It was necessary for Paul to write to the spiritually repressed Corinthians that a husband and wife must practice sexual intercourse, except when they agree together to abstain for a period of time. To reject this is to give an occasion for Satan to tempt them for their "incontinency" (1 Cor. 7:5).

Spiritually mature persons are not only aware of the work of the Spirit in their lives, but they are aware of a Christian flow of history by which they may validate their own experience. As the apostle Paul wrote to the excitable Corinthians, he was determined to know one thing among them, which was Jesus Christ and his crucifixion (1 Cor. 2:2). All spiritual experiences were to be measured by the character of Christ. The explicit measurement is presented in 1 Corinthians 13.

By contrast, spiritually isolated persons are intoxicated with their own message and seek no approval from the body of Christ. Their feelings take precedence over apostolic faith (although some confuse the distinctions by asserting that *they* are apostles). "Superior" intuition substitutes for awareness of their feelings about others and the feelings of others about them. The apostle Paul used a stern warning against those who do not "recognize the meaning of the Lord's body" when they drink the cup of the new covenant, for they think only of their own appetites and disregard the needs of others (1 Cor. 11:26–34). The warning of the apostle is still applicable to the painful pretensions and socially inept perceptions of many co-dependent people. Their own history of isolation has made them so afraid of interpersonal relations that they cannot relate to a faith that is built upon the continuity of disciplined relationships.

Spiritually sensitive persons are aware of the uniqueness of God's movement in each person. They pay attention to personal characteristics and varied circumstances. Ambiguity and mystery are accepted and appreciated.

In contrast, imprudent (unrealistic) converts are not "apt teachers." They present their own mountaintop experiences with God as the answer for everyone and fail to recognize that God speaks in a unique way to each person.

The spiritually mature are growing persons, and their growth is within a Christian fellowship. The direction of the growth both in themselves and in those around them is steadily in the direction of compassion, patience, and courage.

By contrast, those who are spiritually stunted know all things and have no need to be taught of anyone (1 Cor. 4:8–21). They are often in power conflicts with those who do not accept their judgments and consequently are isolated from most believers in Christ.

The spiritually mature welcome correction and seek instruction (Pss. 1:2, 12–13; 3:12–16). There is a spirit of graciousness in their ability to learn from others (Phil. 1:15–17).

In contrast, the spiritually insecure are moved only, as they think, by God himself and then only when he shows them some "sign." They will not change their opinion unless they receive some special warning from God or the Devil, and the warning must come on their terms. Our Lord continually warned against seeking after such signs (Matt. 12:38–42; Mark 13:4, 21ff; Luke 17:20–21).

The spiritually discerning look for the gifts of the Spirit. What attitudes and actions follow from the work of the Holy Spirit—or the evil one? Whenever someone asks about the presence of the Spirit, the spiritually discerning will look for those personally identifiable characteristics mentioned in Gal. 5:22ff.

In contrast, those who dread authentic selfhood are fascinated with showy gifts and pay little attention to personal conduct or character. In fact, the apostle Paul had to warn the Corinthian church, which prided itself on spiritual gifts, that it tolerated gross sin in the membership and seemed unconcerned about this (1 Cor. 5:1–13).

When we look at a list of attributes such as this it is easy to think only in terms of one column or the other. However, it is more realistic to admit that many of us combine qualities from both columns. In some areas we are spiritually alert and in others we are lacking. May balance be our goal![5]

When Is the Account Settled?

Whatever lists we follow, there will be disappointment both in ourselves and in others. The ethical ledger of justice for ourselves or of grace toward others is continually going into arrears. At least that is what I was taught by a wise friend, Carlyle Marney. When he became pastor of a large church with many powerful and influential members, he told me of his prayerful admission of his own weakness:

Lord, you have called me to manage hard-headed people. Control my temper—even if I can't help but cuss at least once a week.

A year later I asked Carlyle if the prayer had been effective. "Oh yes," he replied, "although I'm already ten years overdrawn on the weekly cussing."

We're continually overdrawn on some accounting to ourself, others, or God. The wisdom literature is a continual reminder that we never catch up before death overtakes us. So what are we to do?

Allow wisdom to dwell with prudence (Prov. 8:12). Prudence is our ability to see life as it really is, and wisdom is the gracious perspective that makes sense out of the nonsense that we observe in ourselves and others. Prudence teaches us that there is never enough strength in us or in our relationships to bear all the shocks of betrayal, uncertainty, temptation, sickness, disaster, and death that we face in this life.[6] But there is an inner source of strength that keeps faith with us despite all these forces of alienation (Luke 13:1–5; 2 Cor. 11:23–29; Rom. 8). The inner strength is "blessing." This is the bestowing of God's Spirit upon us so that we will retain confidence in our integrity as his children in all circumstances of life (Rom. 8:18–39; Phil. 1:12–30). The blessing is an attitude of fellowship with God and others in our choices, rather than an isolated confidence that we can always get what we want.

This is an attitude some counselees desire, but it is difficult to teach among people who are need-oriented. Without superficial reassurance, how can we realistically accept their anxious need for "peace with God" and acceptance in a community?

Begin with the assumption that anyone's prayerful motivation may be amiss (James 4:1–3). Do we really know ourselves? All of us can become quite anxious about natural needs and allow the most troublesome ones to dominate our perception of life (Matt. 6:24–34).

We may suggest some differences between our desires and God's will. How have our deprivations shaped our demands upon God? Do we know how to identify the ways by which God will actually meet our basic needs (James 1:16–18; Matt. 7:7–11)? Warn that much of what we desire in prayer seems to be according to our own convenience (Matt. 5:23–24) and we assume that it can be achieved through the magical use of words (Matt. 6:5–8).

Will these questions only intensify introspection? In the midst of our inner journey we must move out of ourselves toward God. The greatest "blessing" is God's presence as our honest companion and realistic guide. Without this continual encouragement to see ourselves and the world in a larger and more accurate perspective, we fall prey to the deceit and secrecy that discredits instinct-oriented spirituality.

The challenge of spiritual direction is to create a prudent atmosphere in which persons may be blessed through honest knowledge of self-limitations and realistic knowledge of God. Then we pray in a relationship with God that sheds steady and confident light upon our basic needs, no matter how unfulfilled they may be. This was the discovery of William Barry at the Center of Religious Development in Cambridge. When he and colleagues began to help people pay attention to what happened to them when they prayed, he found that their desires became much clearer. One woman began this process of open prayer with a statement about her difficulty in reading the Bible. She felt that it was always an exercise in guilt, especially when she read Hosea and thought about how bad she was. As she gradually developed a more contemplative attitude in prayer she began to challenge the self-preoccupation that was evident in her assumption of "badness." Her most basic problem was an obsession with righteousness and perfection. Would she be willing to look at this need in the light of the biblical teaching concerning forgiveness?[7]

Self-preoccupation, with our own definition of "need," is challenged to a more spiritual direction by emphasis on God's knowledge of us as we really are. This is accomplished in wise counsel through contemplative prayer, a gradual awareness of our inner structure and the way in which it can make sense before God. There is an insistence upon more than disclosure of our disappointments and deficiencies. There also must be definition of our expectations and needs in the light of God's revelation concerning our individual purpose and the friendship by which we are strengthened and directed to live for his glory in this world. There is an insistence upon dedication of our desires to his will in a fellowship of faith. It is a reorientation of our private inner structure to transform our way of thinking into conformity with the mind of Christ. We enter a process of deliberately directive counsel, even though it proceeds with patience and with admonition against attempts to force the human will into any preconceived mold of spirituality.[8]

How can this directiveness be justified in a tradition of Christian counsel that depends upon acceptance of another person without coercion or manipulation? If we follow the biblical evidence about prayer, we know that anxieties must be shared, distortions must be revealed as we move toward faithful communication with our heavenly Father. The challenge for counselors is to allow godly control of our own anxieties, so we may enter with realistic and faithful persistence into the motivation of another for prayer.

The search for blessing through worship is part of the tradition of a "soul friend."[9] The emphasis is upon "in-spiriting," the ability of a person to internalize the vision of God. Our purpose as spiritual guides is not to implant our own image into an individual but to draw out the hidden parts of the self in a way that will avoid self-deception in submission to the divine will of God. It is the biblical tradition of listening and understanding with wisdom (Isa. 54). It is imparted between friends of God through prayer.

After masterful and systematic presentation of the structure of theology, in his final volume Karl Barth came to the inner meaning of spiritual wisdom.

How is it possible to have an encounter with God? I have heard his word, I wish sincerely to listen to it, and yet here I am in my insufficiency. The Reformers were not unaware of other difficulties, but they knew that such hindrances are all implicit in the following reality: I stand before God with my desires, my thoughts, my misery; I must live with him, for to live means nothing other than to live with God. Here I am, caught between the exigencies of life, both small and great, and the necessity of prayer. The Reformers tell us the first thing is to pray.[10]

NOTES

1. Is the devil an objective presence? Arguments for a positive answer are given by M. Scott Peck, M.D. in *People of the Lie* (New York: Simon and Schuster, 1983) and by Graham Twelftree, *Christ Triumphant* (London: Hodder and Stoughton, 1985). Walter Wink leans more toward a subjective answer—demonic feeling rather than objective presence—in *Unmasking the Powers* (Philadelphia: Fortress Press, 1986) and *Naming the Powers* (Philadelphia: Fortress Press, 1984).

    Demonology became prominent in Jewish writings between the times of Old and New Testament writings. The teaching was rejected by the Sadducees because they were strict followers of Torah and would not accept the newer teaching about demons and a cataclysmic ending of the world because they were not specifically identified in the Old Testament, as they read it.

2. See the discussion of *epithumia* in Gerhard Kittel, ed., *Theological Dictionary of the New Testament* (Grand Rapids: William B. Eerdmans, 1954), tr. Geoffrey Bromiley, III, 170–71.

3. See Heinrich Schlier, *Principalities and Powers in the New Testament* (Edinburgh: Nelson, 1961). Marguerita Schuster, *Power, Pathology and Paradox* (Grand Rapids: Zondervan, 1987).

4. See "Satan, Beelzebul, Devil, Exorcism" in Colin Brown, ed., *New Testament Theology* (Zondervan, 1971), vol. 3, pp. 468–77. The connection between human desire and demonically rooted evil occurs when the impulses of the heart are at the point of desertion from God. Helmut Thielicke, *Between God and Satan*, p. 17.

5. Any attempt to define maturity in spirituality is hazardous. We know that it means "to be strong in our inner selves" (Eph. 3:16), to have "the mind of Christ" (Phil. 2), to demonstrate the "fruit of the Spirit" (Gal. 5:22–26). All this is to be based upon the record of the life and teaching of Jesus in the Gospels. Just what does this mean in terms of modern conditions and the understanding of personality in our own time?

The pioneer of spiritual direction in the Western church, Ignatius of Loyola, provided some criteria in his day by defining the characteristics of good and evil spirits. Hugo Rahner, *Ignatius the Theologian* (London: Geoffrey Chapman, 1968), pp. 168–69.

The earlier tradition of the Eastern church set forth four requirements for maturity: openness and readiness to accept another into one's heart, a thorough knowledge of one's self, patience with frankness and honesty in the relationship, willingness to embrace solitude and cultivate detachment. Alan Jones, *Exploring Spiritual Direction* (New York: Seabury Press, 1982), pp. 77–79.

Spiritual guidelines have been especially helpful in warning against the reduction of spirituality to criteria that will build up the individual ego. This is a continual Western temptation. Tilden Edwards, *Spiritual Friend* (New York: Paulist Press, 1980), p. 79.

6. In *Should Anyone Say Forever?* (Chicago: Loyola University Press, 1985), John C. Haughey provides many scriptural illustrations of the mistakes, misunderstandings, and possible mutual hardship that may be a part of any commitment in friendship, marriage, and/or church.

7. William A. Barry, "Prayer in Pastoral Care: A Contribution from the Tradition of Spiritual Direction," *Journal of Pastoral Care*, Vol. XXXI, no. 2, June 1977, p. 93.

8. For a guide to self-awareness and devotion to God through prayer without deception, see Gerald G. May, *Care of Mind: Care of Spirit* (San Francisco: Harper and Row, 1982), pp. 84–92.

The approach of May to prayer is apophatic, a willingness to know God behind, beyond, or hidden in all sensory or intellectual representations. It is seen in the silent way of the Quaker, the mysticism of Meister Eckhardt, the self-emptiness of Zen Buddhism.

Another approach is described by May as evangelical or charismatic. A prayer is seen in these groups as a search for deeper realization of God through visions, feelings, words, symbols (May, *Care of Mind*, pp. 10–11).

Edward E. Thornton applies the first of these approaches to Christian counsel and spiritual discipline through a discipline of relaxation, centering upon the inner self before God and contemplation of the meaning of God that is beyond intellect. Edward E. Thornton, *Being Transformed: An Inner Way of Spiritual Growth*, (Philadelphia: Westminster Press, 1984).

9. This ancient Irish view of spiritual direction has been redefined for modern Christian life by Kenneth Leech, *Soul Friend* (San Francisco: Harper and Row, 1977).

10. Karl Barth, *Prayer*, tr. Sara F. Terrien (Philadelphia: Westminster Press, 1952), p. 20.

Index

Index

Index

Index